Augsburg College
George Sverdrup Library
Minneapolis, Minnesota

D0777055

LIBEL AND ACADEMIC FREEDOM

Libel
and Academic
Freedom

A Lawsuit against Political Extremists

by Arnold M. Rose

FOREWORD BY PAUL A. FREUND

UNIVERSITY OF MINNESOTA PRESS   *Minneapolis*

© Copyright 1968 by the University of Minnesota. All rights reserved
Printed in the United States of America at the Lund Press, Inc., Minneapolis

Library of Congress Catalog Card Number: 68-19743

PUBLISHED IN GREAT BRITAIN, INDIA, AND PAKISTAN BY THE OXFORD
UNIVERSITY PRESS, LONDON, BOMBAY, AND KARACHI, AND IN CANADA BY THE
COPP CLARK PUBLISHING CO. LIMITED, TORONTO

KF
228
R6

Foreword

JUDGE LEARNED HAND once remarked that he could not think of a more terrible personal ordeal, apart from a serious illness, than involvement in a lawsuit. The uncertainties, the unexpected turns, the continuing emotional drain, and the risk of heavy financial loss all combine to make the experience one not lightly or ill-advisedly to be entered into. When the lawsuit is brought for libel these elements are greatly intensified. Such an action is the subject matter of this absorbing book, written by the victim of the libel and yet presented in the third person with remarkable objectivity and detachment, as befits a scholar in sociology.

To describe the book as the story of a lawsuit is, however, to miss its special texture. It is at once the dispassionate, engrossing account of a trial and a discerning analysis of the phenomenon of right-wing extremism in contemporary America. Professor Rose, on leave from the University of Minnesota while serving a term in the Minnesota legislature, found himself the object of abuse from certain local and vocal votaries of this persuasion. As a member of the Democratic-Farmer-Labor party, he espoused measures that his accusers associated with a "welfare state." He was an academic and a Jew; but his principal vulnerability as seen by his detractors was that some nineteen years before, he had served as a principal assistant in the preparation of Gunnar Myrdal's landmark study of the Negro in America, *An American Dilemma*. For this he was called a Communist collaborator and security risk. When, on his return to full-time teaching at the conclusion of the legislative session, these labels gained greater currency and seriousness because of a movement to investigate the university, Professor Rose finally sought legal counsel and instituted suit.

v

89506

At this juncture two great public issues converged, and they form the double motif of this volume. The one, already adverted to, is the theme of right-wing extremism, which the author is at pains to distinguish sharply from genuine anti-Communism. Its roots in American history and its specific manifestations in the Middle West are coolly and carefully dissected. The other theme is the law of political libel — the rules governing defamation leveled at a public officer or a public figure.

Less than two months after the case of *Rose v. Koch* was filed, the United States Supreme Court handed down its decision in *New York Times v. Sullivan*, a ruling that greatly restricted the libel laws of the states in the interest of full and free political debate. False and defamatory statements about a public officer, the Court held, are privileged unless uttered "maliciously," that is, with knowledge of their falsity or in reckless disregard of their truth or falsity. This doctrine placed a heavy burden of proof on the complainant in *Rose v. Koch*, insofar as he was libeled as a public officer, and it also enabled the defendants to introduce into evidence a whole spate of scurrilous documents, not otherwise relevant or admissible, to negate "malice" and show the underpinning, however murky and preposterous, for the defendants' honest belief.

Actually, as Professor Rose has written, the latitude thus given to the defense may have been its undoing. Much of the time of the three-and-a-half-week trial was consumed in efforts to establish the Communist party as a front for such groups as the Federal Reserve Banks and the Council on Foreign Relations; and when Professor Rose during the trial received an invitation to attend a White House conference on race problems the event only served to confirm for the defense the existence of a general conspiratorial web that reached into the highest echelons of military and political life. Evidently the members of the jury were not without a sense of humor; they returned a verdict for Rose in the amount of $20,000.

The victory was short-lived. On appeal the Minnesota Supreme Court reversed the judgment, on the ground that the trial judge had not instructed the jury on the issue of "malice" in precise accord with certain intervening decisions of the Supreme Court of the United States concerning the libel of public figures as well as public officers. Nothing in the reversal affected in the slightest the jury's finding that the accusations against Rose were false; but public figures were now fair game for damaging defamatory falsehoods if uttered out of simple-mindedness, carelessness, or stubborn irrationality.

Foreword

This is the issue of law and policy that is finally raised by the book: have we reached the wisest balance between the interest in reputation and the interest in free public debate? To be sure, the press must be protected against half-million-dollar judgments for minor inaccuracies that cause no demonstrable harm, as in the *New York Times* case. But full and free public discussion is a two-way street; those who contemplate entering the arena of political debate may themselves be deterred if the law leaves them virtually remediless against personal calumny.

Other resolutions of the issue seem possible without sacrificing the values of fearless debate of public issues. The victim of libel might be denied legal redress if a suitable retraction is published; in any event, he might be limited to compensatory damages, including his counsel fees and other legal costs. And disparaging comment, as distinguished from misstatements of fact, ought to be privileged, as in literary and artistic criticism. The good name of the victim could at least be vindicated under these suggested principles.

In preparing for trial Professor Rose drew up a memorandum essaying a point-by-point differentiation of his case from that of the *New York Times*. With a characteristically inquiring mind he wondered how the Supreme Court of the United States would respond to his analysis. Tragically, he was destined never to know. On January 2, 1968, Arnold Rose died, aged forty-nine. What had been undertaken as living testimony will stand as a testament.

PAUL A. FREUND

Harvard Law School
January 1968

vii

Acknowledgments

THE libel suit described and analyzed in this book could not have been carried on without the generous help and support of many people: faculty members from the University of Minnesota and from other colleges in this and neighboring states who contributed their time and money to the Faculty Legal Protection Committee; ordinary citizens who made financial contributions and gave encouragement and support; friends who gave of their valuable time to appear as character witnesses; and, of course, lawyer Norman Newhall and his staff. If *Rose v. Koch* has contributed to the strengthening of academic freedom, these friends and colleagues are equally responsible along with Arnold Rose.

The entire manuscript of *Libel and Academic Freedom* was read and corrected in galley proof by Arnold Rose before his death on January 2, 1968.

CAROLINE B. ROSE

Minneapolis, Minnesota
January 1968

Contents

LIBEL AND ACADEMIC FREEDOM

1

Overview

Big issues mirrored
in little events

THE great events of the world are mirrored in the small. In a libel suit tried in a Minneapolis courtroom in November 1965 were reflected the worldwide struggles between constitutional government and arbitrary government, between internationalism and the narrowest nationalism, between race hatred and respect for man regardless of race, between religious fanaticism and religious tolerance, between supporters and opponents of academic freedom. The case brought to public attention other important issues: the effort of right-wing extremists to make a shambles of American institutions such as the courts and the universities; the abuse of "freedom of the press" by reporters who distort and falsify in order to provide "newsworthy" stories for their readers; the need to clarify what from a legal standpoint constitutes "libelous criticism" of public officials and other "public figures."

The case was that of *Arnold Rose v. Gerda Koch et al.*, heard in Hennepin County District Court, Judge Donald T. Barbeau presiding. At various times between 1962 and 1965, Gerda Koch had published and distributed leaflets saying Rose was a collaborator with Communists or Communist fronters and was a "security risk." Rose was now suing Miss Koch and her associates for libel. But much greater persons and institutions than these were actually on trial: Gunnar Myrdal, eminent Swedish economist and government official; Ralph Bunche, United Nations Undersecretary General and Nobel Prize winner; former Presidents Franklin D. Roosevelt, Harry S. Truman, Dwight D. Eisenhower, and John F. Kennedy; President Lyndon B. Johnson; "50–70 per cent of

3

Eisenhower's administration"; "100 per cent of the military leaders of the United States"; the United States Supreme Court and especially Chief Justice Earl Warren; the University of Minnesota, where Rose was a professor; the Minnesota State Legislature, to which Rose had been elected as a representative; and dozens of prominent American social scientists. All these were labeled Communists, Communist collaborators, or Communist fronters.

The defendants were members of a species currently known as "right-wing extremists," and the trial provided an unusual insight into their motives and ways of operating. It is the purpose of this book to reveal to the public what they revealed of themselves in the courtroom and in their publications. Some of this is tragic, some amusing, but all of it highly significant for understanding an important aspect of American life. A number of valuable studies have recently been made on the right-wing extremists (and these will be discussed in Chapter 3) but few of them provide the drama of a confrontation in a courtroom before a jury of average American citizens. Rarely has the mind of the right-wing extremist been so fully put on public view as in this lawsuit.

The author of this book is the plaintiff, the man who claimed he was libeled and therefore brought the right-wing extremists into court to defend their accusations. The reader might properly inquire whether the author is so biased that he cannot report accurately what occurred. Of course he is biased, but all of his biases will shortly be laid bare, so the reader may judge for himself just what distortion might creep into this report. More important, everything that is reported here — except for some background information — will be quoted directly from the transcript of the trial, from the exhibits entered in evidence, and from newspaper reports. The author is a social scientist, trained to report accurately and to separate his own feelings and speculations from the facts. This is a document of participant observation; the full facts can be reported only by a participant.

The history of the case goes back more than thirty years. In 1931, Newton D. Baker, who had been Secretary of War in President Wilson's Cabinet, joined the Board of the Carnegie Corporation of New York, a philanthropic foundation. He persuaded his colleagues on the Board to undertake a comprehensive study of the status and problems of the Negro in America. In the words of Frederick P. Keppel, then president of the Carnegie Corporation:

4

Mr. Baker knew so much more than the rest of us on the Board about these questions, and his mind had been so deeply concerned with them, that we readily agreed when he told us that more knowledge and better organized and interrelated knowledge were essential before the Corporation could intelligently distribute its own funds. We agreed with him further in believing that the gathering and digestion of the material might well have a usefulness far beyond our own needs.[1]

Even the prescient Mr. Baker could not have foreseen all the consequences of the study he got the Carnegie Corporation to undertake.

The story of the study itself will be reported on in the next chapter. Suffice it here to say that the Carnegie Corporation in 1937 selected as director of the study Dr. Gunnar Myrdal, "a scholar who despite his youth [he was then thirty-eight years old] had already achieved an international reputation as a social economist, a professor in the University of Stockholm, economic adviser to the Swedish Government, and a member of the Swedish Senate," [2] to quote Mr. Keppel again. Myrdal sought the advice of fifty-one eminent social scientists and hired thirty-seven experts on the Negro to write specialized memoranda for him (they in turn hired thirty-six assistants to help them). Myrdal and his two assistants — Richard Sterner and Arnold Rose — did independent research and wrote the main product of the study, a book of 1483 pages titled *An American Dilemma.*

Shortly after the book was published in January 1944, the United States Supreme Court opened a new era in race relations in this country by deciding, by a vote of 9 to 0, that the "white primary," employed by the southern states as the major legal device to exclude Negroes from the ballot, was illegal.[3] According to John Gunther, some of the members of the Court had read *An American Dilemma*, and it had impressed them.[4]

It is difficult to assign causes in history, and certainly most social scientists agree that technological, economic, political, ideological, and sociological factors are most important for explaining the major changes which any society undergoes. But it can scarcely be doubted that the Supreme Court led the way after 1944 to a more equalitarian treatment of Negroes in America. In a series of more than thirty decisions, nearly all by unanimous vote, during the ensuing twenty years, a Court of constantly changing membership gave the Negro his full legal rights as a citizen of a democratic society. In the most important of these decisions, that of *Brown v. Board of Education of Topeka* (1954), the new Chief Justice, Earl Warren (formerly Republican governor of California), broke precedent and cited a few of the studies which influenced the Court's thinking. The famous footnote 11 closed with these words: "And see generally Myrdal, *An American Dilemma*, 1944."

It was this 1954 decision which sparked strong southern opposition, although changes encouraged by Supreme Court decisions had already been going on for ten years. Southern whites who sought to maintain the traditional subordination of the Negro now organized and acted in various ways to stop the social changes. One of their leaders, Senator James O. Eastland of Mississippi, chose a then-familiar tactic of attributing the Supreme Court's decisions to Communist influence. In a speech to the Senate on May 26, 1955, he said, among other things:

The Court cited and adopted generally, and without reservation, as its leading authority on modern psychology, Myrdal's book An American Dilemma when it said — and I quote from Chief Justice Warren's opinion: "And see generally Myrdal, An American Dilemma, 1944." . . . This is purely Communist propaganda, which was cited by the Supreme Court, and on which the Chief Justice of the United States based a very far-reaching decision looking to the destruction of our form of government. I have often wondered what was the source of the pro-Communist influence in the Supreme Court.

It was this speech, offered by Senator Eastland with congressional immunity from libel charges, which provided one of the important bases during the following decade for right-wing extremist attacks on thousands of important and unimportant Americans, who were labeled Communists or Communist sympathizers.

In November 1958, Gunnar Myrdal — who, after finishing the Negro study, had served as Minister of Commerce in the Swedish government and as executive secretary of the United Nations Economic Commission for Europe, and was now engaged in a large-scale study of South Asia — was invited to give a lecture at the University of Minnesota. Arnold Rose — who, after finishing the Negro study, had served in the United States Army and had taught at Bennington College and at Washington University, and was now professor of sociology at the University of Minnesota — was asked by university officials to be chairman at Dr. Myrdal's lecture. The subject of the talk was "Nationalism and Internationalism in the Rich and Poor Countries," and Myrdal stressed his recent observations in South Asia. There was a question period at the end, and six or seven of the audience of some three hundred persons chose to ask questions.

6

The fourth person to raise a question was a well-dressed woman of about fifty years of age. She asked, "Dr. Myrdal, when you were directing the study of the Negro in America, why did you hire Ralph Bunche, a well-known Communist?" [5] Myrdal was taken aback, and responded: "Why do you ask that question?" The questioner then began to read from a publication which described Bunche as a Communist. After a moment of this, Rose went to the podium and said to the woman, "Your question is not relevant to the subject of this evening's lecture, and unless you can ask a question that is pertinent, I shall ask you to sit down." She continued to read out loud about Bunche, and Rose put whatever tone of authority he could into his voice and shouted, "Please sit down!" She did. The rest of the audience seemed to be either shocked or amused at the incident. A few more questions were put to Myrdal, and then the evening was over. This was the first encounter between Gerda Koch and Arnold Rose, although neither knew who the other was at that time.

Almost four years later, in the fall of 1962, Rose was running for a seat in the Minnesota State Legislature. Late in the campaign, he became aware that one of his opponents [6] was calling him a Communist and was even apparently distributing a leaflet labeling him a Communist collaborator. At a candidates' meeting, the campaign manager of this opponent stated that Rose was a Communist sympathizer and gave as the basis of his accusation Rose's association with Myrdal and others in writing *An American Dilemma*. What struck Rose as odd at the time, in this vigorous and bitterly fought campaign, was that the opponent and his campaign manager were not persons who ordinarily would be aware of scholarly books.[7] It was not until after the election, which he won, that Rose saw two leaflets attacking him as a collaborator with Communists and Communist fronters. One had been printed at the order of the political opponent but he was not named in it and it was apparently scarcely circulated at all.[8] The other was mimeographed, consisted of two pages from a periodical pamphlet called *Facts for Action*, and was written and distributed by Gerda Koch, now director of what she called "Christian Research, Inc." [9] (She was also a substitute teacher in the schools of a Minneapolis suburb.) The second leaflet identified Rose as the chairman at the Myrdal lecture in 1958, where Gerda Koch had been told by Rose to desist from following up her question to Myrdal regarding Ralph Bunche. The two leaflets were similar in content, though different in format. They later became plaintiff's exhibits in the libel suit of 1965.[10]

After the election, Miss Koch reissued the mimeographed leaflet, adding only these sentences:

— and now (Dec. 5 '62) Rose is elected. Will our state legislature and Minnesota citizens grant him a seat in our honored Minnesota legislature? — that depends upon what you will do!

Minnesotans, write our Governor and your state representative, and protest the seating of Arnold Rose in the legislature — and get at least five others to do the same. If you do not know who your representative is, call your city hall, library or newspaper.

In March 1963, Miss Koch both mailed and distributed by hand this revised sheet to most members of the Minnesota State Legislature, of which Rose was now a member. She and her followers also, on several occasions, came to testify at committee hearings of the legislature, and in two or three instances influenced the outcome of the committees' votes. At this juncture, Rose took the floor of the House to warn his fellow legislators about "revolutionaries who pretend to be conservatives," to deny the validity of their charge that he was pro-Communist, and to suggest that he might sue them for libel. A full report on this was carried in the Minneapolis newspapers, which also published an editorial supporting Rose, and a local television station that night showed Rose reading his statement. Rose declined to mention his adversaries by name, but Gerda Koch and her associates had been given due notice.

About a month later, a new issue of *Facts for Action* was mailed and hand-distributed to most members of the legislature.[11] This eight-page document was devoted entirely to an attack on Rose, containing such headings as "ARNOLD ROSE, MINNESOTA UNIVERSITY PROFESSOR AND STATE LEGISLATOR, COLLABORATES WITH COMMUNISTS AND COMMUNIST FRONTERS" and "CLEAN OUT THE UNIVERSITY!!!" (Six others from the University of Minnesota — including the president and a former president — were mentioned as Communists, fronters, and collaborators.) Rose made no response to this piece, even after it was distributed widely at the Minnesota State Fair the following September and at other public gatherings. His attitude at the time was that no responsible person was paying any attention to the attacks on him, and he was busy trying to catch up with his research after a year of campaigning and of work in the legislature. But this complacency was shattered in December 1963.

On October 22, 1963, Rose had received an invitation to lecture on "American Public Opinion toward Communism" at the Anoka County

Public Library [12] sometime in January. This invitation stemmed from a committee meeting of university faculty members, chaired by Dean Julius Nolte of the Extension Division, two years earlier. Dean Nolte and his assistant, Professor William C. Rogers, director of a branch of the Extension Division called the World Affairs Center, had argued that the faculty had an obligation to inform the American public about world Communism, since it was a subject of great public concern and a number of demagogues were exploiting this concern without providing factual information or rational suggestions on how America might cope with an aggressive and imperialistic worldwide Communist movement. Rose did not consider himself an expert on Communism, but he felt he should respond to Nolte's plea, and so he signed up to lecture on American public opinion toward Communism because he was something of an expert on public opinion. When the invitation to speak at Anoka arrived, Rose was not enthusiastic about driving some fifteen miles on a cold Minnesota winter night to give a public lecture, but he could scarcely refuse when he had previously offered to give such a lecture and the invitation was for any weekday evening in January, at Rose's choice. Besides, there was an honorarium of $50, and Rose had almost never before been paid for a local public lecture. So he accepted, and a chain of events was begun which led inexorably to a fantastic lawsuit.

Not mentioned in the Anoka invitation was the fact that two other university professors were also being invited to speak during the winter — Mulford Q. Sibley of the Department of Political Science and Raymond B. Nixon of the School of Journalism. Sibley was one of the few colorful personalities in an otherwise staid university: He was a socialist, a religious Quaker, an outspoken pacifist, an advocate of certain "unscientific" causes such as spiritualism and extrasensory perception, a superb lecturer, and a person much admired by many students. He could always be counted on by students to support their "testing the limits" of free expression and avoiding administrative restraints, even if he himself did not always agree with their cause and was inclined to be rather conservative in his personal habits. His "standing up" to the university administration was probably not always appreciated by the latter, but university officials — in their rigorous adherence to the principles of academic freedom — never took any action to restrain Sibley. Sibley also annoyed some faculty members by his attack on empirical and quantitative methods in social science, by his advocacy of extrasensory perception, and by his willingness to serve

9

as faculty sponsor for student radical clubs. Sibley himself was strongly opposed to Communism because of its connection with political dictatorship and repression of individual freedoms, although he once called himself a "communist with a small *c*" because of his anticapitalist economic ideology, but he felt that Communists should have freedom of expression. In short, Mulford Q. Sibley was an unusual personality and he provided the stimulus to the chain of events that were about to take place.

Sibley lectured at the Anoka County Library on November 21, 1963. The lecture was uneventful, except for the fact that a Mr. Adolph Grinde distributed outside the lecture hall several pamphlets, some of which he had obtained from Gerda Koch, attacking Sibley and Rose. Grinde ran a small furniture- and rug-cleaning establishment in Anoka County, and for several years had been associated with a local movement of religious fundamentalism. He was a subscriber to Gerda Koch's *Facts for Action*, and occasionally he distributed her literature as well as leaflets from other right-wing extremist groups.

At 9 A.M., Monday, December 2, 1963, Anoka County Board Chairman Edward Fields called to order a regular meeting of the Board.[13] Present were the five commissioners, the county attorney, Robert W. Johnson, a clerk, a *Minneapolis Star* staff writer named Gordon Slovut, and a few local citizens. While the clerk was organizing some routine business, Commissioner Fields opened a bulky envelope, and — after reading for a few seconds — exclaimed to his fellow commissioners, "Listen to this!" He read the following letter aloud:

> 1708 2nd Avenue South
> Anoka, Minnesota
> November 29, 1963

Edward Fields, Chairman
Anoka County Commission
Anoka, Minnesota

DEAR MR. FIELDS,

A series of lectures is being given at the Anoka County Library, 8411 Center Drive, Spring Lake Park. According to the announcement in the Anoka County Union the stated purpose of the lectures is "to learn more about the political and economic systems which oppose us in the world conflict". These lecturers are being paid with a grant from the federal government which is to be used for educational purposes.

The three selected speakers are Mulford Q. Sibley, Professor of Political Science, Raymond Nixon, Professor of Journalism and Arnold Rose, Professor of Sociology. They are all of the University of Minnesota.

10

In a recent letter to the Minneapolis Tribune Mr. Sibley admits he is a communist. Arnold Rose is co-author with Gunnar Myrdal (a notorious Swedish communist) of the book "American Dilemma". I am also enclosing material on the background of both Mr. Sibley and Arnold Rose.

I attended the lecture by Mulford Q. Sibley which was given November 21. As I had feared, he said the American free enterprise system is "decadent" and that socialism is inevitable. The audience was predominantly young people and therefore I feel they were very likely to be influenced by his praise of the socialist-communist system.

I do not see why the taxpayers must pay to denounce free enterprise and promote the socialist-communist system. I feel there has been gross negligence on the part of the Anoka County Library Staff and Board in choosing to spend this grant in this manner. There has been no intention of having anti-socialist speakers also.

I would like to know if you have any jurisdiction over these library matters. If not, who does? I believe the lecture series should be stopped.

Thank you.

Sincerely yours,

/s/   ADOLPH GRINDE

Enclosed with the letter [14] was an unsigned sheet attacking Sibley as a Communist, Gerda Koch's first mimeographed attack on Rose, and a pamphlet labeled *The Suppressed Report* by SPX Associates, which, among other things, called Gunnar Myrdal "a notorious Communist."

The Board members were startled. They took no formal action, but asked the county attorney to check into the characters of Professors Nixon and Rose — the two who were yet to speak at the Anoka Library. They also called in the librarian, who explained that the three professors were invited to speak on Communism and had been recommended by the university's World Affairs Center. One of the commissioners suggested to the librarian that the remaining two lectures should be postponed until the county attorney could check the loyalty of Nixon and Rose. When the Board turned its attention to its regular business, reporter Slovut got up, announced that he had his story for the day, and left the room.

That afternoon County Attorney Johnson telephoned the university and the local office of the FBI, both of which informed him that there wasn't the slightest basis for questioning the loyalty or reliability of Professors Nixon and Rose. That evening, he conveyed this information to a reporter from the *Minneapolis Tribune*. He reported the same information the next morning to the commissioners, and that evening — December 3, 1963 — the Anoka County Library Board met and reaffirmed its invitations to Professors Nixon and Rose. The commissioners themselves, at their next meeting the following Monday, apologized for their role in the incident. Nixon gave his lecture in December and Rose gave his lecture in January, without further trouble from Anoka. The public officials involved behaved most responsibly in seeking both to protect their constituents from any possible subversive influence and to prevent the spread of false and inflammatory charges against the university and its professors. Nevertheless, because such charges were "good copy" for a Minneapolis newspaper the fire lit by Grinde was fanned into a blaze that aroused fear throughout the state during the next six months and had the potentiality of seriously damaging its university.

Gerda Koch wrote several libelous and inflammatory leaflets, but they had almost no effect by themselves. Adolph Grinde used Miss Koch's false and vicious material to incite the Anoka County commissioners to restrict freedom of speech, but the commissioners — after quickly checking on the validity of Grinde's charges — took no action. However, *Minneapolis Star* reporter Gordon Slovut published Miss Koch's libels and added a few falsehoods on his own. Other *Star* reporters picked up the theme in the next few weeks and published further false and harmful statements. The *Star* did not report County Attorney Johnson's "clearance" of Nixon and Rose, nor did it report the re-invitation to lecture extended to Professors Nixon and Rose, nor did it report the Anoka County commissioners' apology, even though it was expressly mailed to the newspaper. The *Star* ignored two letters from Rose asking them to stop printing the false statements about him. Rose and his attorney then visited the *Star*'s managing editor and vice president to ask for a retraction, but — in effect — they refused to print one.

In the meantime, events at the university involving Professor Sibley were used by the *Star* to further excite the population of Minnesota. Demands were made that the state legislature investigate "Communism at the university," and the Senate later did hold a brief and desultory "investigation." Sibley and Rose were subjected to all kinds of threats and harassment. The major events of December 1963 through May 1964 will be detailed in the following chapters: They would be hilariously funny if they did not also hold ominous implications for the civil liberties of individuals and the very existence of a great state university. This blow-up — as distinguished from the ineffective attacks by Gerda Koch during the preceding year — was stimulated by the *Minneapolis Star*.

12

Big Issues Mirrored in Little Events

Within a few days of the Anoka County commissioners' meeting, Rose sought the services of an attorney in connection with a possible libel suit. Because he himself was identified as a Democrat, Rose sought an attorney who was not in partisan politics. Because he was a Jew, and because he correctly anticipated that anti-Semitism would later be involved in the case, Rose sought an attorney who was not a Jew. He also sought someone who he thought was highly competent, highly respectable, and could be "educated" to understand the dangers posed by the right-wing extremists. He chose Norman Newhall, Jr., with whom he had once served on a citizens' committee dealing with municipal problems, and he never had occasion to regret his choice. Newhall's performance and his growth in knowledge and awareness during the period leading up to the trial, and during the trial itself, provide testimony to the decency of the American citizen once he learns what the issues are. The two men — Rose and Newhall — were about as different as two educated persons in their late forties could be, but they developed considerable mutual understanding.

Newhall advised Rose that he had a strong case for libel against Gerda Koch and her associates. This opinion was checked informally with three University of Minnesota law professors, who concurred — with the proviso that "one can never be sure of what a jury might do."

When Rose first went to see Norman Newhall about initiating a libel suit, he of course asked the attorney about the cost. Newhall put a ceiling on legal fees through the trial at $3000. Rose did not believe that, even in the event of a favorable verdict, he could collect a penny from Gerda Koch. She was no longer employed as a substitute schoolteacher, and she seemed to earn her living by selling extremist literature. Rose told Newhall that he was willing to spend up to $3000 for the suit, and Newhall accepted the case.

Several weeks later, as word spread among the faculty that Rose was planning to sue those responsible for the attack on the university, a number of professors offered Rose small sums of money to help pay for the lawsuit. More important, a highly respected member of the faculty, Harold Deutsch, chairman of the History Department, offered to organize a committee that would raise a legal defense fund. He was soon joined by Professor Robert H. Beck of the College of Education, and they formed a committee which included Francis M. Boddy, professor of economics; Richard K. Gaumnitz, professor of business administration; Donald Hastings, chairman of the Psychiatry Department; Richard C. Jordan, head of

13

the Mechanical Engineering Department; Stanley V. Kinyon, professor of law; William P. Martin, head of the Department of Soil Science; Alfred O. C. Nier, chairman of the School of Physics; and Grover C. Stephens, professor of zoology.

On the same day that the suit was filed, January 30, 1964, the creation of the Faculty Legal Protection Committee was announced, and an appeal for contributions was sent to each member of the Minnesota faculty, along with an explanation of what the lawsuit was about.[15] Hundreds of contributions were received. Some came from outside the university, especially from Democratic politicians who knew Rose (including the governor and lieutenant governor of the state), but outside contributions were not solicited, for the Faculty Committee wanted to be free to control the funds if any were left after the Rose case was paid for. Faculty members at other colleges and universities were encouraged to send messages of support rather than money, since the latter might best be spent for similar purposes within their own institutions. Within a month after the announcement of the lawsuit, more than $7300 had been contributed for its prosecution. With the expressions of moral support that also poured in, these contributions meant a great deal to Rose. They indicated to him that he was not alone in fighting the right-wing extremists who had attacked him and the goals of the institutions of which he was a part — independent scholarship and academic freedom. The support meant more to him than even most of the contributors then knew, for about a week after the Anoka County incident, and before the Faculty Legal Protection Committee was formed, Rose learned from his physician that he had a serious illness. Through those difficult four months in which Rose was repeatedly the subject of false stories in the *Minneapolis Star*, and when he was trying to get the lawsuit underway, he was undergoing a painful medical treatment, the effectiveness of which was then deemed uncertain. Needless to say, he felt sustained by his friends in academic life and in politics. By May 1964, Rose was almost well again, and by September he was strong enough to begin a lecture tour of South Asia (under the auspices of the State Department).

Such were the main events leading up to what must be one of the more bizarre trials in modern American history. Gerda Koch chose as her attorney Jerome Daly, who was as involved in right-wing extremist activities as she was. Together they made the court into a spectacle for three and a half weeks. Their factual position was that there was a gigantic but

14

secret Communist conspiracy afoot in the United States, in which Rose played a leading role. At the center of this alleged conspiracy were the Federal Reserve Banks and the Council on Foreign Relations, with the chairman of the latter organization being the head of the whole operation. Presidents Eisenhower and Kennedy were stated to be "conscious tools" of the conspiracy. The majority of Eisenhower's administration and all of the military leaders of the United States were said to be Communists by Miss Koch and her followers on the witness stand. President Kennedy, whose acts were "shown" in detail to "favor" the Communist cause, was assassinated because he went to New York, just before he went to Dallas, to inform the Communist leaders that he would no longer play their game. Rose was said to have had a hand in ordering the assassination of Kennedy. Most of the United States Congress, according to Miss Koch and her associates, had shown itself at various times to be pro-Communist by passing laws for the income tax, the Federal Reserve Bank System, "socialized medicine, urban renewal . . . trade expansion . . . federal aid to education, disarmament, etc." And, of course, "the Jews" played a leading role in the Communist conspiracy — at least those Jews who "worshipped the Golden Calf." [16] Rose was said by Daly, in court, to be a "Shylock Jew usurer."

These are merely a few of the highlights of a serious courtroom trial, in which the "Communist conspiracy" theme was used by the defense to educate the public, just as the plaintiff sought to educate the public by the lawsuit itself. To substantiate his case, attorney Daly adduced evidence that certain Communists had been consulted or quoted in the preparation of *An American Dilemma* and that Myrdal had acknowledged in his "Author's Preface" that Rose "collaborated" in writing this book. He further claimed, for legal reasons, that Miss Koch had no "malice" in her attacks on Rose, but was merely performing the role of good citizen in exposing as a "Communist collaborator" one who was a professor in the state university and a representative in the state legislature. In a counterclaim, Daly showed that Rose had said, first on the floor of the state House of Representatives and later to the newspapers, that those who were attacking him were "subversives, revolutionaries, and just as dangerous as the Communists" — and Rose acknowledged on the witness stand that he had said this and that he had had Gerda Koch in mind, although he had not mentioned her by name. Daly then brought in character witnesses to testify that Gerda Koch was a loyal American citizen and very devoted

15

to the Constitution, which she often praised. Despite the "show" that Daly put on, there were several difficult questions of fact and law in this trial, which will be brought out in subsequent chapters.

Rose won his suit against Gerda Koch and Christian Research, Inc., but his claim against Adolph Grinde was dismissed, as were all counterclaims against Rose. After the trial, the judge was quoted in the *Minneapolis Tribune* as saying that the case ought to go to the United States Supreme Court as a test case, to provide a means of clarifying the law of libel when a public official was the one claiming he was libeled. It would be especially interesting to bring this case to the Supreme Court, because the Court itself — by citing *An American Dilemma* in its 1954 decision — would be a "Communist collaborator" in almost the same sense that Rose was said by Miss Koch to be a "Communist collaborator."

It was said by some close observers of the trial that Daly was "stupid," and hence lost the case for his client. A close reading of the transcript shows that Daly was not stupid in the exact sense of that word. It is true that Daly did not always do his "homework," but the case was very complicated and it was extremely difficult to keep all the facts in mind. His client, Gerda Koch, had so many "facts" in mind — she brought into the courtroom well over two hundred government reports and other books as well as dozens of "research files," which were mostly irrelevant and immaterial to the trial — that she was not always ready with the truly relevant facts. Rose, on the other hand, was more aware of which facts were relevant and admissible as testimony because of his partial familiarity with court procedure. He briefed his attorney about most of the important and relevant facts in a number of precise memoranda and by notes even during the course of the long trial.

More important, Miss Koch and Daly were not interested simply in voiding Rose's claim of legal libel. They knew that a simple apology, or statement that there had been a misunderstanding of Senator Eastland's speech, would have ended the lawsuit at any time before the jury went out to deliberate; the *New York Times* decision handed down by the United States Supreme Court in 1964 had made it extremely difficult for a public official to claim successfully that he had been libeled (see Chapter 7), and Rose and Newhall had dismissed from the suit those of Miss Koch's associates who had apologized. Their purposes were obviously far broader: to "educate" the public into believing that many of America's leaders were involved in a gigantic Communist conspiracy and, by winning the

16

suit on a point of difficult law, to discredit the professors at the University of Minnesota, the liberal Democrats, and others with whom Rose was associated in the public mind.

Some close observers of Gerda Koch's and Jerome Daly's actions both before and during the trial dismissed them as "mentally ill" or "insane." The author is something of a student of mental illness, having published several studies on the subject, and he will aver that Miss Koch and Daly are not mentally ill, at least no more so than the great majority of the German government under Hitler, or the majority of those who seized control of the Republican party in the United States in the period 1962 through 1964. Some of Miss Koch's followers are probably mentally ill, and there is a paranoid quality [17] throughout the extremist movement that has a practical interest for the psychologist and the sociologist. But to say that Miss Koch attacked Rose, or Daly lost the suit, because of psychiatric disturbances is both technically inaccurate and a misunderstanding of one of the central facts about contemporary American society.

Miss Koch and Daly are in revolt against contemporary American society; they are deliberately working very hard to subvert many of its basic institutions. They want to create a new form of American government different from any this country has ever before known. And they are not alone in this effort but collaborate — by their own testimony — with at least a dozen national organizations to this end. They are "subversives, revolutionaries, and just as dangerous as the Communists," as Rose repeatedly said in public, and as the jury — after listening to over three weeks of testimony — found in dismissing the counterclaims of *Koch et al. v. Rose*, for truth is an absolute defense against libel. Unless the reader understands this last paragraph — no matter how much he may sympathize with Rose or find Miss Koch's and Daly's actions reprehensible — he will have missed the point of this book.

Immediately after the trial jury awarded the victory to Rose, Miss Koch began taking steps to get the decision reversed. She and her associates in the right-wing extremist movement successfully raised funds for an appeal; she hired an additional lawyer; they went through all the legal processes to bring a formal appeal to the Minnesota Supreme Court, which heard the case on March 19, 1967. Three months later, on June 20, 1967, a simultaneous decision of the United States Supreme Court — in the cases of *Curtis Publishing Company v. Butts* and *Associated Press v. Walker* — changed the law of libel by further weakening it. It was the third time since

17

the Rose-Koch case began that the libel law in the United States had been changed. The upshot was that the Minnesota Supreme Court in its decision of October 20, 1967, reversed the trial decision on legal grounds, even though it stated that the jury had clearly found that Rose was not a Communist sympathizer or Communist collaborator. (United States Supreme Court decisions concerning libel apply retroactively to a case still under appeal since a constitutional issue is involved.) The Minnesota Supreme Court faithfully followed the United States Supreme Court in holding that any public official or any "public figure" is subject — without the protection of being able to institute a libel suit — to "defamatory and untruthful attacks" unless he can prove that the defamers acted with malice. Malice is narrowly defined, and the trial judge may not cite examples in instructing the jury what the definition means.

Since the narrow definition of "malice" is that the defamatory falsehood must be stated "with knowledge that it was false or with reckless disregard of whether it was false or not," and it is virtually impossible for a defamed person to prove what was in the mind of his defamer when he printed false charges, there is — in fact — no longer a libel law in the United States to protect public officials or "public figures" against any type of false statement unless the courts are willing to accept a liberal or reasonable definition of "reckless disregard of whether it was false or not." The implications of these recent decisions of the United States Supreme Court have not yet reached any sector of the American people, but they will gradually reduce the access of the public to correct information in the press or other mass media, and they will open political campaigns to false charges such as the country has never before experienced. Only the most unscrupulous politicians and irresponsible people generally can ultimately benefit from these court decisions. Rose believes that the United States Supreme Court — while reaching correct findings in "bad cases" — through the language of its decisions has opened a hornet's nest of future political crises and moral cleavages throughout the nation.

2

A Study

"America's single
most important
domestic problem"

FOR the past several years, the Gallup Poll has shown that the American people most frequently name "civil rights" or the "race problem" as America's single most important domestic problem. President Lyndon Johnson has also made the same observation. Newspapers throughout the country devote a great deal of space to reports about race conflict, Negro problems, and Negro progress. Scores of books, of every type, appear every year on the subject, as do innumerable television and radio and film programs. But until about twenty-five years ago, there was practically nothing on the Negro problem in the mass media. In fact, little mention was made in the press of Negroes except for occasional stories about crimes, and in the other media the highly stereotyped figures of "Amos 'n' Andy" or "Stepin Fetchit" were the only reflections of this minority group. Public officials seldom made reference to the Negro, except for the southern demagogues who, during election campaigns, regularly referred to myths of Negro domination in the post-Civil War days. From about 1876 to about 1940, there was a "conspiracy of silence" surrounding the Negro in public though not in private communications. The agreement to avoid discussion of the Negro had been deliberately organized in the first place as part of the political compromise of 1876, and in revulsion against the public prominence of the Negro problem from the 1830's through the early 1870's. But after a few years, the public silence about the Negro, and his occasional appearance in only stereotyped and distorted forms, even in

19

the history books,[1] entered into the folkways of American society. Until the 1940's, few white Americans would have publicly stated that the Negro was the most important domestic problem for this country.

Does that mean there was little by way of a race problem before 1940? Many white southerners would like to think so, and most right-wing extremists state this was the case. But the facts speak otherwise: Considerably less than half the Negro males had full-time employment in the 1920's and 1930's, and there were few occupations they were allowed to enter at all. The average Negro family income was less than a third that of the average white family, even during the great depression of the 1930's. Peonage (practically slavery) continued to exist on the turpentine farms, and even on many of the cotton plantations, in the southern states, although by the 1930's many Negroes were being driven out of southern rural areas. There were almost no legal protections for the 80 per cent of the Negroes who lived in the southern states: In eight of those states during more than fifty years, not one case has been discovered where a white man was arrested, tried, and punished for committing a crime against a Negro. And yet white violence against Negroes was frequent, and far outweighed Negro violence against whites, which was severely punished. In the 1890's, a Negro was lynched someplace in the South nearly every day; and through the 1930's, flogging of Negroes was a common, everyday practice in the South. Only a few thousand Negroes were allowed to vote in all of the southern states, despite a constitutional requirement that they be allowed to do so. Government agencies, at every level, discriminated against the Negro, and discrimination by white organizations and individuals was all but universal. Not least painful to the Negro was the fact that he could not communicate either with his white oppressors in the South or with well-intentioned but ignorant whites throughout the country. The American Negro was as in a glass cage, where he could occasionally be seen but never heard, where he could beat his head against the walls of this cage but appear only funny to those who observed him from the outside.[2] To any halfway impartial observer, it is clear that no minority in the modern Western world, other than the Jews under the German Nazis, were so maltreated and oppressed as were the Negroes in the United States.

Thus, there was a serious American problem through the 1930's regarding the Negro, and almost nobody said anything about it publicly. Even the sociologists, scholars of the social scene, wrote evasively about "invasion-succession cycles" and other "race relations cycles," as though

20

they were talking astronomy. Except for an interesting little book by Ray Stannard Baker,[3] published in 1908, nothing on the Negro appeared from any of the thundering muckrakers or other American reformers.

The 1940's changed all that. Socioeconomic forces were developing over many decades to create rapid social change in American race relations, and World War II accentuated and precipitated them. Most of the important forces were impersonal ones — such as the changes in the cotton economy and the rise of a great demand for labor in industry — but some were influences that worked through public opinion and the American conscience. One of the latter influences was the new literature that now found its way onto the bookshelves of literate Americans. There were horrifying novels like Lillian Smith's *Strange Fruit* (1944) or Richard Wright's *Native Son* (1940). There were penetrating essays like W. F. Cash's *The Mind of the South* (1941) and Claude McKay's *Harlem: Negro Metropolis* (1940). There were scholarly studies like J. G. St. Clair Drake and H. R. Cayton's *Black Metropolis* (1945) and Myrdal-Sterner-Rose's *An American Dilemma* (1944).

It is perhaps safe to say that most Americans are today roughly aware of this nation's shortcomings in its treatment of Negroes. Educated people especially — including leaders in government, industry, unions, churches, and voluntary associations of many kinds — have been made aware of the plight of the Negro in the United States. The new literature was a major factor in bringing about this awareness. Powerful efforts have been made over the past twenty-odd years to reduce racial discrimination, and the nation has even begun to tackle the blighting heritage of past discriminations. Providing some of the motivation behind this effort, by creating new insights and moral confrontations, was the new literature. Sometimes today we — both whites and Negroes — are so blinded by the race problems still facing us that we neglect to recognize how much more serious these problems were in 1940, and how much progress we have made to provide some semblance of an American life for the American Negro. The new literature was one factor in creating these significant changes. It helped to "redefine" the situation for many Americans.

So *An American Dilemma* was not merely a social science study; it also became a footnote in history. It is impossible to describe a scholarly work of almost fifteen hundred pages in a few paragraphs, and only those aspects of it pertinent to the Rose-Koch lawsuit will be singled out for discussion.[4] There are two parts to *An American Dilemma*: One is an orderly

21

compilation of nearly all the facts available on the American Negro and on race relations in the United States as of around 1940, published and unpublished, integrated in a framework of social science theory and benefiting from several methodological analyses (the major ones described in the appendixes). This part of the work makes up the bulk of the pages, and was compiled and written almost equally by Myrdal and Rose, with Sterner contributing the factual portions of the chapters on economics. The other part was written almost solely by Myrdal, and represents a work of genius: It is an analysis of American culture in terms of the values and the structure of that complex and heterogeneous society. While Rose does not agree with every single sentence of it, he believes it to be one of the most insightful analyses of American society available, paralleled only by the work of Tocqueville over a hundred years earlier. It is permeated by an admiration — even love — of American society, although it also contains much that is critical in detail. Considering Rose's attitude toward this work, he can be expected to have registered some indignation when Gerda Koch described it as having been compiled by more than a hundred Communists and Communist fronters.

Actually it is doubtful whether Gerda Koch ever read much of the book before she wrote her attacks on Rose for his "collaboration" in writing *An American Dilemma*. On the witness stand, she said she had read "small portions," but she probably had reference to the "portions" referred to by Senator Eastland in his speech of May 26, 1955. These were references to the names listed in the "Author's Preface," plus three half-sentences on pages 12 and 13. During the entire trial, the three paragraphs in which these half-sentences occur were the only "portions" of the 1483-page work that Miss Koch could specifically mention as reflecting its "Communist nature," although she claimed to have read about 30 per cent of the work as of November 1965. These paragraphs, from Chapter 1, are reprinted here in their entirety, and the "portions" described as "pro-Communist" by Senator Eastland and Miss Koch are italicized:

These ideological forces — the Christian religion and the English law — also explain why America through all its adventures has so doggedly stuck to its high ideals: why it has been so conservative in keeping to liberalism as a national creed even if not as its actual way of life. This conservatism, in fundamental principles, has, to a great extent, been perverted into *a nearly fetishistic cult of the Constitution*. This is unfortunate since *the 150-year-old Constitution is in many respects impractical and ill-suited for modern conditions* and since, furthermore, the drafters of the document made it technically difficult to change even if there were no popular feeling against change.

The worship of the Constitution also is a most flagrant violation of the American Creed which, as far as the technical arrangements for executing the power of the people are concerned, is strongly opposed to stiff formulas. Jefferson actually referred to the American form of government as an experiment. The young Walt Whitman, among many other liberals before and after him, expressed the spirit of the American Revolution more faithfully when he demanded "continual additions to our great experiment of how much liberty society will bear." Modern historical studies of how the Constitution came to be as it is reveal that *the Constitutional Convention was nearly a plot against the common people.* Until recently, the Constitution has been used to block the popular will: the Fourteenth Amendment inserted after the Civil War to protect the civil rights of the poor freedmen has, for instance, been used more to protect business corporations against public control.

But when all this is said, it does not give more than one side of the cult of the Constitution. The common American is not informed on the technicalities and has never thought of any great difference in spirit between the Declaration of Independence and the Constitution. When he worships the Constitution, it is an act of American nationalism, and in this the American Creed is inextricably blended. The liberal Creed, even in its dynamic formulation by Jefferson, is adhered to by every American. The unanimity around, and the explicitness of, this Creed is the great wonder of America. The "Old Americans," all those who have thoroughly come to identify themselves with the nation — which are many more than the Sons and Daughters of the Revolution — adhere to the Creed as the faith of their ancestors. The others — the Negroes, the new immigrants, the Jews, and other disadvantaged and unpopular groups — could not possibly have invented a system of political ideals which better corresponded to their interests. So, by the logic of the unique American history, it has developed that the rich and secure, out of pride and conservatism, and the poor and insecure, out of dire need, have come to profess the identical ideals. The reflecting observer comes to feel that this spiritual convergence, more than America's strategic position behind the oceans and its immense material resources, is what makes the nation great and what promises it a still greater future. Behind it all is the historical reality which makes it possible for the President to appeal to all in the nation in this way: "Let us not forget that we are all descendants from revolutionaries and immigrants."

What the reader may fail to understand is that Gerda Koch and Jerome Daly, among others, really believe that the statement above is pro-Communist.[5]

However, the main case made by Miss Koch and Daly against *An American Dilemma*, as a "Communist book," was based on the "Author's Preface." In this preface, Myrdal courteously acknowledges the advice and information provided him by some 125 persons. When he first came to the United States, on the invitation of the Carnegie Corporation, in 1938, Myrdal knew almost nothing of the American Negro problem or of the scholars in the field. Mr. Keppel of the Corporation recommended that he consult with three of these scholars — Donald R. Young of the Social Science Research Council, Charles S. Johnson of Fisk University, and Thomas J. Woofter, Jr., of the Works Progress Administration, all quite conservative gentlemen. They, in turn, gave him a list of about 50 "scholars and experts," to whom Myrdal sent his "first memorandum on the planning of the research" for "criticisms and suggestions." This list included Ruth Benedict, Franz Boas, Melville J. Herskovits, Ralph Linton, who were America's leading anthropologists; E. Franklin Frazier, Guy B. Johnson, George Lundberg, Howard W. Odum, Robert E. Park, E. B. Reuter, Dorothy Swaine Thomas, W. I. Thomas, Rupert B. Vance, Louis Wirth, who along with Johnson and Young were among America's leading sociologists; Ralph J. Bunche, Allison Davis, John Dollard, W. E. B. Du Bois, Abram L. Harris, Otto Klineberg, Frank Lorimer, Frank Notestein, Charles H. Thompson, Edward L. Thorndike, Jacob Viner, who were leading scholars in the other social sciences; W. W. Alexander, Jackson Davis, Edwin Embree, Eugene Kinckle Jones, Thomas Jesse Jones, Frederick Osborn, Faith Williams, L. Hollingsworth Wood, who along with Woofter were leading government officials or top officers of philanthropic foundations. On the witness stand, Gerda Koch presented a copy of this list as one of "Communists, Communist fronters, or Communist collaborators." Next to Bunche and Du Bois, she had most to suggest about Frederick Osborn as a "secret pro-Communist." To anyone who knows who Osborn is, this is so incredible as to be immensely funny. He was a member of a leading New York public relations firm, a former major general in the United States Army, and president of the American Eugenics Society.

Gerda Koch tried to bring into evidence more than a hundred right-wing extremist publications, as well as comments of witnesses who testified before the House Committee on Un-American Activities and the Senate Internal Security Subcommittee, to support her claims about "Communists" or "Communist fronters." The congressional committee

24

reports were not findings of these committees, but merely testimony presented by witnesses who volunteered information before the committees, and many of the witnesses were right-wing extremists who were no more reliable than Gerda Koch herself. She was able to get much of this hearsay testimony into evidence in court, not as proof of her statements, but as "influences on her state of mind when she prepared the leaflets" attacking Rose. Of course, she got some of the names confused: The "evidence" against Franz Boas, who died several years before the House committee came into existence, turned out to be that claimed against one Frank Boas; the Eveline Burns cited by Miss Koch from her "documents" was not the same Eveline Burns who was the economist referred to by Myrdal; nor was the James E. Jackson Miss Koch attacked the same person Myrdal mentioned.

Nevertheless, Gerda Koch had most of the names correct when she labeled them "Communists or Communist fronters" in her major pamphlet attacking Rose and later repeated and expanded this accusation on the witness stand. Her reasoning that Rose was a "Communist collaborator" was based on his alleged collaboration with those from this list. Her evidence of collaboration was that Rose was an assistant to Myrdal and that Myrdal expressed appreciation to those fifty-plus persons who provided him with "criticisms and suggestions" when he presented them with his "first memorandum on the planning of the research." She neglected the fact that Myrdal, as he mentioned in the preface, sought this advice in January 1939 and did not employ Rose as his assistant until September 1941. Actually, Rose did not know, nor had he ever met, most of those on this list, or those mentioned in the "Author's Preface" as "persons who undertook various research tasks" for Myrdal in 1939 and their research assistants, several of whom were also claimed by Miss Koch to be "Communists or Communist fronters." It is, in fact, highly doubtful that more than two persons among the 125 mentioned by Myrdal in his preface were ever really Communists or even "Communist fronters," by which Rose understood Miss Koch to mean members of Communist-front organizations. One problem with labeling a person a "Communist fronter" is that an organization can at one time be genuinely seeking, say, to improve conditions for Negroes, then be infiltrated and taken over by Communists, whereupon the non-Communists become disgusted and renounce their membership. Persons who actually fought the Communists in the organ-

25

ization, but lost, are thenceforth labeled by people like Miss Koch as "Communist fronters."

Before the two whom Rose acknowledged to be real Communists are considered, Rose's own connection with the study must be clarified. It has already been mentioned in the first chapter that Myrdal was invited by the Carnegie Corporation of New York in 1937 to undertake a major study of the American Negro problem. He arrived in the United States in 1938 and did a great deal of traveling, observing, and interviewing. In 1939, he hired a small staff and a larger number of experts around the country to prepare specialized research memoranda for him (and many of these employed graduate-student research assistants). He also continued his personal observations, but did no writing other than the memorandum mentioned. When World War II began in September 1939, it must have personally disturbed him, for he was a European and Europe was beginning to explode. In May and June 1940, the Germans seized France and it appeared that nothing could stop them from overrunning the rest of Europe, as they almost did later. Myrdal suddenly decided to go home to Sweden, so that he could be in his own country if it should be invaded by the Germans (he was still a member of the Swedish Senate, and close to the Social-Democratic government of Sweden). It must also be mentioned that staff morale was low, and many of the experts hired by Myrdal were nowhere near finishing their commitments to provide him with research memoranda by September 1, 1940.[6]

At this critical juncture, Mr. Keppel and his assistant Charles Dollard decided to employ Professor Samuel A. Stouffer of the University of Chicago to take over the direction of the study and wind up the phase of memoranda production. Stouffer was a capable sociological methodologist and administrator, and not an expert on the Negro problem, so he would not be involved in the rivalries and recriminations that had developed among the memoranda writers. Stouffer was employed for only four months, and his major task was to cut off the preparation of the memoranda, whether the authors were finished or not, by September 1, 1940.[7] He brought with him to the project office on the forty-sixth floor of the Chrysler Building in New York City two of his graduate students, Felix E. Moore, Jr., and Arnold M. Rose. They were to serve as "shock troops," he told them — that is, to work with senior researchers who had made much progress but were not likely to complete their work by September 1 unless they had more assistance. These two young men received a higher rate of pay than

26

was customary in those years, in return for which they were expected to work evenings and some weekends to bring certain studies to a finish. They were employed for only two and a half months, and both returned to their graduate studies at the University of Chicago in September.

Rose was then just twenty-two years of age and on his first trip outside the Chicago area, where he was born and had been raised. He worked with Richard Sterner to produce memoranda on Negroes in public assistance programs, and with Paul H. Norgren to produce memoranda on Negroes in the meat-packing industry and in the service occupations. He also assisted Stouffer with various minor tasks. These were the only persons with whom he collaborated that summer of 1940. Sterner was a Swedish economist whom Myrdal had brought with him when he first came to the United States in 1938. Sterner reluctantly decided not to return to Sweden with the Myrdals that summer because his wife was Jewish, and he was afraid of what might happen to her if the Nazis should invade Sweden. Paul Norgren was an American labor economist. Many years later he published a book which had a foreword by Vice President Richard Nixon, and Rose was pleased that he could write a favorable review of it. Rose met several other members of the staff, but all were working so furiously that there was no time for any discussions or social life. He remembers going to lunch once with Ralph Bunche and he remembers having been introduced to Doxey Wilkerson — both of whom were cited as "Communists" by Gerda Koch at the 1965 trial — but he did not know much about either of these men in 1940. Wilkerson did not bother to come to the office very often and when September arrived he turned in a brief fragment of what he had been employed by Myrdal to produce. Bunche produced full, brilliant memoranda that proved very useful in subsequent work on *An American Dilemma*, but unfortunately these memoranda were never put into such shape that they could be published.

In Gerda Koch's libelous attacks on Rose in 1962 and 1963, she mentioned Myrdal, Bunche, and Du Bois as the "Communists" with whom Rose collaborated on *An American Dilemma*. If Rose knew little about Bunche in 1940, except that he was then a professor at Howard University and had been a football player when a student at the University of California at Los Angeles in the 1920's, he learned much about Bunche later. Ralph Bunche joined the Office of Strategic Services after the United States entered World War II, and served effectively there and later in the United States State Department, where he rose to high rank. In the late

1940's he joined the United Nations as executive secretary of the Trusteeship Council. In this capacity he became the U.N. mediator who settled the Arab-Israel war of 1948 — for which he was awarded the Nobel Peace Prize. Later he was appointed Undersecretary General of the United Nations, the highest staff position which any American has held in that international body. In 1963, at the time he was being labeled a Communist by Gerda Koch, President Kennedy selected him as one of a very limited number of persons to receive the highest American medal of honor that could be given to a civilian. Kennedy was assassinated just as the award was announced, and President Johnson personally made the award to Bunche. Between 1940 and 1963, Rose met Bunche on four or five occasions to renew a friendly but minor relationship.

W. E. B. Du Bois was in no way associated with the Myrdal research project, and Rose never met him. In the late 1930's he was perhaps the most distinguished Negro in the United States and an acknowledged leader of the civil rights movement. He was a renowned scholar, the first Negro to obtain the Ph.D. degree from Harvard University, and a former professor at Atlanta University; it was in this capacity that Myrdal had asked him in 1939 to comment on the research plans for the Negro study, and Du Bois' name appears in the "Author's Preface" to *An American Dilemma* in acknowledgment of his reply. Du Bois' career had had nothing to do with Communism; in fact, all through the 1930's and 1940's Du Bois had worked with the National Association for the Advancement of Colored People in its strong attack on Communism for attempting to subvert the civil rights movement. But in the 1950's, when Du Bois was about eighty-five years of age, newspapers published accounts of his participation in certain Communist activities. Some years later, when Du Bois was ninety-three, he publicly announced that he was joining the Communist party, and he exiled himself to Ghana (where he died at ninety-five in 1963). Rose testified from his secondhand knowledge of Du Bois at the trial (see Chapter 8).

Rose never met Doxey Wilkerson after his momentary encounter with him in 1940, but heard — sometime in late 1941 or in 1942, probably through some Negro acquaintance — that he had become a Communist; there were newspaper reports to this effect in 1943. Later Wilkerson wrote the "Introduction" to a small book entitled *The Negro People in America*, published in 1946. This book was written by Herbert Aptheker, an acknowledged leading official of the American Communist party, and issued by International Publishers, a publishing house for radical books in New York City. The entire book was a denunciation of *An American Dilemma,* and indicated clearly what the real Communists thought of the Myrdal-Sterner-Rose book. In his "Introduction," Wilkerson speaks of "pseudo-scientific literature,"

and of this there is no more pretentious and dangerous an illustration than Dr. Gunnar Myrdal's two-volume, corporation-financed, so-called "monumental and definitive" study of the Negro in America, published under the highly revealing title, *An American Dilemma.*

This is the study which Aptheker here subjects to thorough and painstaking analysis and evaluation. With fine scholarship, brilliant Marxist insight, and (happily!) a strong sense of righteous indignation, he demonstrates conclusively that the philosophical premises of *An American Dilemma* are superficial and dishonest, its historiography distorted and false, its ethics vicious, and its analysis of the Negro question, "weak, mystical, and dangerous." [8]

In attacking Rose in 1962 and 1963, Gerda Koch made no mention of Doxey Wilkerson, and it is possible that she might never have known that Wilkerson was the one person who became a Communist after having earlier been associated with Myrdal if Rose had not mentioned his name in his sworn deposition on May 16, 1964, in response to attorney Daly's question whether Rose had been "aware that any of the people listed in the preface of your book belonged to Communist organizations or fronts." In the trial, Newhall stressed that the Communist party — including Doxey Wilkerson — denounced *An American Dilemma,* whereas Daly was claiming that the Communist party "adopted and praised" the book. Rose has no knowledge of whether Wilkerson continued to be a Communist in later years, and so indicated in his deposition.

Of course, Doxey Wilkerson never wrote any portion of *An American Dilemma,* nor was his unsatisfactory manuscript cited more than a few times (for some statistics) in the book. It was difficult for Rose to make clear to Daly that none of the persons listed in the "Author's Preface," except Myrdal, Sterner, and Rose, wrote *An American Dilemma.* Myrdal states this in his preface (page xv):

The second stage of the study began when I returned to America on March 6, 1941. In writing the present book, which has been produced during this second stage, I have utilized the unpublished manuscripts, prepared for the study during its first stage, in the same manner as I have used the printed literature. . . . In September, 1941, I was joined by Richard

Sterner and Arnold Rose, whose names rightly appear on the title page as assistants.

When Myrdal returned to Sweden in May 1940, most of his associates said he was running away from his big task of writing a book. At that time Rose had not read anything of Myrdal's earlier writings, except the typescript of the plan for the Negro study, and after he joined the office staff in June 1940 he was inclined to accept the generally unfavorable image of the man that prevailed there.[9] When Myrdal returned to the United States in March 1941, after reading all of the memoranda that had been prepared during his absence, he went to Chicago to consult with Stouffer, who had wound up the business of the New York office. For the writing of the book later titled *An American Dilemma*, Myrdal was allowed by the Carnegie Corporation to hire only one assistant and a secretary. He had apparently been favorably impressed with Rose's memoranda prepared during the summer of 1940, and Stouffer strongly recommended Rose to Myrdal. So Myrdal offered to employ Rose as assistant and Stouffer's secretary, Miss Ruth Moulik, as his own secretary. By this time, Rose had completed his preliminary examinations for the Ph.D. degree but was bogged down in his effort to gather data for a thesis. On the advice of Professors Stouffer, Louis Wirth, and Everett Hughes, Rose accepted Myrdal's offer, at the then-munificent salary of $4000 a year.

When he joined Myrdal in late August 1941, he found that Myrdal had employed the intervening months in reading some of the published and unpublished literature on the Negro problem, and had not written any of the proposed book. Carrying over the negative attitudes toward Myrdal that he had picked up from the office staff in 1940, Rose was prepared to be critical of Myrdal. But he made a number of discoveries: Myrdal accepted Rose's criticism with good grace and was receptive to many of his ideas even though Rose was only half Myrdal's age and much less experienced. Moreover, Myrdal was a genius, with brilliant insights into human behavior and American society, and his knowledge was worldwide, so their frequent discussions became a tremendous educational experience for Rose. There developed a friendship between the two men, which continued through the subsequent decades, although they never worked together again after 1942.

Richard Sterner, Myrdal's long-time friend and the associate he had brought with him from Sweden in 1938, was now working for the State of Virginia Planning Commission, although still trying to complete in his spare time a monograph of his own on benefits to the Negro from welfare programs.[10] Since it now appeared that the Nazis were unlikely to invade Sweden, he had decided to return to his home country with his Jewish wife. But Myrdal persuaded Mr. Keppel to allow him to rehire Sterner so the latter might assist him on *An American Dilemma* as well as finish up his own monograph. The Sterners therefore joined the little team of Myrdal, Moulik, and Rose shortly after they moved to Princeton, New Jersey, about October 1, 1941.[11] That winter Myrdal arranged to have his wife, Alva, come from Sweden and join the group at Princeton, although Mrs. Myrdal had no connection with the Negro study and devoted her working time to writing her own significant book, *Nation and Family*,[12] a report on the Swedish welfare and population program. Rose had gotten to know Sterner in his earlier work on the Negro study in 1940, and now in 1941 and 1942 they also became close friends.

The three men were very different: Myrdal was a brilliant cosmopolitan, constantly erupting with ideas and speculations, manifesting a self-assurance that made him seem arrogant to those who did not know him well. His optimistic exuberance made him seem very unlike the stereotype of a Swede, although he always tempered it with a willingness to modify his ideas in the light of facts provided by others. He loved debate and welcomed criticism; he must have been a wonderful teacher and senator, although one can see how such a personality might get into difficulties in an administrative post if he had no subordinate who would criticize him. Sterner was quite different: He was a careful statistician and precise economist, who would never stray beyond the facts. While he also had strong enthusiasms, he insisted on keeping close to social reality in a way that sometimes made him seem cynical or pessimistic. He would have made a superb administrator, but he devoted most of his working life to research. Rose was somewhere between the two: While trained to be cautious about facts, he was also attracted by ranging speculation. His main difference from the others was that he was a sociologist, rather than an economist (although he had also done all the work for his bachelor's degree in economics at the University of Chicago), and the study at hand was primarily a sociological study. Myrdal described their work together in his preface (page xvi):

About the contributions of both Sterner and Rose I want to add the following. The size of the book, and still more the scope of the problems involved, will make it understandable even to the reader who is not himself

31

familiar with many of the specific fields, that the work done has been immense. We have had to dig deep into primary sources in many fields of social science and a major part of this digging has been done by them. The collaboration, which stretched ruthlessly over evenings and weekends, has been a sheer pleasure to me, as I have felt more than I have ever experienced before the stimulation of an ideal cooperation where we not only added together the results of our labor but imagined that we in our concerted endeavors sometimes reached higher than an arithmetical sum. A similar outlook on the methodological problems of social science and a mutually shared scientific curiosity in seeing our structure of hypothesis, data, and conclusion rise, have given to our collaboration a spirit of intellectual exploration which I will not soon forget.

The work progressed rapidly, and in September 1942 the Myrdals and Sterners departed for other tasks in Sweden, leaving Rose to finish up the book. This meant writing Chapters 43 and 44, on the Negro community and culture, and much of Appendix 10 on "Quantitative Studies of Race Attitudes." It also meant completing the editing, gap-filling, and revision, for which he had assumed responsibility throughout. Of Rose's editing, Myrdal wrote in the preface (page xvi):

His editing work has included much more than polishing the English. It has, rather, been a most conscientious checking of basic data as well as of inferences, and a critical consideration of arrangement, viewpoints and conclusions. Both his criticisms and suggestions have, with few exceptions, led to changes in the final manuscript, and many of these changes are important. His wide knowledge of the social science literature and his sound judgment on methodological problems have, in this critical work, been significant.

Quoting this, Daly charged at the trial that Rose was the "real author" of *An American Dilemma.* The reader can judge that Rose's work with Myrdal and Sterner was a most valuable and exciting experience for him.

Working with the assistance of Caroline Baer, who shortly afterward became his wife, Rose completed the manuscript for *An American Dilemma* in January 1943. They worked in an office in New York City which was a replica of that once used by Andrew Carnegie, sitting at the great entrepreneur's own desk, and under the eye of an official painting of that Calvinist. For some time, Rose had had an invitation to rejoin Professor Samuel Stouffer, who was directing — out of the Pentagon in Washington — the United States Army's research on morale and soldiers' problems, and he now accepted it. While employed at this task through 1943, Rose did the proofreading on *An American Dilemma.*

32

"America's Single Most Important Domestic Problem"

Most of the reviews of *An American Dilemma* were favorable, although some readers were shocked by the evidence of oppression of the Negro. Only the overt racists and the Communists wrote strongly unfavorable reviews. Some of the sociologists expressed doubts about the open espousal in the book of value premises from the American Creed, such as liberty, equality, and justice. Social scientists were not supposed to have values, but Myrdal led the way in getting them to see that they should make their values explicit and show how these might color the selection and organization of facts, for the values would be there nevertheless and, by remaining hidden, would bias the research.[13] While there had been scholarly studies of race relations published before *An American Dilemma*, the subject had seldom been treated as a social problem before. It had been something to describe, as an anthropologist describes the marriage customs of a primitive society. Many sociological experts on the Negro did not like this innovation in the book. They also did not like the interpretation of the Negro problem as a "moral dilemma" — ideological factors seemed so softheaded — and this aspect of the study remains misunderstood to the present day.[14]

But it could not be denied that the work was one of comprehensive scholarship; it reported facts carefully, and it dealt with vital issues and theories. So the book was widely read, despite its length and ponderosity. More important, the book had an effect. Many people who were in decision-making positions read it, or portions of it, or one of its several condensations.[15] If the sociologists doubted whether there was really an ideological American dilemma, most of the readers recognized their personal dilemma regarding the Negro and their own democratic ideology while reading the book. Thus, it was no accident that the Supreme Court should refer to *An American Dilemma* in its epoch-making decision on May 17, 1954, and that Senator Eastland should choose an attack on the book as his means of encouraging resistance against the civil rights movement and the Supreme Court decisions. And it was historically appropriate that the right-wing extremists — as part of their major effort to identify liberalism as Communism — should use *An American Dilemma* to libel its authors.

Whether the Negro in the United States is to be given his constitutional rights and treated as a full member of American society remains a question today. The book gives the fullest recognition to the economic, political, and social structural forces affecting the answer to that question, but it further recognizes that the decision is being made in the mind of every

American, white or Negro. Myrdal and Sterner made up their minds personally, but they are Swedish citizens living in Sweden, so the decision is not one of great consequence for them. Arnold Rose is an American citizen, living in the United States, and he long ago decided that he would do what he could to induce his countrymen, white and Negro, to accept the Negro as an American in every sense of the term. He would recognize that different strategies might appropriately be chosen to effect different aspects of this goal under varying circumstances, but he could never accept any compromise on the goal itself.

Gerda Koch chose better than she knew when she decided to attack Arnold Rose. For her kind — the right-wing extremists, those who would subvert American institutions in the name of fundamentalist religion and political authoritarianism — Rose was an enemy. Rose had abhorred Communism — its political dictatorship, its concentration of the economic tools of production in the state, its ideological absolutism — all his life. But Gerda Koch and her associates paid no attention to Rose's opinions on these matters. They were opposed to Rose because he was an intellectual teaching at a university, a liberal member of a state legislature, a Jew, a person who explicitly favored social justice for the Negro and others deprived of the full opportunities available in American society, and one who explicitly condemned their authoritarian approach to religion and politics. So Gerda Koch chose to make the worst accusations against Rose she could think of — she called him a Communist collaborator and a "security risk." And when he realized that the Minneapolis newspapers were making Gerda Koch's words dangerous to the university and to humane legislation in his state, Arnold Rose struck back by suing Gerda Koch for libel. The contest was — in miniature — an expression of the American dilemma: the aspirations toward democracy versus the practiced resistances against democracy.

3

The Right-Wing Extremists

An Upper Midwest variation

GERDA KOCH and her attorney, Jerome Daly, are what are called, in this book, "right-wing extremists." Other writers have used such equivalent terms as "members of the radical right" or the "revolutionary right," "new conservatives," and "pseudo-conservatives" to categorize them. Senator Barry Goldwater, the nominal current leader for most of them, seemed to have accepted the appellation "right-wing extremists" for this segment of his followers in his famous speech accepting the nomination for the presidency at the Republican National Convention on July 17, 1964.[1]

This chapter is about the political and social movement of right-wing extremism, but not everything in it applies to Gerda Koch or Jerome Daly or any other individual who can be categorized as a right-wing extremist. There is considerable variation in the movement, and the various subgroups do not agree with each other on many matters. Miss Koch and Daly will be personally described in Chapters 8 and 9, but there is much about them which the author does not know. Miss Koch is director of only one subgroup, local to Minnesota, called "Christian Research," and she testified that she was the regular distributor for the publications of a dozen other groups that have their headquarters outside of Minnesota. Her testimony at the trial indicated that she was more or less in agreement with these groups, but there are about a hundred additional groups operating throughout the United States which may be called "right-wing extremist" that she may or may not be in agreement with. This chapter will attempt to characterize what is common to most of them and note some of their major variations.

35

There are some common mis-impressions of what right-wing extremism is. It is not a new movement. The historian Richard Hofstadter [2] traces it back to the earliest days of the American Republic, and parallel movements are to be found in many other countries besides the United States. Its history in this country includes the Know-Nothing party in the 1850's, the American Protective Association (anti-Catholic) and the Greenback party in the 1880's, large segments of the Populist movement of the 1890's and of its various successors, the Ku Klux Klan after 1915, the Social Justice movement of Father Coughlin in the 1930's, the hundred or so organizations developed in the 1930's in sympathy with the German National Socialist party, and the Joe McCarthy phenomenon of the 1950's. The movement has had its ups and downs: The present period — beginning in 1961 — is one of the strongest in its history. Not only does it have a significant number of active adherents — estimates range between 2 and 15 per cent of the adult population [3] — but it is better organized than it has ever been before. Since 1964 it has had control of the majority of the Republican party's state organizations, and it would have dominated a Republican National Convention if one had been called in 1965 or 1966, just as it dominated the 1964 convention. This does not mean that all right-wing extremists support or vote for Republican candidates. A significant minority vote for Democratic party candidates, particularly in the southern states; in New York there is a separate Conservative party, in South Dakota the Christian Coalition party, in several parts of the South the States' Rights party, in Indiana and elsewhere the Constitution party; and in other parts of the nation there are other small "third parties" which are right-wing extremist.

Right-wing extremism is not to be thought of solely as a political movement, although this is its dominant expression and the political aspect of it will get particular attention in this book. It is closely associated with religious "fundamentalism" of both the Protestant and Roman Catholic varieties.[4] A considerable number of the leaders of right-wing extremism are Protestant fundamentalist ministers — notably Billy James Hargis, Carl McIntire, and Fred C. Schwarz.[5] The Christian fundamentalist leaders of right-wing extremism often claim their religion as justification for their political and economic doctrines. For example, a pamphlet distributed by Christian Research, and published by the American Council of Christian Laymen, states: "Joseph and Son [that is, Jesus] were entrepreneurs, what Karl Marx would call petit-bourgeoisie. The father and son fixed their prices in competition, low bidder to win. They bought lumber and findings from the caravans, from the hardest and shrewdest of traders, who would do them out of their eye-teeth unless themselves were equally hard and shrewd." [6] This does not mean that every right-wing extremist is a fundamentalist — some are atheists, some belong to the regular denominations of Protestantism, Catholicism, and Judaism. Nor does it mean that every religious fundamentalist is a right-wing extremist; some fundamentalists are also liberal or conservative in politics. Further, right-wing extremists are to be found in certain "reform" movements that have little to do with politics or religion — such as some parts of the segregationist movement in the southern states and the anti-fluoridation movement in several American cities.

The final term in our list of characterizations of what right-wing extremism is *not*, but which it is popularly thought to be, is anti-Communist. Communism, of course, did not exist when the earlier historical manifestations of right-wing extremism developed. It could be said that almost no right-wing extremists were aware of Communism before the 1920's, and they did not choose Communism as their leading verbal target until the 1950's. But even in the 1950's and the 1960's, Communism has only been a verbal target for the right-wing extremists — a popular label for what they are really against. As Gerda Koch said in her sworn deposition, while answering a question about her opinion concerning the Council on Foreign Relations: "Communism itself is a front really for the ones that are causing the trouble." Their real target has always been the established leadership and organizations of the United States, whether liberal or conservative. Occasionally they have joined up in support of a Democrat like William Jennings Bryan, or in support of a "liberal" economic measure such as price supports for farm products. More frequently they have joined up in support of a Republican like Robert Taft, or in support of a "conservative" economic measure such as the "balanced" budget. But most often they have been against the dominant leaders of both political parties, and against the domestic measures favored by either of them. Some students have claimed that the "softness on Communism" of some of the liberal New Dealers stimulated the right-wing extremists to their attacks on them. This is highly doubtful: The attacks on the New Dealers were not because of their leftism, not even because of their economic liberalism (many of the right-wing extremists tended to favor some of the welfare and price-support measures that were inaugurated by the New

37

Deal), but because of their high level of education and their power in government.

On many issues the right-wing extremists have positions strangely parallel to those of the Communists. On most foreign policy issues today, the two extremes are in substantial agreement: Both right-wing extremists and Communists today are against American military or economic involvement in Asia, Africa, and Europe (the Communists would also have the United States abandon its commitments to Latin America, but the right-wing extremists usually favor our military involvements there). Both left and right extremists agree that there is a conspiratorial "power elite" — led by bankers and industrialists in the eastern states — in secret control of the United States. Even Barry Goldwater — who has been on the fringes, not in the center, of right-wing extremism — has denounced the domination of "the eastern money interests, the large banks, the financial houses" of Wall Street. These are almost the same terms used by Communists and Trotskyists. In their various attacks on alleged "Communists," right-wing extremists very rarely mention the names of any Communists. They will, of course, denounce Marx and Lenin, but these men are safely dead, and their chief fault seems to have been that they were atheists. They will also denounce Alger Hiss and Harry Dexter White, but one of these is dead and the other apparently does not now have an active functioning role in the Communist apparatus, and their chief fault according to the extremists is that they were highly educated and once worked for the State Department (the extremists do not distinguish between these two and the conservatives Dean Acheson and John Foster Dulles, who were also educated men and of the State Department "establishment"). The names of active leaders of the Communist party — Kosygin, Gomulka, Aptheker, to give three top examples from three different countries — are practically unknown in the statements of the right-wing extremists. Senator Joseph Mc-Carthy used to flourish papers on which he said were lists of names of Communists in the United States government, but he never mentioned a single name.[7] Senator James Eastland has been more willing to mention names of alleged Communists — when he speaks with immunity from libel suits in the United States Senate — but the names he mentions are simply those who have been accused by volunteer witnesses before his Senate Subcommittee on Internal Security, and against whom no evidence is formally presented that they are Communists. Most of the right-wing extremists today label as "Communists" those who are actually anti-Communist liberals and some who are anti-Communist conservatives. They, like the Communists, are primarily "anti-establishment."

The observations above should not be taken to mean that the right-wing extremists are pro-Communist, but rather that they are not particularly concerned with Communists as an effective threat to their own values. The only help the right extremists give the left extremists is accidental: They camouflage the real Communists by denouncing everyone they disagree with strongly as "Communists"; and like many other groups in the society they occasionally favor a stand on an issue which is the same as that favored by the Communists. They find it expedient in these days of cold and hot war with Communist-dominated nations to call their enemies "Communists." In this respect, the right-wing extremists are eminently rational.

In most other respects, the right-wing extremists are highly irrational. They have a belief system which scarcely coordinates with the known facts about the real social world. They differ among themselves about who the "chief enemy of the American people" really is, but in nearly all cases it is a most unlikely "enemy": the Federal Reserve Banks, the national trade union leaders, the Jews,[8] the general staff of the military services, "Wall Street," the President of the United States.[9] Sometimes these are grouped together and called a "conspiracy," and in all cases the conspirators are said to operate secretly in devious ways to work against the American people. A President or a governor has great powers to work for good or for evil, but why he should choose fluoridation of the water, or raising the income tax, as his chief secret tool for destroying the American people is never rationally explained. This "paranoid style" in the speeches and writings of the right-wing extremists (to use Richard Hofstadter's phrase) is an exact parallel to the "Newspeak" in the speeches and writings of the Communists (to use George Orwell's phrase). Both extremist groups are likely to explain the evils and problems of the world as due to the actions of deliberate and self-seeking conspirators who use insidious and fiendish techniques. The distinctive language and conspiratorial world-views of both groups of extremists indicate that both are living in mental worlds that deviate sharply from the world of the majority of the population. They have a deviant subculture, which needs to be studied in sociological terms, as well as in the terms in which extremists are usually studied — as a historical development or as a political movement.

Another irrationality of the right-wing extremist is to make what is really complex seem simple, and what is really simple seem complex.[10] The great complexities of international relations will be portrayed as merely a struggle between Communism and free enterprise and readily solvable by a strong military posture. The complexities of government finance will be portrayed simply as a plot of the rich to steal money from the poor, and readily solvable by the government's creating "cheap money" and credit. On the other hand, all sorts of nuances and hidden meanings will be found in the fluoridation of water, in Jewish religious ceremonies, or in rock-and-roll music. Their achievements with the latter indicate that there is no lack of imagination among the right-wing extremists.

This passion for rhetoric, for fighting their enemies with words, has been one of the non-rationalities of extremist movements in their early stages. But, as earlier in Russia and Germany, the extremist movement has discovered the rational basis of real power in the United States: political and para-military organization. Once discovered, the techniques of organization are ingeniously developed and manipulated by extremist leaders. Their rank-and-file followers prove to be devoted and hard-working soldiers in the cause. Because of widespread apathy, laissez-faire philosophy, and gentlemanliness in politics among the majority in most democratic countries, extremists often prove themselves unusually adept in seizing political power once they discover the techniques of organization. In all countries where Communists rule today, political power has been seized by small minorities. The fascists seized political power in Italy, Germany, and Spain without a majority. Extremist groups throughout the history of the United States have been poorly organized and ineptly led. Since 1961 they have learned the techniques of political organization (partly they have learned them from the Communists in their use of "cells," para-military activities, and infiltration), and already they have seized control of the Republican party in the majority of states.[11]

They still lack able and fully committed top leaders. Some of the second-string leaders have considerable organizing ability and are fully committed, but are not well known enough to gain any but local attention. Others among the secondary leaders are opportunists who are in the movement for personal financial gain and have little sense of commitment; still others are emotionally unbalanced and hence cannot be counted on for sustained organizational leadership. There is a rivalry and suspicion characteristic of the right-wing movement which makes it unusually difficult for secondary leaders to rise to the top. The only national leaders in recent years who have surmounted the subgroup rivalries have been Senator Joseph McCarthy, who had little interest in organization, and Senator Barry Goldwater, about whom there is some question of deep and exclusive commitment to the revolutionary cause. The next national leader to emerge may not have these weaknesses. (A likely prospect for national leadership at the time of writing is movie actor Ronald Reagan, elected governor of California in 1966. He seems to have qualities his predecessors lacked in one measure or another.)

In one sense, the right-wing extremists' claim to be called "conservative" is justified. They would like to return the country to something like what it was supposed to be in the early nineteenth century, with its lack of involvement in foreign affairs, its lack of controls on free enterprise, the absence of the income tax, its rural social structure, the relative absence of immigrants from South and East Europe, its "benevolent" enslavement of Negroes, its strong emphasis on states rights in government, etc. But there is a lack of realism about this ideal in at least two respects, which destroy the claim to "conservatism": (1) The supposedly admired leaders of the early nineteenth century were either radicals like Jefferson and Jackson or forward-looking and responsible conservatives like Adams and Hamilton. The true conservative heritage of America has always been a liberal one; the authoritarian qualities of the contemporary right-wing extremists are partly drawn from an alien European tradition of absolute monarchism and fascism.[12] (2) Society has become urbanized and industrialized since the early nineteenth century and hence can support one hundred times the population of that period; it would be necessary to kill off about 95 per cent of the American people to restore an agricultural society — which no doubt many of the right-wing extremists would like to do, but for which they are unlikely to get much support. Further, it is unlikely that such a society could survive external Communist aggression.

The heritage of right-wing extremism in America is revolutionary, not conservative. Its political philosophy is that, on the one hand, of the European writers about elitism, racism, and *ressentiment* (resentment), Nietzsche and Gobineau, and, on the other hand, of the American activists against the federal government, Jacob Coxey and Ignatius Donnelly and "Coin" Harvey.[13] Even though some of its contemporary exponents have grown wealthy, through the advantages of American prosperity, their identifications are "old" middle class and rural. They resent the rise of the "new" middle class — of children of immigrants and of other ethnic minorities. Their nonpolitical affiliations are with the nondenomination-alized religious sects, with certain agricultural organizations and certain businessmen's organizations that are opposed to the established leader-ship in those branches of economic activity. They help support only a few intellectuals, like Russell Kirk, Clarence Manion, and William Buckley, but all seem to be fascinated by pseudo-scientific "research." They like to maintain files, to chart trends buttressed by mystical lines, to use exten-sive footnoting and bibliographies in their publications, and to report pre-cise statistics such as "The Eisenhower administration was 50 to 70 per cent Communist."

Despite the historical traditions of right-wing extremism in certain rural nineteenth-century movements, there is a certain "rootlessness" about it. The most obvious explanation of this is that the extremists have not grown with the country. While many have personally benefited from social changes, they oppose change unless it can be revolutionary in character. This they also share with the Communists, for whom all "reforms" are meaningless unless they can forthwith bring their Utopia. Their politics are those of frustration and resentment against the established order, and of unrest in the face of orderly change.

What the right wing is fighting, in the shadow of Communism, is es-sentially "modernity" — that complex of attitudes that might be defined most simply as the belief in rational assessment, rather than established custom, for the evaluation of social change — and what it seeks to defend is its fading dominance, exercised once through the institutions of small-town America, over the control of social change.[14]

Their interpretation of orderly change is solely that it represents the break-down of "moral fiber" in the United States. This was, for example, the chief "issue" for Goldwater in his campaign for the presidency in 1964.

The extremists' attitude toward change probably provides the best clue about the sources of the movement. It is a result of the inability to under-stand social change and a feeling that change has dispossessed them, that "America has been largely taken away from them and their kind, though they are determined to try to repossess it and to prevent the final destruc-tive act of subversion." [15] The latter refers to the "gigantic Communist conspiracy" or some other "conspiracy" which is about to take over the country. This interpretation of history as a gigantic conspiracy is central to all right-wing extremist thought: "History *is* a conspiracy, set in motion by demonic forces of almost transcendent power, and what is felt to be needed to defeat it is not the usual methods of political give-and-take, but an all-out crusade."[16] The extremist's reasoning is circular, and hence all events — including successes — leave him dissatisfied:

Nothing but complete victory will do. Since the enemy is thought of as being totally evil and totally unappeasable, he must be totally eliminated . . . This demand for unqualified victories leads to the formulation of hopelessly demanding and unrealistic goals, and since these goals are not even remotely attainable, failure constantly heightens the paranoid's frustration. Even partial success leaves him with the same sense of powerlessness with which he began, and this in turn only strengthens his awareness of the vast and terrifying quality of the enemy he opposes.[17]

Historical change, then, motivates the right-wing extremist, and rapid change involving a conflict of basic values creates the wave in which the extremist surges to the forefront of public activity.

. . . the fact that movements employing the paranoid style are not constant but come in successive episodic waves suggests that the paranoid disposition is mobilized into action chiefly by social conflicts that involve ultimate schemes of values and that bring fundamental fears and hatreds, rather than negotiable interests, into political action. Catastrophe or the fear of catastrophe is most likely to elicit the syndrome of paranoid rhetoric.[18]

The American right-wing extremist movement of the 1960's is not only a specific movement, in which certain organizations can be classified and for which a history can be traced. It is also an expression of a type of political thought, which is also formed in cultural traditions other than the American one. This has been called the conspiratorial mode of thought. It consists of a tendency to assume that public events are to be explained in terms of deliberate and organized plots by individuals who have something to gain through such plots, usually at the expense of the public. While the conspiratorial mode of thought is probably indulged in by most people at one time or another, it is much more regularly found among both left- and right-wing extremists than among others, probably because a belief in the existence of a nest of dangerous plotters naturally leads one to advocate extreme political action and, circularly, a tendency to favor extreme political action encourages the assumption that there are evil people against whom the action should be taken.

Of course, political plots and conspiracies do actually exist, more frequently in some countries and times than in others, and rational political thought must always include the possibility of conspiracy in attempting to explain public events. But the conspiratorial mode of thought assumes the existence of plots when there is no evidence of them and when alternative causal explanations are not only plausible and empirically supported but even quite obvious. A degree of personal alienation from other people, which hinders communication of various facts that contribute toward explanations of public events, encourages the conspiratorial mode of thought. For example, those who do not understand how democratic political parties function, and this includes a large proportion of Americans regardless of educational level, will be inclined to explain the many public events which political parties influence in terms of undemocratic conspiracies. While ignorance and alienation alone can probably explain the conspiratorial theory indulged in by those who resort to it occasionally, they cannot explain the persistent use of the conspiratorial mode of thought, because this is indulged in by those who sometimes or often have all the essential facts. The facts are twisted and misinterpreted — in almost a paranoid fashion, as Richard Hofstadter points out — and there must be some reason for this. It does not do to say that the reason is mental illness or psychic disturbance, which is a danger when the word "paranoid" is used, because those who persistently use the conspiratorial mode of thought in explaining public events are usually as rational as anyone else in carrying on their personal lives. Some of them are even creative people, as exemplified by Barbara Garson, the author of the play *MacBird*, a radical leftist conspiratorial "explanation" of the assassination of President Kennedy as an event engineered by Vice President Johnson. It is far more imaginative and artistically expressed — but no better grounded in evidence — than the explanation which emerged from the defendant's attorney in the trial of *Rose v. Koch*, that the assassination was the result of a plot organized jointly by the Federal Reserve Banks, the Council on Foreign Relations, and Arnold Rose.

Two types of explanations can be offered about those who persistently use the conspiratorial mode of thought to explain public events. One may be stated in terms of status mobility: It has been hypothesized that those who are rapidly changing their position in the social structure have a great personal need to explain in drastic terms the drastically "changing" world about them (that is, it appears to be drastically changing to them largely because their own position is moving rapidly). On the one hand, there are those who are downwardly mobile, and need the concept of a conspiracy to explain the untoward and disagreeable events associated with loss of social status, including wealth and prestige. On the other hand, there are those who have suddenly become wealthy, but are equally bewildered by the new aspects of the social world about them. Only something like a conspiracy is large and dramatic enough to explain the manifold changes or "events" which need explanation, including a reason for the former social submergence of these people.

A second hypothesis offered to explain the persistent conspiratorial mode of thought arises from the existence of subcultures. Groups form among those who tend to favor extreme political action of one sort or another, and through their interactions and their internal group pressures, they tend to accept only extremist explanations of events. He who can contribute a bizarre conspiratorial explanation of a recent and public event is hailed by the group, because the explanation is in accord with the group's goal of extreme political action, while a member who offers a common-sense explanation of the same event is either ignored or laughed out of the group (temporarily until he conforms to the conspiratorial explanation, or permanently and literally out). All groups in a society have subcultures, and the content of the subculture of extremist political groups largely consists of conspiratorial explanations of events centered around a basic dogma concerning the nature of history and social structure.

Probably there is some truth in both hypotheses, and logically there is no opposition between them. Rapid status mobility, possibly coupled with the alienation mentioned earlier, could attract members to the extremist political groups which then rapidly build a subculture which does not tolerate any but conspiratorial explanations of public events. When persons who have the conspiratorial mode of thought are found outside these groups, they are either unwitting candidates for membership, recent rejects from the groups, or so alienated from everyone in the society that they cannot establish enough contact to get into a group where they would find others with congenial viewpoints. This combination of hypotheses, while certainly not proved, would logically suffice to explain the existence of a persistent conspiratorial mode of thought, concentrated mainly in certain groups and at certain periods of history. These hypotheses also can be used to explain the similarity in the modes of thought among right-wing and left-wing political extremists, despite the difference in the specific content of their thought.

So much for what is common to most right-wing extremists. There are also marked variations among them. While most think of themselves as being American as apple pie, others consciously follow European movements, like the American Nazi party of George Lincoln Rockwell. While most are ill-educated, despite their pretensions to scholarship, some are educated and even intellectual, like modified extremists Russell Kirk, Clarence Manion, and William Buckley (Goldwater has usually tried to identify himself with this segment). While most are lower class either in present fact or in immediate antecedents, a few have upper-class backgrounds or connections, like Archibald Roosevelt or General Edwin Walker.[19] Some are persons of great wealth — *nouveaux riches* — who support much of the propaganda and organizational activities of their fellow extremists like H. L. Hunt. A significant number of the larger industrialists of the United States are supporting one or another right-wing extremist organization.[20] In other words, there are many kinds and degrees of right-wing extremism.

Among the important variations of right-wing extremism are regional ones. Right-wing extremism is particularly strong in the Southwest (California, Arizona, and Texas) where it seems to be most closely associated with the social disorientation caused by rapid migration and status mobility, and in the old South (the Alabama of George Wallace, the South Carolina of Strom Thurmond, the Mississippi of Byron de la Beckwith, the Louisiana of Leander Perez) where it seems to be associated with the effort to maintain an older way of life. Right-wing extremism is no longer particularly strong in the Upper Midwest (that is, Wisconsin, Minnesota, North and South Dakota, and eastern Montana and Wyoming), but it was from about 1890 to about 1948 a major center of right-wing extremism, and remnants of the older movement have lingered into the new era and have merged with contemporary forms. The older movement started with Populism, but its forms in the Upper Midwest were somewhat different from the then equally strong movement in the South and the Lower Midwest. The Upper Midwest movement later took on an affinity for European fascism [21] that was not so true in other sections of the country. Some degree of sympathy with the German Nazis was openly expressed by Senator Ernest Lundeen of Minnesota; Charles A. Lindbergh, Jr., son of Congressman Lindbergh of Minnesota; and Congressman William Lemke of North Dakota, presidential candidate in 1936 for Father Coughlin and Gerald L. K. Smith's Union party. Many other leading politicians of the area were part of the extremist movement in some degree and without expressing sympathy for European fascism: Senator Burton K. Wheeler of Montana and Senator Gerald P. Nye, Representative Usher L. Burdick, and Senator William Langer of North Dakota were the best known. Its early philosopher was Ignatius Donnelly of Minnesota, and its latter-day inheritor was Senator Joseph McCarthy of Wisconsin.

The general theme expressed by most of those who were the articulate spokesmen of the movement — despite individual variations — was that there was an international conspiracy, led by Jews and international bankers and later by Communists, to seize control of the world. The American leadership for this conspiracy was centered in Wall Street, where Jewish bankers, munitions industrialists, and socialists conspired together to exploit the farmers and workers. Their fulcrums of power were the Federal Reserve Banks, private large banking firms, and the State and Treasury departments. The political means of opposing these evil powers were isolationism in foreign policy, "cheap money" as a fiscal policy, abandonment of the income tax, price supports for agricultural products, and various social welfare measures to protect the working classes. That this may seem to be a strange combination to most students of politics reflects the fact that our leading political scientists have concentrated on analysis of "rational interest" politics rather than on analysis of symbolic and "status politics." [22] There were variations among these extremists: For example, those from the Dakotas and Montana found much evil in the "big cities" of Minneapolis and St. Paul, whereas the inhabitants of those cities found evil concentrated in New York and Washington. The Protestants among the Upper Midwest extremists often included the Pope as an international conspirator, but the Catholics — concentrated in Wisconsin and southern Minnesota — definitely did not. Those of Scandinavian descent often considered alcohol to be one of the tools used by the conspiracy to debauch the masses, but those of German descent usually did not think this. The trade unionists among the extremists could have only an uneasy coalition with the farmers among them. Some denounced capitalism along with Communism and socialism; others found the enemy only in the latter two. It was, and is today, a strange movement, but thoroughly indigenous to its American midwestern setting.

Numerous attempts have been made to explain the emergence of the pre-1948 protest movements in the Upper Midwest. Generally the explanations have been in terms of the difficult economic conditions imposed on the midwestern farmers during a particular phase of our national development. That is, these movements represented organized attempts on the part of the agricultural Midwest to wage a more effective battle against the urban East, which was presumed to be in control of the grain market, railroad rates, and bank credit. Evidence points to the fact that it was the wheat farmer who spearheaded these protest movements. S. M. Lipset has stated that "An examination of the electoral support of these agrarian movements reveals a consistent pattern. It was the economic and climatically vulnerable wheat belt that formed the backbone of all the protest movements, from the Independent parties of the 1870's down to the contemporary C.C.F. in Canada." [23] The wheat farmer was almost completely at the mercy of the prevailing price system; his life was one of "boom and bust." As such it was impossible to plan for the future or adjust the various community institutions to the impinging economic conditions. The fluctuating character of the wheat belt economy prevented the building of an integrated rural society. In relation to the total society these farmers continued to be a "marginal frontier group." They "developed attitudes characteristic of outcast groups, believing that they did not receive their just . . . share of the national wealth and culture. The cleavage that developed . . . between the economically dominant urban world and the insecure rural areas was sharpened by the fluctuations of the business cycle; and this encouraged conflict between the urban middle class and the farmers." [24]

Not only did the vagaries of the market create difficulties for the farmer, but its complexities were beyond his understanding. In the important realm of economics the traditional meanings and values of the farmer no longer applied. The old principles of a fair price and of business conducted along the lines of traditional ethics, were out of place in dealing with the city-oriented grain dealers, railroad agents, and bankers. As this continued, it engendered an aura of fear and mystery concerning, not only the machinations of certain businesses, but the city in general. The city virtually became "an object of dread and fascination." The city appeared unnatural, and a "plausible" interpretation of its strangeness was its domination by Jews, an urban people par excellence.[25] "They worshipped Mammon, not God." [26] William Jennings Bryan, the great Populist-Democratic leader, referred to the city as "Babylon the great, the mother of harlots and of the abominations of the earth . . . drunken with the blood of the saints, and the blood of the martyrs of Jesus." [27] Ignatius Donnelly, the leading Populist figure in Minnesota, wrote a utopian novel in which he envisioned an ideal society without cities. The fact that many people in the rural Midwest believed that "all trade is treachery" and served as a "manipulation of Satan" and would eventually "dominate all the people of the earth" made fertile ground for anti-Semitism as well as city hatred.[28] It was in the period preceding the turn of the century that the Jew as the urbanite became identified with finance, conspiracy, and the mystery of the city in general. Before this period, Jews had been stereotyped in much the same manner as other immigrant groups when they first arrived in this country.[29] Both Bryan and Donnelly harangued against Wall Street and the eastern bankers. In addition, they expressed some anti-Semitism coupled with a fear and hatred of the city. The attitudes they expressed are the antecedents of similar expressions made by later agrarian leaders like Lundeen and Lemke.

In many respects the midwestern farmers were a disappointed people. The economic and social instability that characterized their lives found expression in radical economics and attacks on the eastern urban world, to which they felt themselves in bondage. During the early periods of falling grain prices, organized groups emerged only to die within a short period of time. By 1920, however, some of the farmers had come to understand the basic processes and issues in the price and market economy.[30] They realized that cooperatives, on which they had pinned their hopes during the first decades of the twentieth century, could not cope with the problem. During the late 1920's the depressed rural groups began to concentrate their efforts on waging battle in the national and state legislatures by means of legislative pressure groups, farm blocs, and organized farm publics.

However, with the onslaught of the depression of the 1930's, Lundeen, Lemke, Burdick, Langer, Nye, and many others dusted off the old epithets and based their campaigns on condemnation of the "eastern bankers," "international cartels," and the British Empire. No new national political parties emerged, except for the ill-timed and ill-fated Union party. The election of 1932 had merged most of the dissident elements in the country into the powerful Roosevelt coalition.

Despite the aims of the New Deal, it failed to aid sufficiently the injured rural groups in the Midwest. The old insecurities remained, and the gulf between rural and urban worlds was unbridged. The conditions of midwestern agriculture had been essentially the same for decades, and this led to a re-emergence of the same old expressions of city hatred as well as to the phenomenon of the attachment of social-welfare-minded leaders to rightist or native fascist groups. When most of the problems of Upper Midwest farmers were solved by government price supports and migration, the old ideology lingered on and in the 1950's and 1960's brought support from that region for Joe McCarthy and Goldwater.

The general proposition can be maintained that the characteristics which emerged in the "liberal" right-wing extremist political movements in the rural Midwest were related to the social disorganization that resulted from the impact of the rapidly changing urban culture upon a rural culture.[31] The urbanization, industrialization, and secularization of America which took place at an ever-increasing tempo following the 1870's created a situation wherein the midwestern farmer suffered a loss of social solidarity. The primary factors resulting in disorganization were five:

1. Economic insecurity resulting from the impact of oscillating prices on a commercialized farm area.

2. Rural-to-urban migration resulting in a segmentalization of the rural family structure and the resultant discrepancy between the meanings and values of the young who went to the city and those of the parents who stayed on the farm.

3. The ineffectiveness of local and state governments as tools for alleviating injustices and economic hardship. This meant the necessity of dealing with a remote national government, incomprehensible and hence presumed to be untrustworthy.

4. The fact that a large portion of the population were immigrants who had left a peasant culture in Europe with traditions and values that were inapplicable to the economic and political forces which played on the new commercialized agricultural system.

5. The insecurities which beset the midwestern farmers from droughts, hail storms, and other destructive climatic forces. The insecurities thus created gave the individual farmer a sense of isolation and bewilderment in the face of the impersonal forces which appeared to be victimizing him. The popular theory of the "gigantic conspiracy" of bankers, Jews, Communists, government officials, was an effort at explanation — a response to the bewilderment. The discrepancy between the expectations, meanings, and values of the rural areas and those of the eastern urban areas led to the ascription of sinister and mysterious powers at first to the Jews and later to the substitute symbol of "eastern financier," or "international banker."

50

An Upper Midwest Variation

The profusion of cooperatives and other voluntary associations which arose in the rural areas seems to indicate that the new meanings imposed by the price and market regime were not being adequately dealt with. All the agrarian organizations were essentially concerned with exercising some kind of control over the marketing of produce and the borrowing of money. By and large their lack of success in meeting the problems of the farmers was due to the fact that the farmers' associations and protest groups did not become integrated into the over-all national power structure. The consistency of failure may well have contributed to a heightened sense of being manipulated by ominous forces symbolized as banks and trusts.

There were parallels in rural Germany in the 1920's, as Loomis and Beegle testify:

Elements of Nazism became entrenched among those rural, middle-class-controlled areas whose residents were suffering most acutely from economic insecurity and anxiety accompanying loss of social solidarity; individuals with limited experience and obligations as active members of dynamic large-scale political or religious social structures were more prone to become Nazis than others; and during the periods of rapid change, Nazism made its greatest inroads into the groups whose basic value orientation and organizational experience had been of a Gemeinschaft, primary, folk, or familistic nature and whose formal, contractual, bureaucratic obligations and affiliations had been insignificant. Due to their feelings of insecurity, frustration, and longing for the good old days, which resulted from secularization and depression, these groups were more apt to become Nazis than other groups.[32]

Loomis and Beegle also observed that opposition to control from the central government and the ethnocentrism of the folk society played into the hands of the Nazis.

Rudolf Heberle provides further evidence from Germany by quoting a newspaper article from the Dithmarschen area of Germany in 1931. The article made this declaration:

Our farms have dropped to about half the value they had last year because of the low prices of agricultural products and the increased burden of interest. Fifty per cent of the farmers have had to declare their insolvency. . . . The octopus arms of international finance capitalism are extended to us through all banks and savings banks. . . . Long enough we have dissipated our forces because we used to think of ourselves too much as kings on our farms. . . . we cannot afford anymore to live in unconcern

51

over the fate of our neighbor. That way we will go to the dogs one after the other.[33]

This kind of statement can regularly be found in the speeches made by the leaders of the Non-Partisan League in North Dakota around 1915 or 1933. The right-wing extremism they espoused as a solution to their problems can be interpreted as an effort to reintegrate with their respective national societies.

The extremist tradition represented by the Farmer-Labor party of Minnesota died with its incorporation into the Democratic-Farmer-Labor party in 1944; that represented by the Non-Partisan League of North Dakota died with the death of its original leaders around 1960. But there are remnants of the old days in the Upper Midwest who carry on its extremist tradition. Throughout the 1950's, A. B. Gilbert of Mound, Minnesota, published brochures and letters to the editor attacking eastern bankers, industrialists, and socialists-Communists as though they were all working together. Claude Efnor of Minneapolis still publishes his monthly newspaper *The Northwest Industrial News* in the same vein. William R. Mills of Bismarck, North Dakota, in 1959 published a pamphlet, *The Spider Web*, describing how the interlocking control of eighteen Minneapolis and St. Paul corporations throttles North Dakota's economy, working through the Republican leaders of the latter state.

The same themes entered the trial of Rose versus Koch in 1965, as we shall see in a later chapter.

4

The University
Professorial dignity and
student ribaldry

THE University of Minnesota is the largest university in the United States
in terms of student population on one campus. It had over 37,000 full-
time day students on its main campus in fall 1965,[1] plus 16,000 students
in its evening classes. It started as a land-grant institution and became
one of the great state universities of the Midwest. While the midwestern
and the Pacific Coast states have all done well financially by their state
universities, Minnesota has been exceptionally generous to its state university, providing the highest contribution per capita of any state in the
union.

One reason for this is ecological: The University of Minnesota is located in the biggest urban complex in the state (which also happens to be
close to the geographic center of the state), so that half the population of
the state is within commuting distance of the university and can use its
facilities daily if it wishes to. A second reason is administrative: Minnesota has only one state university, and there are no separate administrative units among which the resources must be divided.[2] The third reason
is cultural: The state has had a kind of love affair with its university, and
town-gown frictions have historically been minimal. Minnesota is ex-
ceeded by only one other state in the proportion of its youth who attend
college, and it has the lowest draft-rejection rate in the United States for
reasons of educational deficiency.

Some might say that this good relationship has been due to the Scandinavian ancestry of much of the state's population, but it could just as well
be explained by a series of fortunate historical accidents. For example, a

53

practical process for turning low-grade iron ore into usable pellets, called taconite, was invented by a University of Minnesota professor just as the high-grade ores of the state were becoming exhausted, and half of northern Minnesota was saved economically. Two other professors discovered a cure for brucellosis, a dangerous animal disease, by using milk — which just happens to be the state's leading agricultural product.[3] The Minneapolis Symphony and many other cultural resources of the state are housed on the university campus, where hidden subsidies can make them widely available at low cost (without calling it socialism). The one state legislator who advocated a teacher's oath at the university, during the Joe McCarthy[4] era, had a heart attack just as he was beginning to make headway with his bill, and he was so well treated at the University of Minnesota Hospitals (at no expense to himself — a service to all legislators) that he withdrew the bill and became one of the greatest friends of the university. Truly, fate and sensible administrators have combined to build superb town-gown relationships in Minnesota. Generally speaking, if one is a professor at the University of Minnesota he can hold his head high through the state.

At a strong point in this academic love affair, at a time when other universities throughout the nation were recuperating from a decade of Joe McCarthyite attacks on academic freedom, the University of Minnesota was subjected to the most vigorous and vicious attack in its history. The long-developed reputational capital of the university, the good sense of most of the state's political and economic leaders, and the calm firmness of the university's regents and administrative leaders were the main factors that enabled it to weather the public hysteria of late 1963 and early 1964. But the libel suit started by one of its professors also helped the state to return to its usual decorum and good sense.

From time to time an individual or small group arises in the state of Minnesota to criticize the university. Most of the criticisms contain suggestions for improving its operation or efficiency, and are responsible and justifiable whether or not the suggestions are capable of achieving their goal. We distinguish thus between responsible and irresponsible criticisms: The responsible criticisms are based on some factual deficiency in the university and offer suggestions, realistic or unrealistic, for improving the university. The irresponsible criticisms are based on false assumptions and seek to destroy some vital function of the university, or the whole university itself. The line of distinction is not always clear in specific marginal instances, but at the extremes it is. As already indicated, there have been few criticisms of the irresponsible type in Minnesota — at least few that received a significant amount of attention from the legislature or the public.

The university is a "fourth branch of government" in Minnesota in the legal sense that it is not constitutionally subject to direct control by the legislature or governor. Once the regents, twelve in number, are elected by the legislature or are appointed by the governor when a vacancy occurs between legislative sessions, they have final control over the internal operations of the university. Of course, tradition also gives certain powers to the faculty, and the Board of Regents does no more than give formal ratification to faculty decisions of these types. Nevertheless, a state university must give attention to the wishes of the legislature and of the public, since the latter provide the bulk of the financing for the university.

One of the areas of traditional faculty control, throughout Western society, has been "academic freedom." This is essential to any university, and its elimination would destroy a university. Academic freedom has been frequently misunderstood, not only in relations between university and non-university people, but also sometimes within universities themselves. It means the right of a trained scholar to pursue knowledge within his specialty wherever it leads him, so that the sum of knowledge can constantly be increased, even when the knowledge discovered might be unpopular. It also means the right to teach what has been found, so that knowledge will not be lost but passed along from generation to generation, even if it is unpopular. Only the trained scholar, scientist, and teacher have academic freedom, and then only within the area of their specialization. The scholar, scientist, or teacher has a reciprocal duty not to claim academic freedom outside the area of knowledge within his specialty. For example, no faculty member can properly advocate Communism, or any other ism, in the classroom because this is not a branch of knowledge but a political-economic philosophy and practice. If a question arises whether a certain scholar is abusing academic freedom, this can be judged only by his equally trained peers in the same specialty. It is one of the tasks of a college administration and of a board of regents (sometimes called "trustees") to protect academic freedom. At the University of Minnesota, the administration and Board of Regents have usually done a faithful job of protecting academic freedom, even at the cost of making themselves unpopular with outside groups.

Academic freedom is not to be confused with freedom of speech. In democratic societies, every citizen has freedom of speech — that is, the right to express his opinion on public issues providing he does not disturb public order, incite subversion or violence, or translate his words into actions that are contrary to law. Colleges and universities have no more responsibility to maintain freedom of speech in a society than any other institution: All citizens and organizations are supposed to protect it, and government — especially the police and the courts — is called upon to defend it. Students and members of the public outside the universities sometimes claim academic freedom when their only right is to freedom of speech. The only right of a student within a university, aside from his general right in a democratic society to freedom of speech, is to decide whether he wishes to learn what is offered there or not to learn it. If he decides to acquire the knowledge offered by a university, he must learn it in the way the faculty offer it to him. He has no "academic freedom" to insist that knowledge within a university be taught to him in any way that he may personally choose. However, most universities have liberal "outside-speakers policies" which grant student groups the freedom to invite almost anyone they wish to speak to them on the campus. This is not their "academic freedom," which belongs only to the faculty and other trained scholars, but is a privilege accorded by wise college administrations to expand the students' sense of responsibility and the scope of their experience. The speaker from outside the university has neither academic freedom nor the absolute right to speak on the campus. The University of Minnesota has a liberal "outside-speakers policy."

Both academic freedom and the outside-speaker policy at the University of Minnesota have occasionally been challenged by non-university persons and groups, both in general and in specific instances. In the early 1960's, this was publicly done by the "Americanism chairman" of a district American Legion group and by Gerda Koch, who sometimes worked with each other. The major demand of the Americanism chairman was that the World Affairs Center, a department of the Extension Division at the university charged with teaching about international relations and the politics of foreign nations, and the Student Peace Union be abolished because they were alleged to be pro-Communist. Gerda Koch demanded that certain named professors and the president of the university, whom she charged with being "Communists, Communist collaborators, or Communist fronters," be fired. The Americanism chairman had freedom of speech to make these demands, and he was doing nothing illegal, although he was challenging academic freedom and the outside-speaker policy. Gerda Koch was engaged in libel and slander, which opened the way to either a civil suit or a criminal charge against her. (*Libel* refers to published statements that are untrue and harm a person's reputation and ability to pursue his occupation. *Slander* refers to such charges made orally.) She had made similar libelous and slanderous charges against non-University of Minnesota persons as well. In 1960, for example, she charged Max Lerner, a Brandeis University professor who had been invited to speak to a teachers' association in St. Paul, with being a Communist.[5] The American Civil Liberties Union was described as a "red front," "actively engaged in or sympathetic with the Communist revolutionary movement as directed and conducted by the Communist Party of America."[6] The dean of a small denominational college in the Twin Cities received a letter from Gerda Koch complaining without any factual basis about one of his faculty members. The letter included this sentence: "A college professor can do more for Communism in ten minutes than we can do in a lifetime of research." Gerda Koch was not merely the author and publisher of *Facts for Action*, in which her libelous statements had been made, but she was the leading distributor for the state of Minnesota of the publications of about a dozen right-wing extremist organizations around the country. She ran a bookstore, hired a booth at the annual State Fair, and otherwise distributed these publications at group and public meetings of various kinds. At the 1965 trial, she testified that in 1964 she had distributed free "about 40,000 pieces of literature" and had sold several thousand additional copies. Rose had these facts in mind when he decided to sue her for libel. He did not do this merely because he — among many others — had been libeled, but because her false statements had begun to damage the university by gaining credence among and being repeated by other persons or groups in the community who were widely thought to be responsible. Among such persons and groups were the *Minneapolis Star* and a St. Paul city councilman named Milton Rosen.

The first steps in this process have already been recounted: One of her followers, Adolph Grinde, distributed some of her libelous literature to the Anoka County Board, and the *Minneapolis Star* published some of the Koch-Grinde statements, as well as misinformation about what the Anoka County officials had done about it. There were then several angry letters to the newspapers and to the university. Many otherwise responsible and well-intentioned people believe everything they read in a newspaper to be true. Some emotionally disturbed people get so upset by apparent threats of alleged Communist activity that they create a public nuisance and sometimes engage in illegal activities. During December 1963 and early 1964, while the *Star* was publishing false statements about Rose and reporting events occurring at the university in an inflammatory manner, a significant proportion of the Minnesota populace became excited. Professors Sibley and Rose each received dozens of phone calls, sometimes in the middle of the night or in the early morning hours, from persons who refused to give their names but accused whoever happened to answer the phone with being a "Communist." A whole series of magazine subscriptions were taken out in Rose's name, without his knowledge or consent, and he was billed for them. Postal officials unsuccessfully tried to track down their origin, but they kindly took it upon themselves to return the magazines to the publishers with an explanation. Deliveries of merchandise that had not been ordered by the Roses were made to their home and had to be returned. One delivery was of a bouquet of flowers, which was delivered when the Roses were away from their home and was somewhat faded by the time it could be returned. A funeral hearse was sent to Sibley's home, and he received anonymous threats against his life. One early morning, Rose discovered a workman about to begin repairs on his garage door which had not been ordered. (If the repairs had been completed, Rose would have had to pay for them.) Another workman came to repair an electric dishwasher, which the Roses do not possess. One evening six workmen appeared to "dig an air-raid shelter," after their regular working hours. Since, again, the Roses had not ordered this, these men lost an evening's work. One afternoon, Mrs. Rose discovered on their front porch a man generally known to be a mentally disturbed right-wing extremist who was attempting to post there a sign saying something about Rose being a "Jew-Communist." She ordered him to go away, and he left with his sign. There were a number of other such incidents, some of which were frightening to members of the Rose family. The Sibley family experienced many more such incidents.[7]

Most damaging of all were the denunciations of the university for harboring such professors as Sibley, Rose, and named or unnamed others. Sibley reacted in a manner that Rose believed showed lack of insight into the nature of public opinion and collective excitement. He wrote a letter to the *Minnesota Daily*, the student newspaper, on December 3, 1963, which urged that there be more — not less — expression of deviant opinion at the university in the face of these attacks. The unfortunate part of his letter was the following sentences, which were often quoted in newspapers and in discussions throughout the state in the following days and months:

I should like to see on the campus one or two Communist professors, a student Communist club, a chapter of the American Association for the Advancement of Atheism, a Society for the Promotion of Free Love, a League for Overthrow of Government by Jeffersonian Violence (LOGJV), an Anti-Automation League and, perhaps, a Nudist Club. No university should be without individuals and groups like these.

While the general message of the letter was serious, these sentences, of course, were intended to be semi-facetious. But when the letter was re-printed in other newspapers, including the *Minneapolis Star*, it reached many inflamed minds, and was not taken in the semi-serious, semi-humorous vein in which it was written.[8] Sibley privately acknowledged that the sentence should also have included reference to some right-wing group, but he refused to make any public correction. A Minnesota Poll[9] taken a month after the first publication of the Sibley letter showed that among a cross-section of the state's adults, 60 per cent had heard or read his statement, 38 per cent identified it as coming from Sibley specifically or from a "university professor," and 50 per cent believed that one who made such a statement should not be a professor at the university (43 per cent favored having professors with "unusual ideas" and 7 per cent had no opinion).

An interesting aspect of the public reaction to the letter was that there were not nearly so many criticisms of the reference to the need for a Communist Club on the campus as there were violent denunciations of Sibley's call for a Free Love Society and a Nudist Club. Minnesota has many puritanical people to whom this was terribly shocking. Milton Rosen, an elderly St. Paul councilman, became a leading spokesman of the public reaction against Sibley and the university. After a round denunciation for the newspapers, he spoke to a businessman's group — with excerpts of his speech shown on a television newscast — charging that Minnesota professors (unnamed) took female students into their automobiles, seemingly implying that they then had sexual relations with them. After this broadcast, one anonymous father telephoned Rose to ask him if he agreed with Sibley. He broke down in sobs while telling Rose that his daughter, a university student, had recently told her mother that she was pregnant.

In the climate of opinion then prevailing in the state, Rose could not adequately explain to the father that professors did not do the things Rosen had charged, and that his daughter must have become pregnant with some cooperation on her part. There was much excitement of this nature throughout the state.

The students at the university now jumped into the fray. Sibley had always been a popular teacher, and now he became a campus hero. Some students had large buttons printed with the slogan "I am a member of the Nudist Club," and pinned them to their overcoats and stormcoats worn in Minnesota's winters. The "Free Love" theme became great sport, all in words of course. Some students organized a public debate between Sibley and Rosen: Sibley spoke of the need to examine all kinds of beliefs, and said that groups advocating extreme beliefs should be allowed to form on campus. Rosen, in opposing this, said that academic freedom must be tempered by responsibility, that God was against some ideas and practices, and that the relatively few professors and students who advocated them should be "bounced out of the university like rotten apples." The student audience, about 1200 in number, laughed and booed. The show was televised, and it was estimated that 280,000 people heard it on television and radio. Student leaders arranged to have a Communist, a John Birch Society leader, and Governor George Wallace of Alabama speak on campus (later the list was extended to include George Lincoln Rockwell of the American Nazi party). There was fun on the campus, but fury in the state.[10]

State Senator Donald O. Wright was a leader of the dominant Conservative caucus in the legislature. While himself a graduate of the university's Law School, he had long been critical of some aspects of the university's fiscal policies. He claimed that university officials had refused to give him some financial figures he had requested. Earlier that year he had protested a short story in a student publication, which he claimed was a "dirty story" (many faculty members thought it was poor literature and in poor taste; others defended it), but he had been rebuffed as interfering with freedom of the press. The legislature would not be in session for another year, but now in response to a formal request from Milton Rosen, and other public demand, Wright asked his fellow Conservative legislative leaders to conduct an investigation of the university's hiring and firing policies. The House leaders quietly refused, but the Senate Committee on Education agreed to hold hearings in a few months. Probably Senator Wright meant no long-run harm to the university — he said he did not propose that the committee investigate any individual, or that it become a "trial committee" or look into curriculum matters [11] — but he saw the public excitement as an opportunity to give university officials some comeuppance for what he deemed their arrogant attitude toward the legislature, and toward him personally. Councilman Rosen offered to testify against the university, and there were rumors that Wright was planning to arrange for some of the right-wing extremists to present evidence against some of the professors as "Communists." The Minnesota American Legion, the Minnesota Veterans of Foreign Wars, and some local branches of the Knights of Columbus passed resolutions in support of the legislative investigation of the university.

Most of the faculty was deeply chagrined by all these events, but did not know what to do. They knew that Sibley was not a Communist, not an atheist (although it probably would not have disturbed them if he were), and not an advocate of free love or nudism, but rather a strong advocate of free expression, with a penchant for self-dramatization and perhaps martyrdom. They were annoyed by his unwillingness to correct the impression created by the facetious sentences in his now-famous letter, and by his willingness to engage in public and televised debate with Milton Rosen, whom they thought of as a silly old man and certainly no match for a skilled orator like Sibley. (Not until later was it learned that Sibley was "trapped" into the debate by premature student publicity.) But no faculty members wanted to criticize Sibley publicly when he was under such fire. They knew of no Communists on the faculty and no nudists; if there were any free-lovers they had been most discreet. Many on the faculty were concerned about the students' ribaldry, although they saw the humor in the situation. At first, the only public reactions from the faculty were some dignified letters from faculty leaders in the daily newspapers. But these were not widely understood, and did little to reduce the excitement around the state. One of the most forthright of the letters came from the highly respected chairman of the School of Physics:

Much has been said recently about academic freedom and responsibility. The sorry spectacle of the Rosen-Sibley controversy, culminating in its "great debate," has left many of us sick at heart.

As a member of the University of Minnesota faculty, I am embarrassed that my colleague, Mulford Q. Sibley, in illustrating the need for presenting all sides of a question, has chosen examples so extreme as to be com-

61

pletely unrealistic. Within one's family or circle of friends one can safely exaggerate to illustrate a point, but it seems particularly unfortunate that a political science professor hasn't enough sensitivity to realize that public statements should be made with care, lest they be picked up by crackpots or publicity seekers and distorted to serve only destructive ends.

As a native of St. Paul, I am embarrassed that a high public official who professes to be a good citizen would seize upon what was so obviously trivia, blowing it up all out of proportion, and in the process running the risk of bringing serious harm to a great public institution which by its very nature cannot readily defend itself. If Milton Rosen were as astute and as loyal to the principles of freedom as he professes to be, he, too, would have acted more responsibly and realized that uninformed and grossly exaggerated statements such as he makes will certainly be used by those who would destroy the great institutions upon which the future of America, and indeed the world, rests.

At a time when universities and colleges, more than ever before, provide the means for studying the world's problems and putting into practice moral values taught by the great religions, it is appalling that these two individuals can so mask the great work of the thousands of dedicated faculty, employees and students of the University of Minnesota as to impair the public confidence which is essential if it is to carry out its all-important mission.

The editorial in the Jan. 10 Minneapolis Tribune is one of the better expressions that I have seen on this controversy. I hope it may stimulate other individuals and groups to express views more representative than those of either Sibley or Rosen.[12]

The administrative officials of the university were circumspect in public, although privately they were upset. They arranged to have the Board of Regents issue a lengthy statement defending academic freedom, but this had about as much effect on the public as a drop of water, although it reassured the faculty. The Democratic governor of the state, Karl Rolvaag, and the lieutenant governor, A. M. (Sandy) Keith, issued public statements endorsing the regents' statement, and Keith came to the defense of Sibley as a great teacher. Other political leaders, of both parties, issued statements defending the university. But the public excitement was not easily calmed. Under certain circumstances, an aroused public opinion can turn into a furious collective excitement, and this happened in Minnesota during that winter of 1963–64. To put it mildly, it did not seem as though the prospects were good for an increase in the university's budget, to meet the rising student enrollment, during the next session of the legislature. In fact there were prospects that the coming Senate investigation of the university might turn into a witch-hunt that would destroy faculty morale and much of the academic freedom of which the university was so proud.

It was in the midst of this situation that Rose informed a few of his colleagues that he was planning to sue Gerda Koch for libel. As noted in Chapter 1, the Faculty Legal Protection Committee was quickly formed, and when it distributed a notice of its existence and purpose, about half the faculty — most of whom did not know Rose personally — responded with contributions to pay for his lawsuit. Several hundred faculty members came out on a Saturday afternoon to hear Rose explain the issues in his lawsuit. While Rose appreciated this tremendous expression of moral and financial support, he recognized that it was for the university itself that the support was forthcoming. In fact, the committee set itself up as a permanent group, with the intention of supporting any other university professor who might also need help in a lawsuit for libel or abrogation of tenure. The support for Rose and for the Legal Protection Committee was the faculty's way of responding with dignity, rationality, and vigor to the irresponsible and dangerous attack on the university.

The verbal response of the faculty was almost unanimously in support of Rose and the libel suit. A world-famous professor, then on leave of absence, wrote the Faculty Legal Protection Committee:

Here's a small check to support your admirable and heartening efforts. Most of all, I just want to add a word of congratulation and encouragement for what you're doing. Your fine letter to the faculty is something the whole university can be proud of — and something in which the whole state will also, in due course, take pride.

Another wrote:

Enclosed is a check for $6.00 in support of Arnold Rose's libel suit. I felt pleased and proud to read about the formation of this committee. Libelous, malicious charges are, of course, old stuff for the academic community. I have often wished that someone would fight back, and now I value the opportunity to participate. If it happens that too few faculty share this self-assessment, so that the fund falls short of its goal — an unthinkable eventuality — please feel free to ask us for a more sacrificial amount.

Still another:

I think that Mr. Rose is doing a good thing by suing the libelous parties. I realize that he may not win a cent, but I think the suit a good idea in that it may make name-calling a less popular indoor sport than it has recently been. Accordingly, by being willing to sue, Mr. Rose is taking on the cause of all of us, who would like to get on with the business of teaching — and, if we find time for it, the life of the mind — without senseless interruptions from outside the groves of academe. Please convey my thanks to Mr. Rose when you see him; I know him so slightly that I hesitate to do so in person.

One refugee professor made a comparison between what was currently happening at Minnesota and an earlier event in Nazi Germany:

I cannot help to be reminded of an incident which occurred in 1934 involving the father of a close friend of mine, Professor von Zumbusch, a great dermatologist. He was "rector" (president) of the University of Munich at that time. He was ordered to hoist the Swastika flag on the buildings of the university. Claiming the independence of the university from fear by power, he refused to do it and was promptly removed from office and a brilliant academic career. I know of no colleague of his (but I was only 9 years old at that time) who supported him at that time. There may have been a few laudable exceptions. I have left a country which for 12 dreadful years was in the hands of fanatic, right-wing, paranoid extremists who infected successfully the minds of a very large group of Germans. I want to prevent a similar event with all the power in my hands.

A few students also supported the Faculty Legal Protection Committee and Rose:

Please accept this from a senior firmly entrenched in debt so that unfortunately only a token contribution can be made. A worthier cause there could not be. I sincerely hope a permanent fund will be established.

I wish you much success in your "crusade" and hope that your position will receive continued and widened support. It is good to know that we have professors with the courage and conviction to stand up and argue for what they believe is right. Thank you for setting a fine example for others in our community.

Financial contributions and letters expressing moral support came from academics near and far. The teachers of a Minneapolis high school took up a collection and sent $32.50 to the Faculty Legal Protection Committee along with a letter signed by all who contributed. Almost half the faculty of Macalester College in St. Paul signed a strongly worded statement of support, which read in part:

We wish to join you in working for an end to inaccurate whispers, innuendos and emotional attacks masquerading as free speech to the detriment of individuals and institutions whose purpose is to find and communicate knowledge. At present we recognize that these attacks have damaging effects on persons and society, and are destructive of the highest democratic traditions.

A number of sociologists around the country wrote to Rose. What follows is a small sample:

My wife and I wish to convey to you our deep respect for your forthright stand against those who threaten our democratic values and the ethos of American life. Your many years of intellectual and scientific leadership within the community of sociologists is further enriched by your present role and all of us are indebted to you for having the courage to represent all of us. The acts you challenge may be local in origin but they signify in a larger sense a clear threat to all American scholars, and hence you are acting on behalf of that which we all cherish in a society of free men.

As fellow sociologists and as colleagues in the field of higher education we want to encourage you in the fight in which you are now engaged, a fight which concerns us deeply both because of our high regard for you and also because it is at least symbolic of the threat in our times to academic freedom. While we have some understanding of the personal cost of this ordeal to you we are indeed proud that it can be a man such as you, with your integrity and your professional distinction, who now stands before the public and bears witness for us all in this crucial matter.

I want to add my sentiment of support for you to those expressions I know you have received from your colleagues. And I also want to congratulate you on your scrappy and courageous approach to the scandal-mongering activities of the local cranks. I have often wondered if I would do this kind of thing if I were attacked, and I am not sure. But I think we in the academic world are fortunate to have a few who will bring the attackers into court.

Only to let you know that I am horrified reading about the dirty attacks on you and that you have to fight back before the courts. It is good to know that your colleagues support you actively. Be assured of my full solidarity.

We are sorry that so much of the burden of what is essentially a common battle falls upon your shoulders, and we wish that there was more we could do. If you can think of anything, please let us know. We have had to wage the same battle here over the years and we will continue to do so. Know that we wish you well and will follow the case with the hope that your example will be a source of courage for all those who believe in academic freedom.

We have been following your battle with the super-patriotic far right, and of course our sympathies lie entirely with you. It is with this in mind that I would like to invite you for an evening lecture.

(The last letter came from a priest-professor at a Catholic university.)

One letter to the Faculty Legal Protection Committee from a colleague in the university's Medical School stated a very realistic caution that troubled Rose from the time he began to think seriously of suing until the time the trial verdict was announced two years later:

While I am willing to support the court action to be brought by Arnold, I, nevertheless, wonder about the wisdom of doing so. If the libel suit is lost many people will then draw the conclusion that the accusations made about Rose are true and have so been judged by the courts. Also, if the legal action fails this will encourage other kinds of character assassinations to be made since those who wish to do so will then feel that they will escape legal liability.

Rose wrote a letter for publication in the *Minnesota Daily*, first, to thank the faculty for their support and, second, to inform his colleagues what expert predictions he had received concerning the outcome of the suit:

I have received the independent judgments of three able attorneys that I have an actionable and valid libel suit. This does not necessarily mean, of course, that I shall win the case. The outcome of the case will depend on a jury. If I win, we shall have beaten one of the most serious foes of the university. If I lose, we can still say that we fought back on relevant grounds. The outcome of the suit will help to inform the faculty where it stands with the other citizens of Minnesota.

Only one Minnesota professor criticized Rose during these months. He sent a letter to Rose, with a copy simultaneously to the *Minnesota Daily* for publication. The letter was lengthy, but the gist of it can be gathered from the following sentence: "What if you had written a book with a Communist or two, supposing it a good book?"

If the intention of your suit, and the presumed intention of the proposed "Truth squad," should they come into being, were to purvey to the public an image of the university as "responsible" rather than "irresponsible," as free of "left-leaning," taint, etc., an image, in other words of a university "cleared" like yourself, of grounds for suspicion against it, I would be afraid of the university coming under the influence of a potentially far more dangerous repression — because of its origin within the university, and because it would wear the symbols of "responsibility," and liberalism — than those threatening from the outside, represented by Miss Koch, Mr. Grinde, The American Legion and the Christian Anti-Vaccine Crusade.

66

Assuming that the hypothetical book referred to by the professor was non-fiction dealing with a controversial public issue — which *was* the case with *An American Dilemma* — and assuming that Rose had been sympathetic with the viewpoint of his hypothetical "Communist co-authors" — which he would not have been — Rose would not have had a case against Gerda Koch because she would not then have made libelous statements. Her statements that Rose was a Communist supporter and Communist collaborator would then have been true. Further, Rose does not believe that a social science study by a Communist on a controversial issue can be objective, because the Communist's first loyalty is to his ideology rather than to objective truth. These matters seemed to be of little importance to the writer of the letter.

A libel suit is a serious matter, and most responsible people took it seriously. The *Minneapolis Star* stopped repeating Miss Koch's libels and inventing new falsehoods in its news columns. When the state Senate's committee got around to holding its "investigation," this turned into a matter of merely one day's hearings, in which only Milton Rosen among the outspoken attackers of the university was given an opportunity to speak. Gerda Koch and other right-wing extremists were kept out. Two of the university's conservative regents made an effective defense of the university, and no actions were taken by the committee. Responsibility and calmness returned to the state. When the next session of the legislature rolled around the following winter, the university budget was handled in the traditional fashion and allowed its necessary increase to accommodate the growing number of students and the growing development of research.

The students kept up their antics through that winter and spring of 1964 [13] — among other things, arranging for another public debate between Sibley and a leading member of the John Birch Society on the day before the Senate committee hearing was to take place. President O. M. Wilson of the university ordered this to be postponed until after the hearing, but the students arranged for the debate to be held off the campus as a non-university function. In June, most of the students dispersed for their summer vacations or jobs. When the new academic year began in September there was no recurrence of students' "testing the limits," despite the fact that at other universities around the country, student "revolts" against academic administrations and faculties were frequent (notably at the University of California, Berkeley [14]). Students at Minnesota continued to debate controversial issues, in particular the Vietnam war, and continued to invite outside speakers to discuss these issues, but there was no longer the attitude among them that they were going to have their fun even though it destroyed the university. A sense of balance was restored to the university without any inroads on academic freedom or on the liberal outside-speakers' policy.

Thus there was no longer any excitement at the university when, in October 1965, it was announced that the trial of Rose's libel suit was scheduled for the following month. Students' memories are especially short-lived, partly because there is a certain yearly turnover for a significant proportion of them and two new freshman classes had entered the university since the exciting events of early 1964. Also, young people develop new enthusiasms quickly and discard old ones: They are more likely than older people to believe they can ignore their own past and strike out in new directions without regard to what has gone before. (And older people usually cannot understand the fervor with which many younger people feel the need to strike out in new directions, seemingly without regard to consequences.) With a shorter life behind them, time seems to be elongated, and psychologically a year and a half is a much longer time for a young person than for an older one. The freshman reporter for the *Minnesota Daily* who was sent to interview Rose about the forthcoming trial had almost no background information, and his published articles — while factually fairly accurate — had little relevance to the issues that confronted the university. The faculty, of course, had much more interest in the trial, and asked Rose many questions about it.

The newspaper reports of the trial during its progress — both in the *Minnesota Daily* and in the regular morning newspaper, the *Minneapolis Tribune* — necessarily contained only a small sampling of what was occurring in the courtroom. But the events reported seemed so bizarre that they stimulated much interest on the campus. A student in one of Rose's classes, who was a Catholic nun, wrote a letter to Rose expressing her strong support of his cause and saying that she was praying for his victory at the trial.

When the victory had been won, oral and written expressions of congratulations not only were personally warm but reflected a deep understanding of the significance of the trial for the university and for academic freedom in the United States generally. One professor wrote: "I'm sure you know that I know how much you are fighting my battle too." Another wrote a "short note . . . to thank you for the tremendous contribution you've made to the faculty and the university." Still another: "Your action in prosecuting this matter represents a real service to your professional colleagues in academic life, both here and throughout the world of college and university endeavor." A high administrative official: "We're all in your debt for the courage and determination with which you handled this entire affair. It could not help but reflect dignity and credit on the university and the whole academic community." Another administrator saw the trial in even broader terms: "All of us who believe in clean-minded discussion of important affairs have been grateful to you for calling to account those who have improperly attacked you and thereby our system and society."

Academic men from other institutions wrote in a similar vein. One said: "Every demonstration of this kind that there is recourse, within the framework of traditional American jurisprudence and political process, to the onslaught of those who would destroy those frameworks, builds ever more firmly our necessary safeguards for diversity. Your action seems to me a significant contribution to freedom and will make more easy the resistance of teachers and others everywhere to these fanatics." A priest-professor at a Catholic university wrote: "Congratulations on winning your important court case. . . . It was an important victory for all of us in the sense that the whole profession of education was involved." The secretary of a national scientific society: "Hopefully, the trials you endured may result in sparing others against the onslaughts of idiocy." The secretary of the major professional education association: "Congratulations on your victory. It is really a triumph for all teachers and professors in the United States! They can now teach with greater confidence and security according to the best principles of academic freedom and teaching generally."

5

The Minnesota Legislature

The political response

ROSE was one of those people who could not conceive of running for public office — that is, he was until he was past forty years of age. He felt this way not because he despised politicians; quite the contrary, he thought of politics as the highest of callings, demanding the utmost of its practitioners, and offering the rewards of greatest possible achievement. He considered a legislator a kind of physician to the society. His reason for avoiding active politics was a sense of personal inadequacy for its tasks. Rose had grown up a shy person who had few friends, and he strongly believed he had an unattractive personality. He couldn't dream of doing all the things a seeker of public votes has to do. Of course, having learned to conduct classes at the university, and to give occasional public lectures, he had lost the fear of speaking in public. And having risen to a full professorship (in 1952), having published a number of scholarly books and more than a hundred research articles, having raised a family of three fine children — all had increased his self-confidence.

When Rose came to Minnesota in 1949, one of his first friends on the faculty was Arthur Naftalin, associate professor of political science. Naftalin had welcomed Rose to the university because he knew of *An American Dilemma*, in fact, had used it as a text in a general social science survey course. Naftalin had earlier been a newspaper reporter and then secretary to Hubert Humphrey when the latter was mayor of Minneapolis, before Humphrey's election to the United States Senate. From Naftalin, and others in the Political Science Department with whom he frequently lunched, Rose learned something of the background of Minnesota politics.

The Political Response

Minnesota is the only state in the Union not to have a Democratic party — there the equivalent is called the Democratic-Farmer-Labor party, (or DFL, for short). This party did not form until 1944. Before that, the Democratic party was a small organization, having nearly all of its voters in the city of St. Paul, and existing mainly by grace of federal patronage when the national Democratic party was in power in Washington. The chief opponent of the Republicans was the Farmer-Labor party, a latter-day offshoot of the Populist party of the 1890's. This party included the fullest possible range of political views, from extreme right to extreme left.[1] During the 1930's, it had backed the election to public office of candidates who, on the one hand, had advocated American collaboration with the German Nazis and, on the other hand, had given state jobs to some open Communists. At about the same time, it worked for the election as governor of Floyd B. Olson, a liberal New Dealer identified with the Roosevelt administration then in Washington.[2] It was a strange political party, but not greatly different from other offshoots of the Populist movement in the Dakotas, Montana, Idaho, and Wisconsin. Its basis of cohesion was an antagonism toward the upper class, although more often a mythical upper class supposed to exist in New York City than an actual upper class centered in Minneapolis and St. Paul.

The native fascists and Communists were largely in control of the Farmer-Labor party through the late 1930's and early 1940's, although loss of government offices and internal dissension weakened the party. Into the midst of this confusion stepped Hubert H. Humphrey, then a young political science instructor at Macalester College. Using the University of Minnesota faculty and students as a base, he ran for mayor of Minneapolis in 1943 and lost. He never lost an election again, unless the West Virginia presidential primary in 1960 be counted as an election. In 1944, Humphrey effected a coalition of the small Democratic party with the torn Farmer-Labor party to create the DFL party. He used this weak instrument to get himself elected mayor of Minneapolis in 1945.

But the party still included its Communists and fascists, although the latter no longer openly identified with international fascism because of the entry of the United States into World War II in 1941. Humphrey, still using the faculty and students of the university and various colleges as his working force, moved against the Communists and those supporting them. The struggle was a bitter one for three years. In early 1948, the Humphrey faction of the DFL, supporting President Truman nationally, won a decisive victory in the party caucuses over the Communists and pro-Communists, who then moved out of the party to support Henry Wallace for President under the banner of the Progressive party. Humphrey was elected United States senator later that year, and his new breed of liberal DFLers were simultaneously winning House of Representatives seats in three of Minnesota's nine congressional districts. However, it was not until Humphrey's second senatorial race, in 1954, that the rejuvenated DFL won significant state offices. At that time, Orville L. Freeman was elected governor, a position he held for three terms — until 1960, when he almost became Vice President, but became Secretary of Agriculture instead.[3] Also, in 1954, DFL-supported candidates captured a majority of seats in the state House of Representatives, though not in the Senate. This was the first time in modern history that the Republicans experienced anything but complete victory in elections to the state legislature.

The Republican party of Minnesota, largely controlled by a conservative "old guard," had been fairly typical of Republican parties in other midwestern states until 1938. Then it came under the leadership of a vigorous young man, Harold Stassen. Stassen, a graduate of the University of Minnesota Law School, was elected governor that year, and his efforts within the Republican party gave the state GOP an activist local leadership that was even "liberal" in many parts of the state.[4] To this day, the majority faction in the Republican party is more similar, in its positive and responsible attitude toward public issues, to Republican parties in the East Coast states than to those in other midwestern states. There is room for "young Turks" in the party, especially on local issues, and they have kept up a lively debate on what should be the party's goals.

Even though the "moderate" and "liberal" elements have made up a majority within the Republican party since Stassen's early activity, and have even helped elect liberals like Luther Youngdahl and Elmer L. Andersen as governors, they are not the strongest influence in the Minnesota State Legislature. This is largely because Minnesota elects its legislators on a "nonpartisan" basis, a practice that was instituted in Populist days when there was strong public feeling against the established political parties. Whatever "nonpartisan" elections may have accomplished when they were first instituted, for many decades now they have been a device for fooling the voters. The way they work is this: Any individual may declare his candidacy and run in the primary. There is no party designation on the ballot, although a candidate can seek party support, and if he gets it may — if he wishes to — refer to that party endorsement in his campaign literature and campaign speeches. Usually the two candidates who win in the primary, and face each other in the general election, represent the two major political parties. Every candidate who has won in a legislative election, with no more than one or two exceptions in fifty years, has identified himself with one of the major political caucuses in the legislature. But the successful candidate need not mention his party affiliation publicly if he does not believe it will get him added support from the voters. So the party affiliation of a significant proportion of legislators is not known to the majority of their constituents; not infrequently a conservative Republican will thereby get elected to the legislature in a district where the large majority of the voters are Democrats; less often a Democrat will get elected in a Republican district. Some candidates deliberately fool the voters, and get away with it because of the nonpartisan ballot. In one actual instance, a Republican candidate — let us say his name was Doakes — was running in a working-class district, and much of his campaign literature had on it the following slogan:

*D*oakes
*F*or
*L*abor

The intials DFL stood out, and they mean to every Minnesotan the Democratic-Farmer-Labor party, which happened to be vigorously opposing the candidacy of Mr. Doakes. There is no way for the voter to check up on Mr. Doakes's or any other candidate's party affiliation at the polls.

Perhaps a more important consequence of this system is that an incumbent legislator, who is already fairly well known to his constituency, is not likely to need his party to help him get re-elected. If the party members should decide that he is no longer the best man to represent them in the legislature, and support another candidate to run against him, they have a difficult time convincing the voters of this. The incumbent, now rejected by his party, continues to use the party name in his literature and speeches, and the ballot gives no indication who is the party candidate. Thus incumbent legislators often feel no strong sense of responsibility or obligation to their parties. The result is that Minnesota's political parties are weak when it comes to exerting influence on legislators, and in the legislature itself each party caucus is sharply split into at least two factions.

In recent decades the factionalism has been sharpest in the Republican party. The majority of the Republican legislators have little identification with the Republican party, which is dominated by moderates and liberals, although they probably vote, as individual citizens, for most of its candidates for other public offices. This majority group of Republican legislators even refuses to use the name "Republican" for their caucus; instead they label themselves "Conservatives." In earlier decades the same was true for the Democratic-Farmer-Laborites, who then called themselves "Liberals," but in the last decade or so, most of the DFLers have grown closer to their party and call themselves the "DFL caucus." Nevertheless, there is a minority among the DFL legislators who oppose their party, especially in the House of Representatives. Thus, there are in effect four factions in the legislature; in order of descending size there are the "Conservatives," the Republicans, the DFLers, and the "dissident Liberals." [5] These coalesce into two caucuses usually only to elect legislative officials: the Conservative and the DFL caucuses. But when it comes to voting on issues, they form every possible combination.

The DFLers are the most liberal — in the usual sense of that term — of the four factions. It cannot be said which is the most conservative — in the usual sense of that term — among the other three factions. The "Conservatives," the Republicans, and the "dissident Liberals" take turns in being most conservative, depending on the issue, and quite often all three vote together to pass a conservative piece of legislation. Many of the "Conservative" and "dissident Liberal" factions represent some economic interest group in the state, rather than any ideology. On matters that do not affect these economic interest groups, they often vote in terms of their perceptions of the general welfare of the state, regardless of ideology or party platform. The Republican and DFL factions have ideologies which are reflected in their party platforms, and because their ideologies are different, it is often most difficult for these two factions to vote together on issues defined as partisan. Yet, in some respects the Republican and DFL factions are more similar to each other than they are to the other two groups: A larger proportion of them are young and well educated, and they are more likely to be oriented to national issues and national parties. But generally the DFLers find a closer affinity to the "Conservative" faction, particularly because the latter have greater power than the Republican faction and are more likely to be willing to make political compromises and to follow gentlemanly standards of political behavior. Clearly, the nonpartisan ballot makes the Minnesota legislature a more complicated political body than is found in most other states. With 67 members in the Senate (the largest in the United States), and 135 members in the House (one of the largest), it is obviously a difficult body to work in.

In 1952, Arnold Rose bought a house near the university. This was in the Minneapolis ward (the Second Ward) from which Humphrey had launched the new DFL party in 1944, and where his lieutenant, Professor Arthur Naftalin, was now chairman of the ward club. Rose joined the ward club in 1952, but saw his role as a minor one until late 1957. He went to the monthly meetings when there was a good speaker, gave two or three lectures himself during those five years, and forced himself to ring doorbells just before elections.[6] In late 1957, a small group of ward club leaders asked Rose if he would run for chairman of the club, and he was flattered enough to agree. A threatened contest dissipated, and Rose was unanimously elected chairman of the Second Ward Club, now famous through Minnesota as the home ward of Humphrey, Freeman, Fraser, and Naftalin.[7] Rose surprised himself by enjoying his tasks as chairman and as a member of the Hennepin County Central Committee of the DFL. He was especially proud of his organizational work which helped get a majority of votes for Eugene J. McCarthy, running for the United States Senate, in Hennepin County, and a second victory for state Senator Donald M. Fraser. Real politics seemed much more meaningful than academic politics, and campaigning and organizational work had educational opportunities almost as significant as those of university classrooms.

About the same time that Rose was elected ward chairman, he was appointed chairman of the "Freeway Committee" of a neighborhood group called the Prospect Park and East River Road Improvement Association. The purpose of this committee was to oppose the location of a freeway right through the heart of the only residential neighborhood located near the university. After three years of struggle, the committee won only minor concessions from the State Highway Department and the City Council. But Rose became a sort of neighborhood champion, and came to know the neighborhood very well. In 1959, there was a vacancy in the position of Second Ward alderman, and Rose ran for the office. He was defeated — although by a margin of only 117 votes out of over 9000 cast — mainly because a new state Republican chairman chose the Minneapolis Second Ward as the location of a first election battle where he could show his prowess.[8]

In 1961, Rose ran for office again, this time for one of the seven seats

75

on the Minneapolis School Board. He failed to get the support of a civic committee controlled by a small group of businessmen and, faced with a split in the DFL party,[9] he again lost the election. In 1962, he made a third and "last" try, this time for the state legislature, and he won. The last election was as difficult as the other two, since Rose again had to contend with a labor-liberal split in the DFL party, and he was running in a predominantly working-class district,[10] with a large immigrant population (mainly Poles, Swedes, Norwegians, Lebanese, Syrians, and Italians) who would not be likely to favor the candidacy of a Jewish professor. But the incumbent, an ex-labor leader, had lost much of his support, and the Republican candidate was not an effective campaigner.

So Rose was sworn into the Minnesota House of Representatives on January 7, 1963.[11] As mentioned in an earlier chapter, he had only been vaguely aware of a surreptitious effort to prevent his election by labeling him a Communist or Communist collaborator, and apparently not many voters had paid much attention to the attack. It was not until the legislature had been in session for over two months that he realized that Gerda Koch was distributing her libelous leaflets about him to other members of the legislature, and clearly almost none of the other House members believed what she said about him. So, with one exception, he ignored the libel, and happily went about his business of supporting his own bills, figuring out how to vote on major bills,[12] attending meetings of the five committees to which he was appointed, getting to know his fellow-legislators and learning how to work with them as human beings regardless of party, serving as a junior member but informally influential in his party caucus, listening to some of the lobbyists, attending some of the dinners offered by the lobbyists, studying how some departments of the state government worked, answering letters from his constituents, speaking at public affairs especially when some of his constituents might be present, attending DFL party meetings, preparing a news release for a newspaper reporter on one of his bills occasionally, reading or glancing through the several thousands of government reports and propaganda reports that come across the desk of every legislator. Twice a week in the early morning before his 8 A.M. committee sessions began, and often on a Sunday afternoon, he went to his university office to answer his professional and personal correspondence, and read graduate student examinations and theses. He even completed a research article. It was an incredibly busy five months, but fascinating, exciting, and psychologically rewarding. Perhaps no other profession makes so many demands on a person as that of a legislator, but few others offer so many opportunities for stimulating and creative activity. Rose learned more about American society in those five months than in any other equivalent time period in his life as a student of society. And, obviously, he enjoyed his work.

While he paid no attention to Gerda Koch's continuing attacks on him during this time, except on one occasion to be mentioned, he was concerned about the activities of the right-wing extremists. There was one, also newly elected, member of the House of Representatives who was a right-wing extremist, Daniel Slater. He was an intelligent, rational, hardworking man who had obvious leadership qualities for his group. He was shrewd enough to hold his fire if the situation did not seem opportune for the expression of his opinions, and he never appeared emotional. Although elected from a largely working-class district in St. Paul, he joined the Conservative caucus. Periodically he sent out a short newsletter which was well edited, even though it had the usual right-wing-extremist viciousness of content. Slater was "far out" in his political views, although his Conservative colleagues did not realize it when he first joined them.

Slater and Rose never got into a personal quarrel, but they were destined to differ sharply from one another on certain issues, not simply on issues where there was a defined difference between the Conservative and DFL caucuses but on issues where either Slater or Rose stood out from his caucus. Some of these were important issues, such as whether the state should help support local planning bodies to study and advise on problems of water supply, sewage disposal, transportation inadequacies, etc. Rose was strongly for this, and so were most of the Conservatives and DFLers, but Slater stood out against it. Another important issue was whether there should be local government consolidation — there were some 350 independent units of government in the Minneapolis–St. Paul area, and they were growing in number as small suburban areas tried to avoid paying for public services. An earlier legislature had passed a mild bill to permit annexation by existing units of local government of adjacent unincorporated areas (usually small ones). But now, in a few instances, persons living on this formerly unincorporated land were protesting having to pay for schools (they had formerly sent their children on individual contract to other towns' schools), water supply (they had formerly used cesspools), etc. They wanted the right to remain unincorporated or to vote on which incorporated village they could join, even one that was not adjacent to their land, if its taxes were lower. House members divided on non-caucus, nonpartisan lines on this issue: Rose favored maintaining the existing law and even strengthening it; Slater vigorously opposed it.

It was on some very unimportant issues that Slater and Rose came into really vigorous opposition. Fairly early in the session, the Republican governor's secretary came to Rose to ask him if he would join in co-sponsoring a resolution to the United States senators from Minnesota (Humphrey and McCarthy), the President, and the Senate Foreign Relations Committee, asking them to support the United Nations anti-genocide treaty. Rose understood he was being asked to do this because he was a Jew, and because it was customary in the legislature to have three Conservatives and two DFLers co-sponsor a nonpartisan bill of this type. Two of the three Conservatives chosen by the Republican governor to lead in sponsoring this resolution were non-Jews who had a large number of Jews among their constituents. The only other Jew in the House besides Rose was a DFLer who had many Jews among his constituents. Rose had practically no Jews or Negroes among his constituents, and he guessed that this might have been a factor in the governor's choosing him as a co-sponsor. The resolution was a "good" one, although innocuous: It called on the United States senators to vote for a United Nations treaty calling for international sanctions against any nation that began to exterminate its ethnic minorities, as the Germans had done with the Jews in the 1930's and 1940's. This kind of treaty has always proved to be a mere expression of pious intentions; nations decide in terms of their national interests at the moment whether to use effective international sanctions against another nation. Furthermore, Rose was sure that Senators Humphrey and McCarthy favored such a treaty anyway, as a mere expression of international good will and cooperation, and did not need the Minnesota legislature to tell them what to do. When Rose agreed to co-sponsor the resolution, he assumed it was noncontroversial and would pass the House without debate. Probably everyone else involved made the same assumption: Otherwise why should Conservative Representative Robert Johnson, with a large Jewish constituency, agree to be the chief author of the resolution?

But the governor and the legislative leaders did not understand Daniel Slater at this time. At the committee hearings on the resolution, Slater arranged for some forty or fifty citizens to appear in the committee room, and some of them spoke in sharp opposition to the resolution, the others murmuring their approval and applauding at the close of each statement.

78

One elderly lady folded her hands and lifted her eyes heavenward, while apparently engaged in silent prayer, during the whole committee hearing. The burden of Slater's argument was that the anti-genocide treaty was simply another step in the United Nations' plan to seize control of the United States. After Johnson had made his opening statement explaining the resolution and urging its passage, Rose made a supporting statement to explain why the treaty was desirable and that it had practically no effect on American sovereignty. The other committee members were not so much concerned about the arguments as they were about the forty or fifty citizens gathered in the audience. One of them might be a constituent of theirs, and could make trouble in the next election campaign if they voted for the resolution. The presence of such a large number of anonymous citizens is one of the most persuasive arguments that can be used on legislators: Here is the "voice of the people" itself, which legislators are supposed to represent. Slater was truly impressive in getting them out. Probably the entire AFL-CIO or the Chamber of Commerce in Minnesota could not organize themselves in one day to get that many citizens to attend a legislative hearing. Most citizens have jobs or are otherwise "busy," they don't want to be bothered about something that doesn't concern them personally, and they probably do not believe that legislators will pay much attention to them if they merely express their opinion in a legislative hearing room. But citizens are wrong about the latter point; all the majority Conservatives and those in the "dissident Liberal" faction voted to kill the resolution; only Rose and a few other DFLers voted for it (Johnson, the chief author, and the other Conservative sponsors of the resolution, were not members of the committee). It did not concern Rose that the resolution was beaten, because it was not important. It did not concern him that there was some anti-Semitism in the audience, because there was none evident in the committee (in fact, the committee chairman, an elderly rural gentleman, made a personal apology to Rose for the committee's action). What did concern him was that Dan Slater could, all by himself, muster so many people for a committee hearing, and kill a piece of legislation.

Slater's small crowd (up to 60 in number) thereafter appeared at hearings on several other bills and usually got them killed also. Most of these bills were also not important: [13] Slater was shrewd enough to avoid attacks on important legislation supported by Conservative or even DFL leaders in the House, and he was also clever enough not to employ the crowd tactic in pushing *for* a bill that he favored since this would expose his goals too clearly. Most of the other legislators were confused about Slater. On the one hand, he appeared to be an ordinary Conservative on most matters, but he had some unique angles and he had a peculiar following that was increasingly showing up in committee hearing rooms and in the lobbies of the legislature. One ardent follower went so far as to push the minority leader, a diminutive man, while having a heated discussion with him in the lobby. Meanwhile, over in the Minneapolis City Council, a major zoning ordinance was almost beaten by the same group of extremists, led by an able friend of Slater's, and was saved only by the organization of a counter-group of citizens. Rose resolved to expose to his legislative colleagues, on an opportune occasion, the nature of the right-wing extremist movement, for most of the legislature was misinformed or confused about it.

At none of the committee hearings where the extremists appeared was Rose attacked personally. The only incident was in a hearing when Rose mentioned that many important civic groups, such as the League of Women Voters, favored the bill under discussion. A lady stood up in the audience and shouted, "That's a Communist group!" The chairman gaveled her into silence, and nothing more was said about Communism. Gerda Koch was occasionally in these audiences but she seldom spoke up. An exception occurred in an Education Committee hearing on a minor bill sponsored by a Conservative freshman whose star was rising in the House, Salisbury Adams (Rose was also a co-author of this bill). The bill would have permitted public schools around the state to charge a small admission fee for performances by the Minneapolis Symphony Orchestra; the money was to pay for the expenses of the orchestra as it traveled around the state. After a brief committee discussion, in which it was apparent that the members were disposed to vote in favor of the bill, the committee chairman asked the traditional question whether any in the audience wished to speak on the bill. Gerda Koch stood up (none but Rose among the committee members knew who she was) and announced her opposition to the bill because it would permit "the Communists" among the musicians to spread their pernicious doctrines around the state. The committee members were amused, the chairman called for a vote, the bill received unanimous support. The bill later passed the House, but never got out of the Education Committee in the Senate and so never became law.

Rose had another major confrontation with Slater during the legislative session. Rose was the author of a bill to require that illegitimate children be issued the same type of birth certificate as was given out to legitimately born children, so as to avoid the stigma of illegitimacy when the individual applied for entrance to schools, entered the armed services, sought jobs, etc. The current practice was to issue a full birth certificate to legitimate children, stating many facts, including parents' names and the legitimacy of the birth. But illegitimate children were issued only a brief notice, stating the name of the individual and the place and date of birth. The bill included a controversial item: In order to get a father's name on the birth certificate, the applicant was permitted to invent a fictitious father's name, subject to approval by the judge to whom the application was to be made, in which the last name had to be the same as the mother's. The sensitive issue was whether the applicant might seek to use some prominent citizen's name as his putative father's name, even though he was severely limited by the requirement that he have no control over the last name.[14] Rose sought to meet this objection politically by getting two legislators — John T. Anderson, Conservative, and Reuben Nelson, a highly respected DFLer, who had the most popular last names in the state — to sign as co-sponsors of the bill. The bill was approved in committee without much trouble, but when it came to the floor of the House, Dan Slater attacked it because he said it would promote immorality. He made quite a rousing speech on this issue. Rose had prepared for this kind of attack by asking all three of the women representatives — two DFLers and one Conservative, the latter also being a co-sponsor of the bill — to speak on the issue, which they did to good effect. The bill passed, by a vote of 103 to 14.[15]

Thus as the session moved along, with occasional skirmishes between Slater and Rose, Rose was acquiring a stronger conviction that the legislature and the public had to be informed about the goals and tactics of the right-wing extremists. They were having a pernicious influence on some legislation, mainly because the good, honest people of the state did not understand the nature of right-wing extremism. Rose had read about their growing movement in the *New York Times, Newsweek*, and *Commentary* magazines, and other reliable sources of this kind, but most Minnesotans did not read these, and the local press did not carry much national news. Rose had become aware that the right-wing extremists had made significant inroads into government in California, Texas, Alabama, Indiana, and perhaps other states, and now carried significant weight in the Republican party in many other states of the West, South, and Midwest. He resolved to do what he could to prevent this from happening in Minnesota.

Obviously he had to proceed carefully, for he was in the legislative minority, and the Conservative majority would find it difficult to distinguish between their brand of traditional conservatism and the pseudo-conservatism of the right-wing extremists. Whenever Slater and his crowd made one of their "peculiar" forays in the committee hearing rooms, Rose tried to explain to his colleagues — both Conservatives and DFLers — what was happening, and what were the national issues involved that made these people act in a way that seemed so odd in Minnesota. He kept close to the facts, and avoided emotional appeals. His major opportunity to confront the extremists in an all-out way came when Gerda Koch distributed her leaflet accusing Rose of being a Communist collaborator and a security risk. This occurred when the session was about two and a half months old, and most House members had had an opportunity to get to know Rose personally and to learn that he was a loyal citizen and strongly opposed to Communism. After debating with himself for a few days about whether he should do it, he decided to read a brief statement in which he would defend himself and express his concerns about the right-wing extremists. He showed his statement to a close friend, to the DFL minority whip, and to the speaker of the House (who was also the leader of the Conservative caucus). They all cautioned him about possible damage to himself, and said that Gerda Koch's attack would blow over, but he decided to go ahead. On March 20, 1963, he arose on the floor of the House:

Rose: Mr. Speaker.

The Speaker: For what purpose does the gentleman from Hennepin arise?

Rose: I wish to speak on a point of personal privilege.

The Speaker: The Chair recognizes the gentleman from Hennepin. You may proceed.

Rose: Thank you, Mr. Speaker. Ladies and gentlemen of the House: Some of the members of the legislature have been receiving letters accusing me of being a Communist and making other libelous charges against me. I rise to state the facts and also to warn other members of the House of the danger these scurrilous attacks create. I first want to make a matter of public record certain facts about myself.

I have never been a Communist, and I reject completely what Communism stands for. I have a long personal history of anti-Communist activities, and out of my fights with Communism I have learned perhaps better than many members of this House the true evil character of Communism. I have served in the United States Armed Forces and in several governmental positions of trust. This has involved several clearances by the FBI. I do not crow over my record of consistent anti-Communism, as I am aware that some innocent people have been made dupes by the Communists, and I believe that past mistakes — if truly corrected — should be forgiven.

As a strong defender of the basic values of American society, I also want to call your attention to the fact that those who are attacking me are just as subversive and just as revolutionary against American society. They want to change everything that is; they want to revolutionize all the valued aspects of American life. And, of course, they have all the answers to all problems — they want to destroy democratic processes so they can take over power themselves and do what they want with our cherished institutions. They parade falsely under the name of "conservatives" when their real goal is to destroy most of what we in this legislature admire and hold dear. I say that they are dangerous revolutionaries, and no different from Communists in this respect.

Some of these revolutionaries have appeared at several of our committee meetings and have already succeeded in influencing a few pieces of legislation. They are a very tiny minority of the population. I doubt that there are more than 200 of them in the whole state; but they are dedicated and fanatic, and they are devoted to making trouble in all established governmental processes — particularly legislative ones.

I have accumulated enough of their filthy literature to sue them for libel with easy success. Some day I may get around to doing this. My purpose is to warn this legislature against these subversives. They have appeared at some of our committee hearings and have even succeeded in finding influential spokesmen.

I do not pretend to be a Conservative, but I have respect for the true conservative — one who wants to conserve and maintain what he considers good and valuable about the existing society. I am, rather, a Liberal, who believes that social forces are constantly modifying the conditions of our existence, and that government must regularly make adjustments to these social changes so that the basic values *can* be conserved.

In the terms in which I am speaking today, the Conservatives and the Liberals of this legislature have much more in common than either has with the revolutionaries — whether of the left or of the right — who are attacking us. Let us stop giving the name of "conservatives" to these right-wing revolutionaries, and let us familiarize ourselves with what they are trying to do to us and to some of our legislation. We shall save ourselves much trouble in the future if we

83

make just a little effort now to find out about these right-wing sub-versives, who are just as dangerous as the Communists, and who seek to label and libel those who oppose them with the name of Com-munist.

It could probably be honestly said that Dan Slater had less influence in the latter half of the legislative session than he was developing at the beginning. When the 1964 election campaign rolled around, the DFL party made an all-out effort to defeat him, and they succeeded as early as the primary election. The Republican party, and his colleagues in the Conservative caucus of the House, made no effort to help him. As already mentioned, during the early 1964 uproar over "Communism and free love" at the University of Minnesota, when a request was made that the legislature investigate the university, the House Conservative leaders re-fused and the Senate was left to conduct the "investigation" by itself. As will be reported in a later chapter, Dan Slater was the only legislator or ex-legislator who could be found to testify against Arnold Rose at the 1965 trial. Three other Conservative legislators — including Salisbury Adams, who had since become a leader in his caucus — testified in Rose's behalf. In their own way, the Conservatives of the Minnesota House of Representatives had learned to distinguish between true conservatism and the pseudo-conservativism of the right-wing extremists.

6

The Irresponsible Press

A deeper problem

THE Cowles publications are among the most respected in the United States. And rightly so. These publications are organized in two branches headed by brothers John and Gardner Cowles. John Cowles is president of the Minneapolis Star and Tribune Company. Gardner Cowles is president and publisher of the *Des Moines* (Iowa) *Register* and *Tribune*, and also heads *Look* magazine. The policies of these publications have generally shown a high level of social responsibility. Editorially they usually support the Republican party, as do the great majority of newspapers in the United States, but occasionally the *Star* and *Tribune* editors will support Democrats, as when they endorsed Lyndon Johnson in 1964 and Hubert Humphrey and Orville Freeman at some elections. They take what is usually called "an enlightened businessman's point of view," which means that when social needs become significant and obvious, they will support proposed government action intended to satisfy them, but that they will usually not be among the first to see a social problem, or attempt to head it off. They strongly support educational institutions, such as the University of Minnesota.

How did it happen, then, that in December 1963 the *Minneapolis Star* set off the greatest public attack on the university that had ever occurred? It should be clear by now that the *Star* did not itself attack the university. Rather, it reprinted attacks on certain professors made by right-wing extremists, and — probably unintentionally — manufactured more falsehoods through careless reporting. These inflamed certain segments of the public, who then sent letters to the editor which the *Star* published — which further excited the public. The dangerous attack on the university was from the public, which the *Star* brought to fever pitch, rather than from the tiny group of right-wing extremists that initiated the charges. Before trying to explain why this occurred, let us first see exactly what the *Star* did.

In the first place, serious news stories were published about the right-wing extremists, which may have created favorable impressions among some readers. On August 10, 1963, for example, there was a feature story about Gerda Koch and her bookstore. The article was entirely factual — describing the bookstore's location in an apartment (giving the address), indicating the contents, naming the respectable-sounding backers, telling of the growth of the business. The titles of four pamphlets were listed, but the only interpretation in the article came from Miss Koch:

"America and Minneapolis aren't awake to the Communist menace. The biggest challenge for us is to break down the Iron Curtain and get our message to our churches and their people.

"I've been called a crackpot quite a few times, but I'd rather be called one than be one. I've had to get over being afraid to stand up and say what I think regardless of the names they call me."

The only other interpretation in this two-column article is a statement of purpose of Christian Research, as quoted from its articles of incorporation: ". . . to teach, promote and support true patriotism and loyalty to basic Christian and political principles upon which our nation was founded." These statements provided the pro-extremist headlines for the news story: "RIGHT-WINGERS SEEK TO TEACH LOYALTY," "AMERICA ISN'T AWAKE." It apparently never occurred to the reporter to indicate factually what "loyalty" meant to Gerda Koch, or what specific "principles" were being advocated in her literature. The amount of space given to the article would be the envy of any local elected official, and the headlines were chosen to draw attention. The article was printed just about the time the Americanism chairman of the local American Legion was developing his attack on the University of Minnesota for "harboring Communists" and if the reporter had asked Gerda Koch about her association with him, he would readily have found out that they saw eye-to-eye about "subversives at the university," as they called them.

This was by no means the only news story in which the *Star* gave favorable publicity to the extremists. For example, referring to Kennedy's assassination, the *Star* on December 22, 1963, carried an article saying that the right-wing extremists have been the ones calling the attention of the country to the danger of Communists like Oswald. In fact, the extremists did not expose Oswald, and seldom did they refer to any actual Communist.

When the Anoka County incident occurred, the *Star* published a whole series of false statements — many of them quotations from the right-wing extremists — that were damaging to the university. On December 3, the *Star* printed a prominently featured news story — under the byline of reporter Gordon Slovut — headlined " 'U' PROFESSORS FACE PROBE." The article begins with this announcement: "The Anoka County Board Monday ordered an investigation of the backgrounds of two University of Minnesota professors who were invited to speak at a county lecture series." This is false; there was no action by the Board ordering a probe or investigation. The *Star* reprinted this falsehood on at least four occasions during the following three weeks, even though the Anoka County Board sent an official notice to the *Star* saying the story was false. The same news story cited a false and libelous accusation that Gunnar Myrdal, with whom Rose collaborated, was "a notorious Swedish Communist." There was nothing in the news story to indicate that Myrdal might not be "a notorious Swedish Communist" aside from the quotation marks.

On December 4, the day after the Library Board, in a special meeting, reaffirmed its invitation to Rose and Nixon, the *Star* printed another story — by the same reporter — under the headline "ANOKA TALKS 'WOULD HAVE BEEN CALLED OFF,' " and in it the chairman of the County Board, Edward Fields, was quoted as saying that he was considering stopping the library lecture series, in which Professor Sibley had already appeared and Professors Nixon and Rose were scheduled to speak. This is false: The chairman of the County Board denied having made these remarks and said that he knew that the lecture series *could not* have been called off by the County Board, since the series was under the control of the Library Board, not the County Board. The same article quoted a tendentious statement attributed to Chairman Fields: "There are some questions about Rose" in the context of alleged pro-Communist activities.

These news stories provoked some criticism of the Anoka County officials from responsible citizens, and the next Monday, December 9, the County Board officially issued the following news release, which denied the *Star*'s statements as well as reacted against the criticisms:

In order to clarify an apparent erroneous impression, the Board of County Commissioners of the County of Anoka wishes to factually report that they have not at any time taken action in regard to the Anoka County library lecture series. Criticism of the lecture series was received at a regular County Board meeting and its authenticity was routinely checked.

The Board of County Commissioners of the County of Anoka do now issue the following statement.

"The Board of County Commissioners of the County of Anoka have not in the past and do not now attempt to advise or interfere with the University of Minnesota, its policies, or its operation. They believe in the need for academic freedom. They believe, however, that they too have the freedom of choice, the freedom to make decisions, and the freedom to express themselves in matters affecting county government."

The *Star* did not publish this statement, although the St. Paul newspapers and several suburban newspapers did so. Yet it was the *Star* stories of December 3 and 4, presumably based on the Anoka County "probe," which was actually never requested or made, that started the whole furor over academic freedom and "Communist professors at the university."

While publishing his distorted story on two days of *Star* issues (December 3 and 4), Gordon Slovut made no serious effort to reach Rose, who had been libeled, for possible refutation. Even more astounding was the fact that reporter Slovut made no effort to get in touch with Anoka's county attorney, who had been informally asked to look into the matter, as Slovut knew. The *Tribune*, on the other hand, did report, on December 4, the attorney's statement that there was no foundation in fact for the charge made in the Grinde letter, that no probe or investigation had been ordered or had taken place, that the two accused professors were "fine people," and that the whole matter had been blown up out of proportion. The *Star* published Slovut's second false and harmful story *after* the *Tribune* had carried the report of the county attorney's findings. The *Star* reporter never bothered to find out who Gunnar Myrdal was — leaving Grinde's accusation that Myrdal was "a notorious Swedish Communist" unchallenged.[1]

Both County Attorney Johnson and Rose protested the *Star* stories to the managing editor, and expected there would be no further repetition of the falsehoods. The *Star* sent another reporter to interview Rose, a week after the incident. This second reporter, Gary Gilson, was well intentioned, but he did twist Rose's statements and other facts in his story of December 12. For example, he stated that Johnson's report on Rose was "negative." The county attorney never used this word; in fact, the reporter never spoke to Johnson before printing his article, although he put the word "negative" in quotation marks as though it were quoted. Apparently the reporter meant the word "negative" in the medical sense — meaning "having no basis in fact." But that was not the way the readers of the newspaper understood it — the word "negative" sounds bad when it refers to an investigation of somebody.

Gilson also cited Rose as saying that he was being persecuted for his political views. Rose said no such thing. Rose carefully explained to Gilson that he was being persecuted by the right-wing extremists because (1) he had been co-author of a major sociological study, *An American Dilemma*, and because (2) he had once told Gerda Koch, at a public meeting at the University of Minnesota, to sit down when she charged Ralph Bunche with being a Communist, a matter which was completely irrelevant to the subject of the meeting.

What kind of political views was Gilson implying that Rose held that he should be attacked for them? Not in this story, but in other news stories, it was implied that Rose was foisting his "controversial" attitudes on students in the classroom. Yet there wasn't the slightest evidence that Rose ever discussed political issues in the classroom. Rose taught social psychology, and while there are theoretical controversies in the subject matter, there was just no occasion for him to take what is usually called a controversial position on any current political issue. He would probably have done so if the occasion had called for it, but his subject matter did not deal with current political or social issues.

Rose's "controversial" statements outside the classroom dealt mainly with race relations. For over twenty years, Rose has been nationally known as an advocate of equal treatment for the Negro. It is for this reason that Rose was called "leftist" by the right-wing extremists, and the *Star*'s reports in effect aided these extremists by printing their slanders.

On December 20, a third *Star* reporter again repeated the false story that the Anoka County Board ordered an investigation of Rose for "allegedly leftist leanings." This third reporter further stated in his article that Rose was under attack by veterans' groups, by religious groups, and by a St. Paul city official. Rose was never under attack by any of these persons or groups. The *Star* reporter was probably simply careless in confusing Rose with Sibley, but his story nevertheless concocted an additional falsehood.

Rose complained twice to the *Star* about these stories. But the falsehoods were repeated, apparently because they were part of the newsworthy conflict then going on over "academic freedom." There was much else reported in the *Star* about this issue that was erroneous and inflammatory but did not relate to Rose personally.

Because Rose had failed to get any response from the *Star* to two letters he sent them, and because he learned that Anoka County officials had similarly been ignored (a telephone call from County Attorney Johnson to the executive news editor of the *Star* had no effect and the official news release of the Board, which was mailed to the *Star*, was never published by them), he decided to take the first steps toward a libel suit. Under Minnesota law, before one can sue a newspaper, one must send it a "notice of request for retractions." If the newspaper publishes the retractions in five days, there is no basis for a suit. So on December 30, 1963, Rose's attorney, Norman Newhall, sent the *Star* a four-page "notice of request for retractions." After detailing the above-mentioned falsehoods printed in the *Star*, Newhall wrote:

On behalf of Professor Rose we request that the *Star* publish a clear retraction of all of the foregoing libelous material, making clear to its readers in such retraction the following points:

1. The Anoka County Board took no official action of any kind to investigate or probe the background of Professor Rose.
2. The inquiries made by County Attorney Johnson led him to report to the Anoka County Board that Rose and Nixon are "obviously both fine people," "that the affair had gotten blown out of proportion," and "that the accusations as to Professor Rose were false and unfounded."
3. Gunnar Myrdal, with whom Rose co-authored *An American Dilemma,* is not and never has been a Communist; but is rather a Swedish Social Democrat of worldwide distinction who has vigorously opposed Communism for years and has served as executive secretary of the United Nations Economic Commission for Europe, as Minister of Commerce for Sweden, and in other positions of comparable importance.
4. There is no evidence that Professor Rose is a Communist, a Communist sympathizer, a leftist or that he has leftist leanings or connections.
5. Professor Rose has not at any time been "under attack" from any veterans groups nor St. Paul City officials, nor has he been "under attack" by any religious group other than Christian Research, Inc., which engages in exclusively political activity unrelated to religious functions of any kind.

Whereas letters, phone calls, and news releases had failed to get the *Star* to stop publishing falsehoods about Rose, this "notice" had an immediate effect. The day that the notice was received, a *Star* vice president phoned Newhall to ask for a personal conference. At the conference with Newhall and Rose were the *Star* vice president, a legal adviser, and the managing editor who had charge of reporter Slovut's news stories. Rose was surprised to see who the editor was: He had been a reporter for the *Star* three and four years earlier when Rose and his neighbors were opposing the Highway Department's attempts to place a freeway through their neighborhood. The reporter, now editor, had not provided the friendly publicity for the neighborhood which Rose and his friends had hoped for. But the suspicion had never crossed his mind, until now, that the reporter-editor had had any personal feeling against the neighborhood group.

The conference began with Newhall summarizing the contents of his formal "notice." The editor then began a vehement denial or excuse for every one of Newhall's statements. He saw no difference between an "informal inquiry" by County Attorney Johnson and an "official investigation ordered by the Anoka County Board." He had had no space to report the County Board's denial that they had ordered a "probe" of Rose. Since the *Tribune* had reported Johnson's "clearance" of Rose, he said, the *Star* had no need to repeat this (although the *Star* did repeat the original falsehoods twice after that). He said he knew nothing of Myrdal, and merely quoted Grinde's statement that Myrdal was "a notorious Swedish Communist." He recognized that Rose had not been "under attack from certain veterans and religious groups and a St. Paul City official" (as reported in the *Star* of December 20) but said this was simply a way of getting Sibley and Rose into one sentence, and Sibley *had* been so attacked. "What would you have me do?" he inquired, "write two sentences when one would suffice?" (The full sentence was "The statement [by a group of campus and religious advisers] defended Dr. Mulford Q. Sibley of the Department of Political Science and Dr. Arnold M. Rose of the Department of Sociology who have been under attack from certain veterans and religious groups and a St. Paul City official.") It didn't bother him that the sentence was now false. The tone of the editor, as he tried to refute the criticisms, was so acid and unfriendly that Rose was astounded. He had expected that, once the erroneous reporting had been pointed out, the *Star* would be happy to print a retraction to avoid any possibility of a lawsuit.

Newhall and Rose sought to clarify their criticisms of the *Star*'s news stories. There was one amusing interchange over the first point: Rose asked the news editor, "If, as you say, there is no difference between County Attorney Johnson's checking into the backgrounds of the two professors and the Anoka County Board's ordering an official investigation of the two, who then was investigated?" "Sibley and Rose, of course, as we have reported in the *Star* all along," came the prompt reply from the editor. "Wrong," said Rose. "If your reporter had any interest in reporting what actually did occur, he would have indicated that County Attorney Johnson was informally asked to check into the backgrounds of Professors Rose and *Nixon*. Professor Sibley was never checked into, since he had already spoken at the library when the Grinde demand to stop the library lectures was received by the Board. But Sibley makes exciting news, so you bring him into the newspapers whether he's part of the facts or not."

Newhall and Rose got no concession from the editor. But finally the vice president intervened, by saying something like this: The *Star* has no desire to libel Professor Rose, and we don't concede that there has been any libel, only some human carelessness. We won't publish a retraction, but we will publish a new news story that will clarify four of your five points. We'll make this news story seem appropriate as news by printing it on the day when you are to give your address at the Anoka County Library, so that the corrections will appear simply as background for the announcement of your address. The one complaint you make that we cannot bring into such a news story is that we quoted without refutation Grinde's statement that Myrdal is "a notorious Swedish Communist."

Rose was unhappy about leaving Myrdal out of the proposed *Star* story, but Newhall persuaded him he should compromise. Rose also wanted the story to be written as a kind of retraction, even if the *Star* were allowed to save face by not publishing a formal retraction, but again Newhall persuaded him to compromise. Rose realized that he could not quarrel with his lawyer, and that the main thrust of his efforts must be against Gerda Koch and other right-wing extremists. He privately felt that, if he won his case against Miss Koch, he would be in a better legal position to sue the *Star*, which had repeated her libels. If Newhall did not like a legal attack on the powerful *Star*, Rose felt he could later find another lawyer. At that time, he could not know that two months later the United States Supreme Court would issue a decision in the *New York Times* case which would make it impossible for a public official to sue a newspaper for libel unless the newspaper refused to retract and unless the plaintiff could prove actual malice. Rose had no evidence that the *Star* had malice in publishing falsehoods about him, and he did not believe that it had. The culpability of the *Star* in creating difficulties for him and for the university was the only significant point on which Newhall and Rose disagreed during the whole case, and it did not seem they were disagreeing about the *facts* of the *Star*'s culpability, but about whether it was *wise* to sue a major newspaper. Only the subsequent *New York Times* decision pushed Rose into accepting Newhall's position.

A few days later, on January 7, 1964, the *Star* did print the background story on Rose's Anoka Library speech. All the facts which the *Star*'s vice president had agreed to were in it. But it was a story written without grace, without any recognition of all the damaging statements that the *Star* had made about Rose during a whole month. It associated Rose with Sibley and announced Sibley's forthcoming debate with Rosen, which of course Rose had not requested be in the story. It even included a remark that, "In the flurry [over Sibley's controversial letter to the *Minnesota Daily*], Rose was left by the wayside, and Sibley has been the sole target for over a month." In sum, this news story was hardly a response to Rose's formal "notice of request for retractions," and until the *New York Times* decision it left open the possibility of suit against the *Star* at some future date.

Two days after the *Star* printed its "compromise article" it again published a news story referring to Rose as having been accused of "left-wing tendencies," without indicating that the accusation had been made by a right-wing extremist of questionable reliability. Only the *Star*'s false stories about Rose have been detailed here, but these were merely a portion of the inflammatory articles the *Star* printed about the university at this time.

It is difficult to determine why the *Minneapolis Star* published in its news columns stories which were false and inflammatory, and hence damaging to the university and to certain of its professors. The *Star* has generally given support to the university. The *Star* and the *Tribune* are owned and published by the same company, yet the latter newspaper showed itself to be much more responsible in the crisis of December 1963–January 1964. The two newspapers form the "monopoly press" of Minneapolis, the *Tribune* being the only morning newspaper, and the *Star* the only evening newspaper. They have one over-all editor for the editorial pages as well as one publisher, but each has an entirely separate staff of reporters, feature writers, managing editors, and news editors.

There would seem to be two parts to an interpretation of why the *Star* did what it did. The first is particular to the *Star*; the second is applicable to all but the very best newspapers in the United States. It is difficult to prove the first part, because the *Star*'s directors would probably deny it. It is based on certain facts, yet the interpretation of these facts is only a matter of plausibility, not proof. The *Star* was having certain difficulties in the early 1960's: Two of its top editors were dismissed after a disagreement with the publisher, and the direction of the newspaper was taken over by John Cowles, Jr., the son of the publisher. There were sufficient differences between the old and the new management of the *Star* so that a number of reporters resigned shortly after the transition. This left the paper with a largely new and partly inexperienced staff of reporters. This did not happen to the *Tribune* to the same extent, although later dismissal of the chief editor of the editorial pages (for both newspapers) also reduced morale on the *Tribune*'s staff.[2]

In the midst of this trying transition, there was a lengthy newspaper strike. For many months neither newspaper was published. Not only was this a further blow to the morale of the reporters, but it opened an opportunity for a rival newspaper to get started in Minneapolis. The new newspaper, the *Minneapolis Herald*, was an afternoon newspaper and therefore would be in competition with the *Star* when the latter's strike ended. The *Herald* had all the problems of a new newspaper — acquiring the technical competence, attracting advertising, etc. — but it had aggressive leadership and enough financial backing to get underway. Its main advantage was that, for several months, it was the only daily newspaper in Minneapolis, and therefore could attract circulation which might continue after the *Star* and *Tribune* resumed publication. The managers of the established newspapers prohibited their reporters from writing for the *Herald*, of course, and there were rumors that they tried to prevent the *Herald* from getting access to the national news services and to leading advertisers.

The important thing about the *Herald* for our story is that it showed some signs of right-wing extremism, in both its editorial and its news columns. It was not "all-out" extremist, but it was decidedly more so than the *Star* and *Tribune*. And it had a strong dash of the old-time Populism that would appeal to the less well educated, as well as an extremism on certain matters that would appeal to some wealthier but narrow-minded conservatives. Besides, it made an appeal for underdog sympathy, against the monopoly press of the *Star* and *Tribune*. It gained circulation rapidly during the *Star* and *Tribune*'s long-drawn-out strike, and retained a portion of that circulation after those "regular" newspapers first resumed publication. It seems likely that this motivated the directors of the *Star*, which was now in direct competition with the *Herald*, to undercut some of the *Herald*'s appeal to readers with extremist and Populist inclinations. This showed up less on the editorial page of the *Star*, which was staffed by the same old-line liberal-Republican team that also prepared the editorial page for the *Tribune*, than it did on the more flexible news pages of the *Star*. The feature story about Gerda Koch already mentioned, headlined "RIGHT-WINGERS SEEK TO TEACH LOYALTY," is an example of the new style of what might be called "interested objectivity" toward right-wing extremism. Moreover, it was a time when some extremists were gaining control of the Republican party in many states, and while the *Star* and *Tribune* never supported this wing of the Republican party, they may have felt some pressure to bend to the interests of those of their readers and advertisers who did.

It was at this phase of the *Star*'s history that the Anoka County incident broke and the attack on the University of Minnesota began. The *Star*'s partial descent into sensational reporting on this and other public issues may have been its response to competition with the *Herald* and its response to a portion of the public temper which was supporting the Goldwaterites.

The *Herald* ran into increasing technical difficulties, and it had increasing trouble holding advertisers. When a fire destroyed the building in which it was operating, the *Herald* ceased publication "temporarily." For several years afterward, it attempted to resume publication, but gradually the threat of competition to the *Star* disappeared. The decisive defeat of Barry Goldwater in the November 1964 elections also reduced the pressure on the *Star* to cater to the extremist wing of the Republican party. The *Star* increasingly resumed its traditional "responsible" (though perhaps not always thorough) reporting, but to this day it has not fully re-created the highly qualified staff of reporters it had had until the beginning of the 1960's.

The second reason offered here as to why the *Star* disseminated Miss Koch's statements, added falsehoods, and otherwise published materials (such as letters to the editor) which inflamed the Minnesota public against the state university is one which applies to many newspapers around the country. In fact, the *Star* was not alone in disseminating information antagonistic to the university during the crisis period of December 1963 through the winter and spring of 1964: Several of the small-town newspapers in Minnesota also did this. But it is not known that any of the latter published falsehoods. The *Star* is the newspaper with largest circulation in the state, and its circulation extends to some extent throughout the state and even beyond its boundaries. This second explanation requires that we consider the psychology of many newspaper reporters and editors in the United States. They have a conception of what constitutes "news" that involves a selection from, and often a distortion of, the facts. They write the kind of stories which they think will interest and entertain the newspaper-reading public, even though these stories may have little relationship to what actually did occur.

Selection of items to report in the newspapers is necessary and inevitable: Certain personalities, events, and institutions are "newsworthy" while others are not. Many things which occur, no matter how important to the individuals involved, are not important enough for the public as a whole to gain much, if any, space in the newspapers. Events which involve other individuals, no matter how trivial these events may seem to the individuals themselves, receive lengthy and repeated treatment in the newspapers because these individuals are important or interesting to the public. The news editors and reporters must be the ones, in a free society which properly boasts of its freedom of the press, to make this kind of selection. In spite of all this, the newspapers are not justified in publishing false, distorted, and damaging stories. And if significant errors are made by a newspaper's reporter, as errors can be made by any human being, the newspaper should have an obligation to correct them when the errors are brought to its attention, even though the damage has been done.

The problem is not simply one of selecting what is important and avoiding falsehoods. Every reporter will probably agree verbally to these principles, although he may not always put them into practice. But what reporters and newspaper people generally find it difficult to understand and accept is that they have developed a subculture — as every profession does — in which a good newspaper report is *defined* as a dramatic event. If there is no drama — no tragedy or comedy or excitement — in the facts, the newspaper reporters will add it, often quite unconsciously and as a matter of keeping up to professional expectations. In other words, the newspaper is seen by reporters — and again this is something they are not consciously aware of — as an *entertainment medium*. The raw material for this entertainment is, certainly enough, the events of real life. But so is it also for a realistic short story. There are only two incidental differences between a newspaper report and a short story: (1) the newspaper is very "time-limited" in describing events that occurred within the past day, or which had a new development during the past day; (2) the short story does not mention the names of real persons, even though these may provide the underlying facts of the story. It would probably also have to be said that most short stories are more skillfully, more artfully, written than are news reports, if for no other reason than that the short-story writer has more time to prepare his "report." But the essential similarity between the typical news report and the short story is that both are works of drama; both seek to "entertain" their readers, in the broad sense of the term.

It might be objected that the newspapers also seek to inform their readers what is going on in the world. But this is true only insofar as the facts and events can be written in an entertaining manner, which is exactly what the short-story writer is concerned about. True enough, there are events — like a presidential election or a border clash in India — that the newspaper will feel absolutely compelled to report, while a short-story writer may ignore them because they do not seem to hold enough intrinsic characteristics to be made into artistic drama. But the newspaper reporter will still report these events in dramatic form, and since they lack the intrinsic capacity to be made into artistic drama, they will be presented as poor drama, or melodrama.

There is nothing original about the observation above. Nearly anyone who has had firsthand contact with an event that is written up for the newspapers will immediately recognize the distorted and dramatic nature of the report. The newspaper account, if it is of any length beyond two inches, will seem to have only incidental similarity to the event. The citizen who has one or two such experiences will either protest to the newspaper about them, or much more likely dismiss them as aberrations of a reporter or news editor. But they are not aberrations — drama and distortion are the very mind of newspaper reporters and editors; they are the latter's "definitions of the situations" which constitute the subculture of the newswriting profession. Those persons who are in frequent firsthand contact with events written up for newspapers — who are by definition persons in public life, mainly politicians — quickly come to recognize this subculture of the newsman. They see how deep, pervasive, and unconscious it is among newsmen, so they seldom protest against it publicly. It is a rare event when an experienced politician like Richard Nixon inveighs against the distortions in the press before a public audience, as he did immediately after he lost the election for governor of California in 1962. Many were shocked or amused that he did this, but every experienced politician — Republican or Democrat — knew exactly what Nixon was talking about and sympathized with him for what he had had to take from the press. Many politicians berate the press privately, but probably most politicians learn how to adjust to and even to manipulate the subculture of newsmen. It is an easy thing to manipulate a newspaper reporter, once one learns the techniques and the dimensions of the subculture. In presenting a potential news story to a reporter, the politician usually needs to offer it with a dramatic angle before the reporter has a chance to think up one himself. The politician quickly learns the range of dramatic angles appropriate for a given category of news stories, and then offers the one which is most favorable to his own cause, taking care that the dramatic angle does not appear to be too self-serving. Skillful politicians — like Franklin D. Roosevelt or John F. Kennedy — made an art of this, and their images grew in the very newspapers that were editorially opposed to them.[3]

Newspaper reporters are so intent on finding dramatic angles for news stories that they quickly lose touch with the real world with which they seem to have so much contact. This is why the world of the politician — which is probably the most frequently reported world in the news media — is so little known to the average "informed" citizen. The events that occur in an election campaign or a state legislative committee session "make sense" to the public only in terms of the reporters' sense of drama, practically never as the participant experiences it. For example, what goes on in the politicians' "smoke-filled room" is often a pure product of some reporter's imagination. Americans can gain accurate knowledge of the public lives of teachers, grocers, bankers, plumbers, doctors, or of those in other occupations high or low, because their main contact with them is through direct experience, no matter how infrequent.[4] But Americans do not gain accurate knowledge of the public lives of their politicians, because their most frequent experience of them is through the mind and pen of the reporter. One direct visit to a campaign headquarters or to a legislative hearing will temporarily correct for the average citizen the illusions which the newspaper reporters have built around these places and their politician inhabitants. But the day-by-day repetition of the illusions of the reporter — in the newspapers and on the radio or television — will soon outweigh the factual experience of the direct contact. Thus for public events and public personalities the average citizen is forced to some extent to live in the "dramatic world" which has been created by the subculture of the reporters' profession.

An important recent example of the distortion created by virtually the entire press of the nation was the failure of the press to report the organization of the right-wing extremists in the Republican party throughout much of the United States between 1962 and 1964. The newspapers reported political news in terms of the colorful personalities of the possible candidates and the dramatic Republican presidential primaries in half a dozen states. The presidential primary has the dramatic element of conflict, and personalities are always "interesting," but neither help much in understanding why the right-wing extremists captured the Republican National Convention in 1964. This was mainly due to the plodding work of these extremists in thousands of precincts throughout the country — which the newspapers did not report, except occasionally as *local* news within the states where the extremists won control of the state and district conventions. They thus missed the most important domestic news story of 1964. Even after the convention, which should have alerted them, they continued to report the struggles within the top leadership of the Republican party, to the neglect of the controlling forces within the party at the grass roots.

Ordinarily there is no great harm in this neglect of the nondramatic, except that it keeps the public in greater ignorance of public events than is desirable in a democracy. There is too much competition among ordinary politicians to permit any one of them to exploit the reporters' dramatic passion for his own benefit to a danger point for democracy. Many events are one-shot affairs, and event succeeds event, so that the dramatic creativity of the newspaper reporters usually works itself out in a succession of unrelated short stories. In other words, the newspaper or the other mass media present a highly distorted dramatic image of the public world, but there is usually no consistent thread running through their stories that would provide a motive for systematically misguided public action.

This is the "usual" thing, but there are exceptions. In all cultures there are certain dramatic themes that are extremely appealing to nearly all members of the society; in Western culture these include the themes of the Jesus image, the Devil, sin, and conflict. When themes like these are suggested to newspaper reporters by events or by demagogues, the reporters will become unusually inspired to do their most "creative" dramatic writing, just as these themes are the main inspiration for novelists, poets, and short-story writers. But the latter do not pretend to describe the real public world, and anyone who thinks they do is quickly recognized as living in a world of fantasy. Reporters do claim to describe the real, public world, and the *dramatis personae* are flesh-and-blood people. So when an event or a demagogue suggests themes like the Jesus image, the Devil, sin, and conflict to reporters, a strain of consistency appears in their writings. This consistency appears both among the reporters and over a period of time, so that all the interpretations seem to be moving in the same direction. This can work the public up into a condition that sociologists study under the name of "collective excitement." [5]

Collective excitement can be created in any society by the physical coming together of a large number of people, outside of regular institutional auspices such as those of a church, a political party, or some other association. If there is any source of frustration or unrest in the society (and when isn't there in our society?) a provocative idea or an emotion-producing song or symbol can start them in a chain reaction that, if unchecked, will end in a collective frenzy of either senseless destruction or orgiastic expression. In contemporary society, the mass media can set off a similar chain reaction of collective excitement under the proper circumstances. A noteworthy example was the 1938 radio dramatization of H. G. Wells's *War of the Worlds*, in which millions of people in the Middle Atlantic states were briefly convinced that there was an invasion of Martians in their area, and they stimulated each other into a frenzied panic of attempted escape.[6] Extreme examples of this sort of behavior are rare today, although they occurred with considerable frequency in the periods of social disorganization in the late Middle Ages and at the time of the French Revolution. But in less extreme form, involving only a portion of the population, they still occur with some frequency. A number of the recent race riots, student "panty-raids" and other expressive demonstrations of students (including the annual destructive binges in Florida and Sweden), and even crime waves have been set off by dramatic "news reports" that these things are "developing." The news reports, of course, are not by any means the sole causes of these manifestations of collective excitement, but they are contributory and often necessary elements in a chain of causation.

Only a tiny proportion of the population engages in the race riots, destructive orgies by youth, and crime waves, and these are usually terminated quickly — hence they are not dangerous to the society as a whole. But the newspapers (and, to a lesser extent, the radio and television) also set off waves of fear, anger, and excitement that affect larger proportions of the population for longer periods of time. Again there are underlying causes in the society, but without a series of fear- or anger-provoking news stories, the collective excitement would not occur in our heterogeneous, pluralistic society. It is rarely the events themselves that provoke the fear and anger; it is the dramatic presentation of them and their repetition that help to create the collective excitement. If a demagogue should ever be able to seize political control of the United States and turn it into a dictatorship, whether of the "left" or of the "right," it will only be with the aid of a substantial portion of the American mass media. The reporters and editors may personally oppose the dictatorship, but they will create the collective excitement in the public that will make it welcome the dictatorship. Their characteristic penchant for an "interesting" and "exciting" story, regardless of its truth, its context, or its inflammatory character, would — if the situation or the demagogue provided material for "exciting" stories with a consistent theme — create a socially explosive atmosphere. If a demagogue understood and played upon this tendency of news reporters and editors, he could gain his purpose of inflaming the public mind.

The intriguing or provocative element in the dramatic presentation of the news stories differs from society to society: in American society that element most often seems to be, as already noted, the Jesus image, the Devil, sin, or conflict. The build-up of Senator Joseph McCarthy in the early 1950's seems to have largely been accomplished by the press, using especially the first two of the popular themes in the "news stories" about him. McCarthy never produced a single Communist, and his speeches were essentially all repetitions of the theme of fifty-four Communists in the federal government, which he first introduced in a talk at Wheeling, West Virginia, in 1950. But for over four years, most newspapers periodically gave these public statements front-page space and presented them in a dramatic form. This gave the stories the kind of consistency mentioned above as a cause of collective excitement. Of course, the public concern over the Korean war, and the initial failure of President Eisenhower and his top assistants to dispute McCarthy's statements, were also important in the creation of the collective excitement in support of McCarthy. Newsmen apparently found McCarthy fascinating, both when they early dramatized him as an angry Jesus driving the Communists from the temple (the federal government) and later when they dramatized him as the Devil opposing the clean-cut heroes of the Army. They almost never portrayed him as the mediocre senator from Wisconsin, which he was, who had little new to say after his 1950 speech.

It took the newsmen a long while to see the danger McCarthy posed to American institutions and democratic government. Rose remembers attending a lecture by the late Gideon Seymour in 1952. Seymour was the respected and influential executive editor of the *Minneapolis Star* and *Tribune* for many years, and he had basically liberal impulses while serving as a pillar of the local Republican establishment. He spoke at this lecture at the University of Minnesota on "voluntary associations" as a basic strength of American democratic society, echoing a theme which social observers of the United States since Tocqueville had expressed. During the question period after his lecture, Rose expressed agreement with his general views, but asked him whether Senator McCarthy's statements that so many American voluntary associations (including the Parent-Teacher Association) were infiltrated with Communists were not driving many fearful citizens out of these organizations, and otherwise rendering them ineffective. He immediately denied this, and said that McCarthy was a fascinating figure but had no influence in the country. This was in 1952, two years after McCarthy had begun to play his single note on the very guts of the American people, with the aid of the newspapers.

On Monday morning, December 2, 1963, a little-known newspaper reporter for the *Minneapolis Star* heard a sensational letter read at an otherwise mundane meeting of the Anoka County commissioners, and immediately sensed the theme of conflict for a dramatic news story. He did not wait for the commissioners to finish their meeting — which he had been sent to cover — but left the room with the remark "I've got my story for today." Indeed he had, and many other reporters for the same newspaper found that story intriguing enough to repeat and embellish it in the weeks to follow. Conflict followed conflict in the newspaper stories, and, after Sibley's letter was published, the theme of sin — specifically, free love and nudism — became the strong note of variation on the basic theme of conflict. The newspaper reporters, and their editors, were so full of the dramatic themes that they failed to notice the false content of their stories. It was not until a libel suit was threatened that they stopped the repetitions of falsehoods in their news reports.

Even then they pursued the themes of conflict and sin so avidly that they could not get their facts straight. The headlines on the news story reporting Rose's Anoka County talk on January 7, 1964, conveyed almost the opposite of what he said. The headline made him sound like a pro-Communist, so he wrote the following letter to the *Star*, which was published in the letters' column:

Dear Sir:

The headline to your news story about my Anoka County lecture conveyed almost the opposite of what I said. Your headline was " 'U' Professor Flays Anti-Red Extremists."

Almost half my talk was devoted to pointing out that the right-wing extremists were *not* opposing Communism. I quoted one of them directly as saying that she was opposed to "socialized medicine, urban renewal, fair housing laws, metropolitan government, federal aid to education, trade expansion, disarmament, etc." This was her definition of Communism, not mine, and your failure to indicate that this was a quotation from a right-wing extremist led to the misunderstanding of your reader Richard Brostrom in his letter of Jan. 8.

I said that the right-wing extremists were not fighting Communism at all — in Russia, China, or this country — but spent their time fighting Presidents Truman, Eisenhower, Kennedy and Johnson, the University of Minnesota, as well as others who actually were fighting Communism.

Thus for the headline writer to say that I was opposing those who were fighting Communism is quite the opposite of what I actually said. I did oppose the extremists, but I don't believe they are really "anti-Red."

Rose's next local lecture was an explanation of the libel suit he had just filed against Gerda Koch *et al.* He made this speech on February 8 to the faculty of the university, under the auspices of the local branch of the American Association of University Professors, at the Faculty Club. Since the audience was an invited one, and the lecture was not open to the public, there was no necessity to report it in the newspapers at all. But the *Star* would not miss an opportunity to report the latest development in the drama of the conflict between the university and the right-wing extremists, and it reported the speech incorrectly. Rose complained about the errors in the following letter, but this one was not published, perhaps because it criticized the *Star*'s whole policy:

Dear Sir:

Your reporter gets a low grade for her reporting of the faculty meeting at the U. of M. at which I lectured on Feb. 8.

At one point she quotes me as saying about the opposite of what I actually did say. I did not say that our institutions are revolutionary. I said that revolutionaries are seeking to destroy our institutions. Specifically, I said that extremists are attacking our Constitution, our leading public officials (Eisenhower, Kennedy, Warren, etc.), our public schools, our libraries, and our universities. They are trying to destroy all these in order to make over society into their fantastic totalitarian image.

The second error also had to do with the object of attacks by the right-wing extremists. I said that, to the best of my knowledge, there was no one on the faculty of the university who favored nudism, free love, or communism. A combination of right-wing extremists and irresponsible newspaper reporting had conveyed to the public the erroneous idea that such did exist on the campus. I further said that the purpose of the extremists in helping to build this false image was not merely to attack academic freedom, but to destroy the university itself.

The public has been led to believe a lot of nonsense about the university. Can't this be stopped, and straight facts reported?

After this, Rose avoided local speeches, and so he avoided distorted news stories about himself. But the university continued to come under the *Star*'s "dramatic news" policy. The local Veterans of Foreign Wars passed a resolution supporting academic freedom at the university, which the *Star* reported under the headline "VFW BACKS REGENTS 'BUT . . .'" thus falsely implying that the VFW had significant reservations about academic freedom. What the VFW expressed doubts about was the wisdom of Professor Sibley in writing his semi-facetious letter — a position which most faculty members probably agreed with. When the chairman of the Board of Regents, Dr. Charles Mayo, issued a carefully worded statement on the academic freedom controversy, the *Star* published only excerpts from it and elicited off-the-cuff remarks from individual members of the board, which tended to confuse what was actually stated in the official board action.

Further examples could be given of how the *Star* damaged the university in its news columns. All through these hectic months, the *Star* printed letters to the editor which attacked the university. At the same time, there were editorials supporting academic freedom. The best interpretation of what the *Star* was doing appeared in an editorial of a small-town Republican newspaper. The *Winona Daily News*, on February 7, 1964, said:

A Deeper Problem

The Twin Cities news media, by their dogged pursuit of the charges and countercharges that abounded in the Sibley-Rosen affair, blew the entire dispute out of proportion and created a public climate in which suspicion of the university could find a breeding ground. Moreover, the same media, by their seeming inability to judge the worth of an issue, played into the hands of those charlatans who always are ready to exploit mass communications for their own purposes . . .

By faithfully and unquestioningly reporting every irresponsible statement made during the Sibley-Rosen dispute, the Twin Cities media allowed the persons making the statements to add themselves to their staffs. Anything could be said, and it would be spread throughout the state by the media. The whole unsavory affair is uncomfortably reminiscent of the heyday of Joe McCarthy.

Almost two years later, when the controversy had died down, Professor Sibley was given an opportunity to speak at the annual Editors' Short Course at the university's School of Journalism. He asked the following pertinent "questions":

If the press wasn't responsible for making and then arbitrarily ending the controversy over a satirical letter he wrote to the university *Daily*?

Whether the controversy did, in fact, deserve the importance the press gave it?

Whether the press didn't exhibit a lack of humor in failing to note that the tone of the letter was satirical?

And whether the press was, or even ought to be, conscious of the impact of the controversy on his wife? [7]

When the trial of *Rose v. Koch et al.* occurred, the *Star* reported practically none of it. The *Tribune* gave it restrained and objective coverage. The "collective excitement" was over.

7

The Law of Libel

A right decision and
dangerous dicta

MANY people believe that when they have been robbed or swindled or their contracts have been violated, and the offending party is accessible, they ought to be able to go into a court of law and claim restitution. It isn't that simple. In any orderly society, the statutes passed by a legislature are written in a general way to protect all citizens, so they cannot exactly fit every single case. Under the Anglo-American system, case-made law modifies the statutes to take care of the great variation in individual lawsuits and to avoid conflict between statutes. But even the courts cannot take care of all the individual variations, and they never completely succeed in reconciling the inherent inadequacies of laws. Law, like science, is a constantly evolving institution which can never reach perfection. In addition, there are problems concerning "facts" — only in television dramas do all the facts come out and get proved. How can one ever prove "all the facts" in real life? Irrelevancies have to be kept out of a court trial; the judge rules out material or testimony which is "irrelevant, immaterial, and incompetent" according to time-honored rules of evidence, but this is sometimes arbitrary and unjust. The law is a human institution, and therefore has human failings. With the best of cases, there is a risk in going before the law to obtain justice.

Then there is the problem of the jury, which is involved in many court trials in the United States: in nearly all serious criminal cases and in many civil cases involving any sizable amount of damages. The jury consists of twelve [1] men and women whom the parties to the suit do not know personally. They are persons with their own problems and prejudices, hauled out of their jobs and their homes to decide the facts in a case in which they start by knowing nothing. And "knowing nothing" must go pretty far: In the case of *Rose v. Koch*, potential jurors were stricken from the list if they had ever heard or read in the newspapers anything about Rose, Miss Koch, or the lawsuit (Rose's name had appeared in the local newspapers about once a month since 1959; Miss Koch had been the subject of major news stories at least half a dozen times since 1960); if they knew anyone at the University of Minnesota (which employed well over 5000 persons); if they knew anything about the John Birch Society or any of the half-dozen fundamentalist ministers in Minneapolis supporting Gerda Koch; and so on. One must be pretty "ignorant," if one answers honestly, in order to sit on a jury today. Would anyone voluntarily really want to trust his fate or his reputation to such a group of ignorant persons?

Finally, there is the problem of one's attorney. There are so many rules of law and of evidence that only a trained person can effectively present a case in court. Not only that, but under the American "adversary system" of court trials, one needs a friend in court. One can trust one's friend, but inadvertently he may not do the best for one's case. There are only so many hours in a day; the attorney must serve a number of clients simultaneously to earn a living; he cannot possibly know "all" about his client or his client's case to present the case in an ideal way; he must plan his presentation to the court and the jury, taking into consideration the probable outcomes of alternative strategies. One cannot but feel that he faces enormous complexity and difficulty when he places his case in the hands of an attorney.

In a criminal case, of course, one has no choice but to offer oneself up before the law, the jury, and one's lawyer. But in a civil suit, a plaintiff, who voluntarily brings a case to court, must be either mad, unusually aggressive, naive, or very strongly motivated. Whether Rose was or was not mad or unusually aggressive, the gentle reader will have to judge for himself. He was not exactly naive, being a student of the sociology of law. He was strongly motivated, of course. But there were many times between his first serious thought of initiating a lawsuit, in December 1963, and the end of the trial, on November 23, 1965, when he doubted his good sense and rationality for having brought this lawsuit.

The jury remained a puzzle to Rose until the final outcome of the trial, as it inevitably must. His lawyer, Norman Newhall, Jr., was one of the best in Minneapolis, and Rose came to trust him rapidly. But Newhall started with no experience in libel suits, and almost no contact with right-wing extremists or even with the world of social science scholarship. Newhall admitted after the trial that he hadn't realized what he was in for when he accepted the case. From the time of their first discussion about the possibility of a lawsuit, on December 5, 1963, Rose felt a disturbing anxiety about the need to explain to Newhall all that needed to be explained. Throughout 1964 and 1965 Rose presented numerous books, documents, and memoranda to Newhall, but Newhall was too busy with other cases to read them all right away — and of course there was no need to read them all right away.

In early 1965, Newhall had a young assistant prepare a summary of the relevant law cases. The memorandum showed the law to be much more unfavorable to Rose's case than Newhall had earlier believed. The young legal assistant later confessed to Rose that, at the time he finished the memorandum, he didn't think Rose had one chance in 200 of winning the suit. The twenty-three months' lapse of time between Rose's first contact with Newhall about the case and the opening of the trial was a blessing. It permitted Newhall to absorb the mountain of facts which Rose shoved at him, and to discover new facts and law for himself. As late as two weeks before the opening of the trial, Rose had doubts whether Newhall had mastered all the essential facts of the case. And it wasn't until the trial itself was under way that Newhall acquired a full understanding of the mentality of the right-wing extremist who was his adversary and of the defendants generally. But during the last two weeks before the trial, Newhall really studied the complex facts of the case and prepared his case logically, and when they went into the courtroom on the opening day, Rose appreciated and trusted his "friend in court." Newhall performed marvelously all through the trial. He was nervous when he started, but soon he came to enjoy the trial, even though it was taking up much more of his valuable time than he had anticipated, without adequate compensation.

It was the weak law of libel which bothered both Newhall and Rose the most as the trial opened. The United States has had a weaker law of libel than most other countries because of its historic concern about protecting the rights of freedom of speech and freedom of the press. A few states have criminal libel laws, and all states have some kind of law permitting civil suits against libel. But the law is intentionally weak in all jurisdictions, reflecting the historic American belief that a person should be free to speak and publish what is in his mind. If one libels or slanders another and makes any sort of apology at all, there is almost no possibility of winning a suit against him, even when damage has been done. The result is that there have been relatively few libel suits, and fewer still won. In contrast, the British have a stronger libel law, many more successful suits, and yet have just as much freedom of speech and press as the United States does. In October 1967 Prime Minister Harold Wilson won a libel suit against a publication which suggested that he was having an affair with his secretary. A suit of this nature would now be virtually impossible in the United States. Even in South Africa, where militant anti-Communists and fundamentalists run the government in almost dictatorial fashion, one of them was successfully sued for libel by two liberal clergymen advocating religious ecumenicism and racial justice. (The libel was that two unnamed theologians had plotted to overthrow the South African government and had identified themselves with international Communism to destroy white Christianity.) Britain and South Africa offer just two examples of countries which give the individual protection against false accusation. The United States now gives the individual practically no such protection.[2]

One aspect of the American libel law which makes it especially weak is that, in a trial, hearsay testimony can be presented by a defendant accused of libel or slander. In a trial on any other charge, hearsay testimony will be excluded by the judge, and even in a libel suit the plaintiff or his witnesses cannot use hearsay testimony. The rationale behind this unusual privilege for the defendant involves the distinction between compensatory damages and punitive damages. Compensatory damages are claimed by a plaintiff in a libel suit to repay him for losses which he has sustained as a consequence of the libel — either out-of-pocket expenses or damage to his reputation which reduces his earning power or hurts him in some other way. Punitive damages can be awarded by a jury to a successful plaintiff to punish the defendant and to deter him from writing further libels. Punitive damages are used as a deterrent to protect the community as well as the plaintiff from a libeler when the suit is a civil one and no criminal sanctions are involved. Under American law, punitive damages can be awarded by a jury only when the libeler has published his libel "with actual malice." This is a legal term which means "with knowledge that it was false or with reckless disregard of whether it was false or not." Since normally people do not go about making false accusations against someone unless they have some personal motive for doing so, evidence of personal hatred against the person libeled is one kind of evidence of actual malice. If, on the other hand, the libeler can show that he read or heard something which rationally led him to make the libelous charge, even though he later finds out it is false, this is evidence that he had no actual malice. What he heard or read can be pure hearsay, without any reliability whatsoever, but it can be presented in court to show what went to influence his "state of mind" when he wrote the libel, and thus used as evidence to prevent the jury from deciding that he had actual malice and thereby according the plaintiff punitive damages.

When the hearsay "evidence" is presented, the judge makes the distinction for the jury: The hearsay evidence is not to be used to prove the truth of the libel, but merely to show the "state of mind" of the defendant when he wrote the libel. It is doubtful whether most jurors fully understand this distinction when the judge gives them a legal lecture on it. It is likely that when they hear or read the "documents" supporting the libel, right in the courtroom, they are impressed with them, especially if the statements are from some known publication. Most citizens are not trained like lawyers to distinguish between hearsay and direct sources of evidence. In most states, including Minnesota, the plaintiff has no choice when starting a libel suit whether he wants to claim punitive damages or not. Thus the defendant has the right to bring into the trial all kinds of hearsay and other unreliable "evidence" to support the libel, even though the plaintiff has proved it to be false — the only limitation being that the defendant must claim that he saw or heard the hearsay before publishing the libel. It seems that at least the plaintiff ought to be allowed to forgo punitive damages and to claim only compensatory damages — to compensate him as in any other lawsuit for damages he has suffered because of the defendant's action — and thus gain the protection which plaintiffs in any other kind of lawsuits have against hearsay and false testimony.

The law which came to govern the case of *Rose v. Koch* was not even in existence when Newhall accepted Rose's case. Less than two months after the lawsuit was filed, in March 1964, the United States Supreme Court made a historic decision in the case of *New York Times and Abernathy et al. v. Sullivan* (hereafter referred to as the *New York Times* case). Its effect was to weaken still further the law of libel, especially as it applies to public officials and persons known to the public.[3] Probably most Americans would agree that the finding in the *New York Times* case was a just one, but the language in which the decision was couched makes it extremely difficult for a public official ever to sue for libel. There were, in fact, two minority concurring opinions, by three of the judges, which would have wiped out libel suits by public officials and "public figures" completely.[4]

The facts of the *New York Times* case can be summarized briefly. A group of sixty-four citizens placed a full-page advertisement in the *New York Times* on March 29, 1960, to protest the violence against Negroes in the South and to appeal for funds for the civil rights organization of the Reverend Martin Luther King. The advertisement had ten paragraphs, of which two were claimed to be libelous by Commissioner Sullivan of Montgomery, Alabama. The third paragraph read:

In Montgomery, Alabama, after students sang "My Country, 'Tis of Thee" on the State Capitol steps, their leaders were expelled from school, and truckloads of police armed with shotguns and tear-gas ringed the Alabama State College Campus. When the entire student body protested to state authorities by refusing to re-register, their dining hall was padlocked in an attempt to starve them into submission.

The sixth paragraph read:

Again and again the Southern violators have answered Dr. King's peaceful protests with intimidation and violence. They have bombed his home almost killing his wife and child. They have assaulted his person. They have arrested him seven times — for "speeding," "loitering" and similar "offenses." And now they have charged him with "perjury" — a *felony* under which they could imprison him for *ten years*. . . .

Some of the details of these paragraphs were not accurate. For example, as Mr. Justice Brennan noted in his ruling decision for the United States Supreme Court, "although the police were deployed near the campus in large numbers on three occasions, they did not at any time 'ring' the campus, and they were not called to the campus in connection with the demonstration on the State Capitol steps, as the third paragraph implied. Dr. King had not been arrested seven times, but only four." The alleged libel consisted of nine *minor* inaccuracies. The advertisement nowhere mentioned Commissioner Sullivan or anyone else in Alabama, but he contended that the word "police" in the third paragraph implied reference to him as the elected Montgomery commissioner who supervised the Police Department. As to the sixth paragraph, he contended that since arrests are ordinarily made by the police, the statement "They have arrested [Dr. King] seven times" would be read as referring to him, and hence all other references to "they" in the paragraph also referred to him.

On this flimsy basis, Commissioner Sullivan brought a libel suit against four of the Alabama Negro ministers whose names were listed as sponsors of the advertisement and against the *New York Times*. A jury in the Circuit Court of Montgomery awarded him damages of $500,000, the full amount claimed, and the Supreme Court of Alabama affirmed the decision. The defendants then petitioned the United States Supreme Court for relief, and Commissioner Sullivan became the respondent. He made no effort to prove that he suffered actual pecuniary loss as a result of the alleged libel. The four individual defendants denied that they had authorized the use of their names on the advertisement, but it was given to the *Times* and paid for by a responsible Negro leader, and the newspaper's advertising department had accepted the advertisement because they knew nothing to cause them to believe that anything in it was false, although they did not check the specific statements.

The trial judge submitted the case to the jury under instructions that the statements in the advertisement were "libelous per se" and were not privileged, so that the defendants might be held liable if the jury found that they had published the advertisement and that the statements were made "of and concerning" the respondent. The jury was instructed that, because the statements were libelous per se, "the law . . . implies legal injury from the bare fact of publication itself," "falsity and malice are presumed," "general damages need not be alleged or proved but are presumed," and "punitive damages may be awarded by the jury even though the amount of actual damages is neither found nor shown." An award of punitive damages — as distinguished from "general" damages, which are compensatory in nature — apparently requires proof of actual malice under Alabama law, and the judge charged that "mere negligence or carelessness is not evidence of actual malice or malice in fact, and does not justify an award of exemplary or punitive damages." He refused to charge, however, that the jury must be "convinced" of malice, in the sense of "actual intent" to harm or "gross negligence and recklessness," to make such an award, and he also refused to require that a verdict for the respondent differentiate between compensatory and punitive damages. The judge rejected the defendants' contention that his rulings abridged the freedom of speech and of the press that are guaranteed by the First and Fourteenth Amendments to the Constitution.

In affirming the judgment, the Supreme Court of Alabama sustained the trial judge's rulings and instructions in all respects. The United States

112

Supreme Court bluntly reversed the judgment. The ruling decision by Mr. Justice Brennan stated:

We hold that the rule of law applied by the Alabama courts is constitutionally deficient for failure to provide the safeguards for freedom of speech and of the press that are required by the First and Fourteenth Amendments in a libel action brought by a public official against critics of his official conduct. We further hold that under the proper safeguards the evidence presented in this case is constitutionally insufficient to support the judgment for Respondent.

In trying to "determine the extent to which the constitutional protections for speech and press limit a State's power to award damages in a libel action brought by a public official against critics of his official conduct," the Court reached four conclusions:

1. The advertisement was within the realm of free expression envisaged by the First and Fourteenth Amendments to the United States Constitution.

2. "Erroneous statement is inevitable in free debate," and so is "injury to official reputation." If these are "honestly made," they should not be allowed to inhibit freedom of speech or of the press.

3. A public official can recover damages "for a defamatory falsehood relating to his official conduct" only if he "proves that the statement was made with 'actual malice.' " Then the decision devoted several paragraphs to defining "actual malice," showing precedents for its use in several states, and describing how it could be proved. The individual petitioners were not aware of any erroneous statements in the advertisement nor were they "in any way reckless in that regard." Similarly, the *New York Times* had reason to believe that the advertisement was "substantially correct," and — as a matter of fact — "the Respondent's own proofs tend to show that it was." So there was no "actual malice."

4. There were no "attacks of a personal character" in the advertisement, and it was not proved that "the allegedly libelous statements were made 'of and concerning' the Respondent." Nor was there any evidence that the respondent was damaged in any way by the advertisement.

The press was elated by the *New York Times* decision. A *New York Times* commentator said: "The lesson of the case is that we have a living Constitution, one able to meet new threats to a free society. The process seems to me to make for civilization." [5] And the *Minneapolis Tribune* editorialized: "What the court has said is that the discomfiture of individual

113

public officials, or of majority — or minority — groups within our society is not a valid excuse for abolishing our basic freedom of speech."

Arnold Rose would be the last to disagree with the finding of the *New York Times* decision or with the Court's emphasis on the crucial importance of protecting freedom of speech. (There were other cases coming up of like nature in which libel suits had been filed that would have destroyed newspapers and civil rights organizations had they been successful.[6] Thus there was good, practical reason for the Court's decision.) But the *New York Times* decision went far beyond protecting freedom of speech. It took away much of the capacity of a public official to defend himself against any sort of false accusation. Any person in the United States today may freely say that any public official is a homosexual, his wife is a whore, and his son is a murderer, whether or not there is any reasonable basis for such charges, and he may publish his beliefs in newspaper stories or advertisements, without that public official being able to sue for libel unless he can *prove* that the libel was said "with actual malice." It will rarely occur that a person libeled can *prove* that one who libels him did so *with knowledge* at the time that the statement was false or *with reckless disregard* of whether it was false or not. The decision made the press happy, but it should have made every public official and every citizen concerned with the stability of his government shudder.

Senator George McGovern of South Dakota received a public apology from a man who libeled him before the *New York Times* decision was announced. He probably could not have won his suit after that decision, because he would then have had to prove malice, and defeat in the court case would probably have resulted in defeat for re-election. Senator Thomas Kuchel of California was falsely accused of homosexuality in a publication issued by right-wing extremists. He sued for libel before the recent decisions of the United States Supreme Court, and the defendants found his case so strong that they made a public retraction and apology. If Senator Kuchel had sued after the 1964–67 series of Supreme Court decisions, his case would probably have been hopeless, and he could well have lost his Senate seat as the result of the false charge. State Representative John Goldmark, who had been defeated for re-election to the Washington State Legislature because of libels that he was a Communist, had already won his libel suit — with a verdict for $40,000 — when the *New York Times* decision came out, and the verdict had to be quashed because there had been no need under Washington law to prove malice. (Goldmark could have started his trial all over again if he had wanted to and if he could have proved malice.) Goldmark's lawyer observed: "Such a rule [requirement to prove "actual malice"], of course, affords a defendant the right to publish the most wild and outrageous falsehoods concerning a man in public life, so long as he thinks they are true. The burden imposed by this doctrine would be so great, in my opinion, that only the most extreme libel cases of this type should be undertaken at all."

Perhaps highly placed officials do not feel the need to resort to libel suits to defend themselves, especially federal judges who never need to go before the voting public for re-election, but it may be hoped that the Court will modify its decision in future years to liberalize slightly its definition of "actual malice" and thus to give some protection to elected officials.

As in the case of any extreme law, the *New York Times* decision endangers the public under some circumstances as much as it endangers public officials. A corrupt public official who was accused by a citizen or newspaper of his crimes, without a court judgment, used to be told to sue for libel or slander if the accusation were false. The accusation "stuck" a little unless the official sued. (This was not always fair to the official involved since it has always been difficult, even before the *New York Times* decision, to sue for libel or slander successfully.) But now the corrupt public official can simply sit back, point to the *New York Times* decision, and calmly say that the Supreme Court has prevented him from suing for libel or slander. He can even quote Mr. Justice Black's minority concurring opinion: "The *Times* and the individual defendants had an absolute, unconditional constitutional right to publish in the *Times* advertisement their criticisms of the Montgomery agencies and officials. . . . The Constitution . . . grants the press an absolute immunity for criticism of the way public officials do their public duty." The key word here is "absolute." Any "absolute" right — which is so extreme as to permit of no exceptions under any circumstances — will eventually destroy itself, for it is open to absolute abuse.[7]

Mr. Justice Brennan, as well as Mr. Justice Black and all the other justices, was of course talking about the right of citizens and the press to criticize, without malice, public officials in their "official conduct" or in the performance of their "public duties." But the seemingly clear-cut concept of "official conduct" of "public officials" has proved to be more elusive and abstract in the lower courts than even the admittedly vague concept of "malice." The Court did not define "public official" and "official conduct" or "public duties," and that has proved to be a major defect in Mr. Justice Brennan's ruling decision.

Lower courts are now so impressed with the vigorous language of Mr. Justice Brennan's ruling decision and the even more vigorous and "absolute" language of Mr. Justice Black's concurring opinion that they are broadening the term "public official" much beyond the elected category of Commissioner Sullivan to include a city policeman and a candidate merely running for public office.[8] There is even some question among lawyers whether a state university professor or stenographer or janitor might not also be a "public official."

A New York trial judge dismissed a libel suit by the eminent scientist Linus Pauling, a critic of nuclear testing, against William F. Buckley, editor of the *National Review*, for publishing two statements accusing him of "acting as a megaphone for Soviet policy" and giving "aid and comfort to the enemies of this country." The judge dismissed the suit on the ground that Dr. Pauling, while not a public official, had "made himself a public figure engaged voluntarily in public discussion of matters of grave public concern and controversy."[9] The judge also held that Dr. Pauling had failed to prove actual malice, so that the remedy for protection against libel on the part of those in public life was closed to him.

On similar grounds, that they were "public figures," libel suits brought by Drew Pearson, a syndicated columnist, against an Alaska newspaper, and by Frank Pape, a Chicago police captain, against *Time* magazine, were dismissed by the lower courts. In a review of a New Hampshire case, *Rosenblatt v. Baer*, which the plaintiff won in a trial court before the *New York Times* decision, the United States Supreme Court also held that if there was public interest in the plaintiff, the latter would have to prove actual malice to win his suit. The Court held that what is "public interest" and a "public official" is a matter of *fact* for each trial judge or jury to decide. In still another case, Fowler V. Harper, a law professor at Yale, was not precluded from suing the *National Review* for its criticism of his petition criticizing United States Vietnam policy: A New York State court based its decision on the fact that he was a private party.

The *New York Times v. Sullivan* decision has been broadened to require any "public figure," even though not a "public official," to prove actual malice as well as false statement and damages before he can successfully sue on grounds of libel. But there is still confusion in the lower courts about the limits of the *New York Times* case, and on this basis the

A Right Decision and Dangerous Dicta

Yale Law Review has criticized the Supreme Court, in its April 1966 issue, for what it called "inept handling" of the privilege announced in the *New York Times* case.

Lack of definition of "official conduct" leads to similar difficulties. Senator Kuchel was libeled as a homosexual, but have not the FBI, the CIA, and the State Department decided that a homosexual is a security risk in the public service, since he is open to blackmail? Some lower courts might well decide that *not* being a homosexual is a "public duty" and throw out a case like Senator Kuchel's on that ground. Arnold Rose was not accused by Gerda Koch of any malfeasance in public office, or of any legislative activities which favored the Communists.[10] She accused him solely of collaborating with Communists on a scholarly study twenty years earlier. Judge Barbeau ruled that this was still within the framework of "official conduct," since the whole of a public official's life is "official conduct" and if Rose did something culpable in his life as a scholar or professor, the public had a right to be apprised of it. That is, Judge Barbeau ruled that he could not advise the jury to distinguish between Rose as scholar and Rose as legislator. Judge Barbeau was correct in his logic, for — to quote Gertrude Stein out of context — "a rose is a rose is a rose." When Rose went before the voters of the 41st Legislative District of Minnesota to ask them to vote for him, he did not cite his civic accomplishments only — he also said he was a professor who had published many scholarly works, and he said that he had a good wife and three fine children. If some citizen — like Gerda Koch — then said that Rose's scholarly works were Communistic and his wife was a prostitute, such criticisms of his life as a private citizen would be wholly justified *if they were true accusations*. But if they were false, Rose should have the right to sue for libel without having to prove malice.

And so we have come full circle in the consideration of the Supreme Court decision. That decision took away Rose's right to sue — unless he could prove malice — because he was running for public office or was a public official and because "official conduct" was not defined. If Rose had not been able to claim that Miss Koch acted with malice, and if he had still been a public official when she libeled him for the *n*th time in 1965, Judge Barbeau would have thrown his case out of court. But not every public official gives up his office willingly to sue a libeler, and even then giving it up won't help if the libel occurred while he was in office and if it was not malicious. And, as indicated, it is extremely difficult to *prove* ac-

117

tual malice. (It may even be impossible to prove actual malice since the decision in the Walker-Butts cases of 1967; this later Supreme Court decision is discussed in the last chapter of this book.) Rose was fortunate to have such a cooperative libeler, who continued to libel and to demonstrate her malice right in the courtroom. If she or her attorney had shown an ounce of caution, she could have libeled Rose, or any other public official, freely without any danger of being sued.

Since the *New York Times* decision, the falsity of an accusation does not make it legally wrong, nor does the amount or character of the damage it does. The only basis on which a public official can go into court to complain of libel is his ability to *prove* that the defendant used actual malice in publishing the libel — and if Mr. Justice Black's opinion had been adopted by the majority of the Court, that recourse would also have been abolished. The possibilities for damage to the American political system arising out of the *New York Times* decision are enormous. Since few Americans have yet realized the implications of the decision, its dangerous possibilities have not yet been exploited. But no doubt some unscrupulous aspirant to public office will soon take advantage of the decision and arrange for a whole series of signed and testified false accusations against his political opponent. And in practical terms it will matter not whether these accusations concern his strictly public activity or an aspect of his private life; in either case malice would have to be proved against his accuser. The *New York Times* decision opens up the political campaign, and the conduct of government itself, to the rhetoric of shock and confusion.

Not only politicians are endangered by the *New York Times* decision, especially in view of the 1967 decision in the case of *Associated Press v. Walker* which decided that any public figure — even those with no connection to politics and government — comes under the *New York Times* rule. Two books [11] have reported on the instructive case of John Henry Faulk, a popular radio and television entertainer in the early 1950's, whose occupation made him a public figure. Faulk was libeled as a Communist sympathizer and Communist supporter in 1955 by an organization called Aware, Inc., which opposed Faulk's position on certain issues when he was vice president in the New York radio and television entertainers' trade union. He was thereupon removed from all his programs by the opinion-conscious communication and advertising industry, and left unemployed and unemployable in his occupation. He sued for libel and, with the aid of an exceptionally able attorney (Louis Nizer) and after six and a half years of preparation for and conduct of a court trial, was able to win a judgment for $1,250,000 against each of the two defendants (later scaled down by a court of appeals to $150,000). This not only compensated him for his years of poverty (although not possibly compensating him for his loss of prestige and achievement in his chosen profession), but also broke the hold of a vicious organization which blackmailed many other radio and television performers by threatening them with similar exclusion from their occupations.

Faulk's case was settled before the *New York Times* and later decisions, and thus we can only speculate what might have occurred if it had been tried after those decisions. It seems likely that he would have been considered a public figure, and hence required to prove malice as well as falsity in the publicity of Aware, Inc. Faulk was able to prove malice, as evidenced by the award to him of punitive damages as well as compensatory damages, but it would have been a great risk for him to stake his whole economic life on a lawsuit in which he was *required* to prove malice as well as falsehood or else not have been able to claim even compensatory damages. (He would in addition have had to hope that the judge could give correct instructions on a definition of malice which the jury could also understand.) A sensible attorney today cannot conscientiously advise a potential client to undertake a libel suit, even though he has been seriously damaged by false statements, if the client is a public figure. As attorney Nizer points out in his discussion of the Faulk case, it was relatively easy to prove that Aware's published statements were false and that they damaged Faulk. But it took an incredibly lengthy and expensive effort to prove that Aware, Inc., attacked Faulk *maliciously*, as defined by law.

The issue for the American public posed by the Faulk case was whether the two men who organized and ran Aware, Inc., could terrorize an entire industry without possibility of court check. They actually did that — and violated the civil liberties of hundreds of persons — for over a decade until checked by the Faulk decision. The public interest must now force consideration of how much longer they could have done that if the Faulk case had had to be initiated and fought under the handicaps of the *New York Times* and subsequent Supreme Court decisions.

There is a saying among lawyers that "bad cases make bad law." The present libel law of the United States has been fashioned in the cases of

119

Sullivan v. New York Times and *Walker v. Associated Press*, in which the plaintiffs' cases have been "frivolous," in the legal sense of the word. It is easy to understand how the Supreme Court could be misled by such plaintiffs to weaken American libel law. There are two sides to the libel issue facing the United States. The United States Supreme Court has been solicitous of, and has given protection to, one side — the need to protect freedom of speech and of press. The other side is the need to protect the public from false and damaging "information" distributed for private purposes. This should be done, not through censorship, but by permitting the damaged person or group to have recourse to a lawsuit.

It is presumptuous for a non-lawyer to suggest to the Supreme Court how it should have written its *New York Times* decision, and subsequent modifying decisions, but since the Court's reasoning has been criticized here and yet the result of the decision praised, some further comments seem owed the reader. The problem is to find a general rule of law that would allow for the possibility of a public official's suing successfully for libel or slander and at the same time protect the citizen's rights to freedom of speech and publication. Rose would suggest the following guidelines for such a rule of law:

1. There should be a narrow, clean-cut, and specific set of definitions for "public official," "official conduct," and "public figure." But the principle should be accepted that the citizen has greater latitude in criticizing a public official in the pursuit of his public duties than he has in criticizing a private person and is to be held more strictly accountable for an error of fact in the latter situation.

2. An erroneous accusation made against a public official in his official conduct must be substantial and damaging before he can successfully sue. Trial court judges should be empowered, subject to appeal of course, to turn aside lawsuits over trivia or in other situations where the would-be plaintiff suffered no conceivable damage.

3. The person who made the false accusation should be given the opportunity to retract; if he does retract, he must publish his retraction in at least as public a way as he made the original false accusation. In many states (jurisdictions), a suit for libel against a newspaper cannot take place if the newspaper publishes a retraction within a certain number of days after receiving a request for retraction. Such laws could be expanded to protect potential defendants other than newspapers. Error of fact if retracted is not identical with repeated error coupled with refusal to retract.

4. The definition of malice must be made more explicit and more capable of proof than it now is. For example, it should be made explicit that *repeated* publication of charges against a public official in the face of denial by that official would open the accuser to a libel suit, which could be successful if the charges are proved false, because repetition after warning constitutes "reckless disregard" of whether the accusations were false or not.

As soon as he read the *New York Times* decision a week after it was given out, Rose wrote a memorandum to Newhall to distinguish his own case from that of Commissioner Sullivan. He believed that Newhall would have to make these distinctions in court.

1. The allegedly libelous document in the *Times* case is an advertisement inserted in the *Times* which recounts certain "facts" occurring in a race conflict in Alabama, and implying that the law-enforcement officials failed to give full protection of the law to certain (Negro) citizens. The court agreed (32 LW 4185) "that some of the statements contained in the two paragraphs were not accurate descriptions of events which occurred in Montgomery." But it did not find that the *general message* of the ad was in error. I claim that the general message of the *Times* ad is that the law-enforcement officials failed to give full protection of the law to the Negroes — which is true; the general message of the Christian Research leaflet is that I am a "Communist supporter" — which is false.

2. The erroneous "facts" in the *Times* ad reflect on the law-enforcement officials as not properly carrying on their *official* public duties. The contents of the Christian Research leaflets do not mention *any* of my specific legislative activities, although they attack the fact of my being a legislator. Their attack is mainly on me for two of my *academic* activities: (1) participation in the study which led to the publication of *An American Dilemma* in 1944, and certain concomitants thereof; (2) my actions while chairman of a University of Minnesota public lecture in November 1958. The Supreme Court's decision, including the minority concurring opinions, refers only to statements made about public officials acting in their *official* capacities; it does not give license for libelous remarks about public officials in their *private* capacities. There is nothing in the decision which would have permitted the defendants to call the plaintiff a "wife beater" or "Communist supporter."

3. The Court held the defendants *Times* and Abernathy guiltless of malice or intention of error (32 LW 4192–4). It specifically says they were guilty only of carelessness in stating certain *details*. In fact, the *Times* subsequently, in response to a request from the governor of Alabama — but before any court case — published an apology for the ad and said it was not intended to reflect on Alabama. The malice of Christian Research

can be shown in that: (1) it has published the same false accusation against me in *three* separate publications; (2) it has continued to distribute these materials *after* I have publicly denounced them as false and libelous; (3) it has used the libelous leaflets to attempt to prevent my election, to prevent my being seated after election, and to prevent my giving a public lecture at the Anoka County Library; (4) it implies that I continue to be a "Communist collaborator," whereas its "evidence" refers to a book written in 1941–1942, or — at most — an act as chairman of a university lecture in 1958. The Court's decision is pertinent to these facts (32 LW 4192): "The constitutional guarantees require, we think, a federal rule that prohibits a public official from recovering damages for a defamatory falsehood relating to his *official* conduct *unless* he proves that the statement was made with 'actual malice' — that is, with knowledge that it was false *or with reckless disregard of whether it was false or not.*"

Christian Research may claim it was not reckless since it relied on Senator Eastland's remarks about Gunnar Myrdal. But Senator Eastland's remarks were privileged, being made on the floor of the Senate, and they still do not justify calling Myrdal and Bunche "notorious Communists" when much other material is readily available on these two public figures. Senator Eastland nowhere refers to Bunche or me, and he does not specifically call Myrdal a Communist.

4. The *Times* ad nowhere refers to Commissioner Sullivan, the plaintiff, by name. In fact, the *Times* sent Sullivan a letter, in response to one of his, saying "we . . . are somewhat puzzled as to how you think the statements in the advertisement reflect on you." (32 LW 4186) The ad is a general indictment of law enforcement in Alabama, and not a criticism of Commissioner Sullivan specifically. The Christian Research materials attack me, by name, several times.

5. The major defendant in the *Times* case is a newspaper. Freedom of the press is an issue as well as freedom of speech. The *Times* did show itself amenable to correction of the erroneous points in the ad. On the other hand, Christian Research is not publishing a newspaper, and it has repeated the publication and distribution of its libelous materials right through to the present. The *Times* may be said to have made a single error in carrying out its public function of reporting the news and selling ads; Christian Research is engaged in continued malice, and has no public function other than the right of every citizen to have freedom of speech, *provided* he does not engage in libel or slander.

6. The chief audience for the *New York Times* ad was New York, not Alabama. The chief audience of *Facts for Action* is Minnesota. Commissioner Sullivan was not criticized in his home state; I was.

7. There is a difference in *content* of the allegedly libelous material. The *New York Times* ad may be said to have criticized the plaintiff, *by implication*, as having been an ineffective law enforcer in regard to Negro

rights — this could be construed by white people in Alabama as being a praiseworthy characteristic of plaintiff. In *Facts for Action,* I was called a Communist supporter, a security risk, and various other names which could not be considered praiseworthy by the great majority of the citizens of Minnesota.

Among these points, Newhall felt that Rose had a case only on grounds that Miss Koch had shown malice (number 3) and that she had attacked Rose in his capacity as professor and scholar, not in his capacity as legislator (number 2). We have seen that Judge Barbeau could not accept the latter distinction (number 2), which left only the ground of malice on which to fight the lawsuit. This seemed like insufficient ground to Rose, and he continues to wonder what the Supreme Court would think of the other distinctions he made between his own case and that of the *New York Times.*

At the time, and until the trial was half over, Rose did not fully understand Newhall's strategy of getting the jury to decide the case on the *one* most legally solid ground — that of the malice of Miss Koch. Newhall could use the other distinctions in a brief to the appellate court in any appeal. But only the jury could give a definitive and almost irreversible judgment on malice — since it was almost solely a question of "fact," which is in the province of the jury. Judge Barbeau defined "malice" for the jury, and then left it exclusively up to them whether there would be any finding of malice. Fortunately for Rose, the facts supporting a finding of malice in Miss Koch were so strong that the jury seemed to have little trouble in arriving at that finding. But, of course, Rose did not know all these things, from the time of the *New York Times* decision on March 9, 1964, until sometime in November 1965, and he suffered from pangs of strong doubt about the outcome of the trial because of the weak law of libel.

Neither Rose nor Newhall — nor Judge Barbeau, who inadvertently ultimately destroyed Rose's case in defining "malice" for the benefit of the jury — could know about the United States Supreme Court decisions which were to be handed down subsequent to the Rose-Koch trial. Even though Newhall and Barbeau closely followed the *New York Times* definition of "malice," and Newhall built his case carefully around it, the subsequent decisions of the United States Court later forced the Minnesota Supreme Court to reverse the trial jury's decision. What later happened, and the legal and social issues involved, are discussed in the last chapter of this book.

123

Shortly after the *New York Times* decision, Gerda Koch's attorney, Jerome Daly, moved in court to have the plaintiff's suit dismissed on the grounds that there was no malice in Miss Koch and that the Supreme Court's decision made a public official like Rose "fair game for criticism." Judge Barbeau refused to dismiss the suit and stated that the question of malice would have to be determined at the trial. Daly also filed a counterclaim for the three defendants (Miss Koch, Adolph Grinde, and Christian Research), asking $25,000 for each, on the grounds that Rose's lawsuit was "an abuse of process, malicious prosecution, and nuisance generally." He also claimed that Rose's charges in the legislature — which were repeated in the newspapers — referred to his clients, and constituted libel and slander, "motivated by a malicious state of mind."

The *New York Times* decision was only one of many events to keep Rose busy with the libel suit in the late winter and spring of 1964. First he had to explain to the faculty, in a public appearance and in written memoranda, what the suit was all about. The Faculty Legal Protection Committee arranged for these communications. Similarly, he had to communicate with the students through the *Minnesota Daily* and the magazine of opinion at the university, *The Gadfly*.

Second, he had to prepare memoranda for Newhall on (1) the history of Rose's relevant political attitudes; (2) "sensitive" government positions Rose had held; (3) his experiences with the right-wing extremists; (4) material damages resulting from Miss Koch's publications; (5) the aforementioned distinctions between the *New York Times* case and *Rose v. Koch*; (6) the relation of Grinde to Miss Koch; (7) points raised in Miss Koch's deposition; (8) false statements in the libelous exhibits; (9) false statements in Senator Eastland's speech of May 26, 1955; (10) personal employment history; (11) the writing of *An American Dilemma*; (12) brief biographies of Myrdal, Bunche, and Du Bois; (13) suggested character witnesses.

Third, he had to help Newhall prepare "interrogatories" for Miss Koch to answer, and to answer her interrogatories. Then there were the formal depositions of both of them, after a swearing-in ceremony by the court reporter who took down verbatim what they said. There were a number of personal meetings with Newhall, and with members of the Faculty Legal Protection Committee. Finally, there was a search for back copies of *Facts for Action*, Gerda Koch's periodical, and for statements about her and by her in the newspapers of Minneapolis and St. Paul (these paid off handsomely in revealing the mentality of the chief defendant and of the right-wing extremist movement generally). If anyone else is contemplating a libel suit, he ought to examine this listing of all these things that Rose had to do in the five months following the filing of one lawsuit, and decide whether he wants to devote that much time to a lawsuit. Newhall had even more work to do.

The suit had been filed against Gerda Koch, Christian Research, Adolph Grinde, and "John Doe and Mary Roe whose names are unknown to the plaintiff, members of said association." The latter fictitious gentleman and lady were to represent those other members of Christian Research who were responsible for the writing, publication, and distribution of the libelous issues of *Facts for Action*, and Newhall and Rose had the task of finding out who they were. Gerda Koch steadfastly refused to provide a list of members or directors of Christian Research in her answers to the "interrogatories" or in her deposition. But Rose turned up 1959 and 1960 issues of *Facts for Action* in which Gerda Koch had listed the names of persons on her "advisory committee," and Newhall located the incorporation papers for Christian Research in the secretary of state's office in St. Paul which listed the incorporators. Christian Research had incorporated in February 1963, *after* Miss Koch had distributed two of the libelous leaflets (Exhibits A and D), but *before* distributing the libelous pamphlet (Exhibit B), so both she personally and Christian Research were responsible. Several of the committee and incorporators were ministers of fundamentalist churches and one was a well-to-do businessman. These eleven persons were made defendants to the suit in September 1964. They hired lawyers, prepared and answered interrogatories, and made depositions.

One by one, nine of the eleven approached Newhall, either personally or through their attorneys, to deny their responsibility for the libelous attacks on Rose; several said they had no knowledge of being on Gerda Koch's "advisory committee" and two of them said they had advised Miss Koch that they did not wish their names to be used when they saw them mentioned in the 1959 or 1960 *Facts for Action*. Some of them said quite unpleasant things about Gerda Koch. These people did not deny that they had earlier given moral and/or financial support to Gerda Koch, and one — the businessman — had been observed by several witnesses to be distributing the libelous pamphlets. But when they stated under oath that they had no responsibility for preparing the attacks on Rose, or for the direction of Christian Research, and Miss Koch acknowledged this, Newhall dismissed them from the list of defendants. Over half of them provided Rose with letters dissociating themselves from the libelous attacks on him. They all had to go to some bother, and most had lawyers to pay. One of them offered to testify against Miss Koch, but the offer was not accepted.

Two of these eleven refused to apologize, and were kept as defendants until just before the trial began. Newhall did not want them in the suit because he knew that Christian Research was a one-woman operation, and these two were not responsible for the libels even though they refused to desert Miss Koch, as the other nine had. They might complicate the trial, and there was no hope of winning against them anyway — in view of their obvious lack of malice. One of them finally produced a letter saying that he was still supporting Miss Koch and standing by her libelous pamphlets, but he personally knew nothing about Rose and had no part in preparing the libelous pamphlets. Newhall dismissed him from the suit on this basis, and then arbitrarily dismissed the last "minor" defendant since he insisted on acting as his own attorney, and Newhall knew that this could disrupt the trial. Grinde was kept as a defendant since he could be easily proved to have distributed a libelous pamphlet (to the Anoka County commissioners) and because he himself wrote a letter (Exhibit C) — which was the precipitating cause of much of the damage to Rose.

There was one person who asked to be sued but was not — Paul B. Hurley. Hurley was a perennial right-wing extremist, who frequently distributed anti-Semitic literature. He was the local representative of the National Association for the Advancement of the White Race, and a member of several other extremist organizations, and had several times run for mayor of Minneapolis on an extremist platform. Hurley had once been involved with Christian Research, but at least by 1964 Gerda Koch no longer accepted his association. The main reason apparently was that Hurley wrote odd-sounding letters, carried oddly worded signs, and occasionally shouted irrelevancies at meetings. He had been in court several times, had started lawsuits against the judges, but had never been known to engage in physical violence, so he was generally tolerated by the police and the courts. When the lawsuit was announced in the newspapers, Hurley wrote a typical anti-Semitic, oddly worded letter to Rose, demanding to be sued as a member of Christian Research. Rose and Newhall decided to follow the Minneapolis tradition of ignoring him. One day Newhall received a notice from the District Court that Hurley had filed a list of "interrogatories" to Rose and had paid $6 to file them. (See Appendix IV.) Newhall and Rose ignored these interrogatories, since they had no status in law. That was the last Rose saw or heard of Hurley. He didn't even show up at the trial, but he came in for mention: At the trial Newhall introduced into evidence a letter sent by Hurley to the clerk of the Minnesota House of Representatives. The clerk had given the letter to Rose at the suggestion of the speaker. Enclosed with the letter — along with other pieces of extremist literature — was a copy of Gerda Koch's libelous Exhibit A, and Newhall used it to show the jury what sort of activities were stimulated by Miss Koch's libelous attack on Rose. Hurley's typical covering letter is reproduced in Appendix IV; the address on the envelope will give its flavor:

Clerk, for proper processing (House). Attention: Committee Meeting 3-12-63, Subject: Rep. Dr. Arnold Rose, tentative, Room 2, State Capitol. . . . The "Genocide" *PLOT* Bill . . . Purpose: to Silence *4th* Class *Gentile* . . . WHITE Citizens who have documentation to expose the . . . *ETERNAL TORMENTERS of Humanity.* Minn. House of Representatives, St. Paul 1, Minnesotta.

One of the minor issues that had to be decided before the trial was exactly what Gerda Koch had called Rose. She had explicitly, in her literature, called him a collaborator with Communists or Communist fronters and a "security risk." But she never explicitly called him an out-and-out Communist. She merely implied this. For example, in Exhibit A there is this sentence: "No pressure pattern of the Communist global conquest is more familiar than of well-placed Communist and pro-Communist advisors to free government policy-makers and agencies having paralytic potentials." And in Exhibit B, almost all of which was devoted to Rose and his alleged "Communist collaborators" in *An American Dilemma,* reference was made to "Communists and Communist collaborators at our university." Also in Exhibit A was this statement: "Sen. Eastland mentions 17 other Communist fronters and left-wingers as co-authors of the book. He did not mention Dr. Rose, but Dr. Rose may be one of those who keep their names out of Communist fronts but be very useful to them at the same time." In her deposition, Gerda Koch denied that she ever called Rose a Communist. Newhall decided to give her the benefit of the doubt: What she explicitly called Rose was libelous enough. But at the trial, the defendant's lawyer, Jerome Daly, called Rose a "Communist" and a "high-placed Communist" several times; apparently he did not care for Gerda Koch's nice distinctions.

In her deposition, Gerda Koch made it quite clear that she was out to have Arnold Rose dismissed from his university professorship, because of his work on *An American Dilemma*, as well as to keep him out of the legislature:

> Newhall: Is it your contention that Arnold Rose is an improper person to be a teacher at the university?
> Daly: We could say that.
> Koch: Yes. I would say that a man that collaborates with a book that has no respect for our Constitution ought not to be teaching our young people, and that collaborates with so many Communist fronters should not teach at the university and not be a state legislator either in my opinion. In all kindness to him too.

Miss Koch's last remark was also one of her typical niceties. These remarks, and others in her deposition of like nature, set the stage for the trial.[12]

table — was at first occupied by Adolph Grinde, but as the trial progressed, Miss Koch arranged for her young assistant — Richard Landkamer — to sit in the fourth chair to help her with her files, and Grinde was pushed out to a fifth position quite distant from the table. The table was piled high, on Miss Koch's side, with boxes of files and with books and pamphlets. These were the paraphernalia of Gerda Koch's "research" into Arnold Rose and his "collaborators." Newhall, Strothman, and Rose each had a bulky briefcase, but they seemed small beside the great cartons on Miss Koch's side of the table. In fact, the briefcases had to be left on the floor — there was only enough room on Rose's side of the table for notepads and pencils.

Before court opened, attorneys Newhall, Strothman, and Daly had a conference with the judge in his private office, called "judge's chambers." This kind of conference was to be repeated frequently before or after a court session. Later in the trial, Gerda Koch joined the lawmen to argue some point of procedure, but Rose never went into the judge's chambers. When the lawyers returned to the courtroom, the bailiff asked all to rise, and announced the entrance of Judge Donald Barbeau and the opening of the court. This was to be a twice-a-day ritual for the duration of the trial.

The first task was the selection of the jury. About thirty men and women came into the courtroom and took seats on the spectators' benches. The clerk wrote their names on slips of paper which were then placed in a revolving drum. He called out eighteen names, and the persons called took places in the area reserved for jurors. Each side could strike out three names, and so Daly, and later Newhall, interrogated them briefly. Both inquired about personal acquaintance they might have with Rose, Miss Koch, or Grinde. Newhall discovered one man who had been a client of his law firm, and by consent of Daly and the judge, he was dismissed without its counting against the three strikes Newhall could use. Daly asked questions mainly about church affiliation, organizational affiliation, contacts with university personnel, and willingness to believe there is a Communist conspiracy in the United States. Newhall asked questions mainly about knowledge of and attitudes toward the John Birch Society, political activity, and membership in four fundamentalist churches whose ministers were members of Christian Research, Inc. He also asked, "Do you think that in this day and age it is harmful to be called a Communist?" and "Calling a man a Communist doesn't make him one, does it?" After all the questioning was finished, the judge remembered that he had forgotten to ask earlier if any potential juror could not serve for two full weeks, if necessary. To Rose's chagrin, two of the potential jurors who Rose felt would be most favorable to him dropped out and were replaced by two others, one of whom Newhall then decided to strike. After each side made its three strikes, the clerk called two more groups of three names each to provide for two alternate jurors. After each lawyer questioned these, they struck one name each from the two groups, and the panel of twelve jurors and two alternate jurors was sworn in.

The judge made a friendly and informative statement to the jurors, telling them their duties, advising them to pay attention only to the testimony presented from the witness stand and ignore newspaper accounts of the trial, and warning them not to discuss the case with anyone until the trial was over. Newhall made a brief opening statement to the jurors, outlining what he intended to prove and giving some background on Rose's career. The first day was over. Trial hours were from 9:30 A.M. to noon, and from 2 P.M. to 4:30 P.M., with recesses of fifteen minutes during both morning and afternoon sessions. Actually, because of daily conferences in the judge's chambers, this time was cut into.

Newhall started out the second morning by calling Gerda Koch to the witness stand. He established that she had been a substitute schoolteacher in Minneapolis until 1958, when she had accused Carl Rowan, then a Minneapolis newspaper reporter (and subsequently United States minister to Finland and director of the United States Information Agency), of pro-Communist attitudes at a public meeting. Then she substituted in St. Paul schools until 1960, when, as noted earlier, she accused Max Lerner, a Brandeis University professor, who came to give a talk to a St. Paul teachers' association, of being a Communist. Then she substituted in suburban Bloomington schools until the lawsuit began. Miss Koch commented: "I didn't have one call [to teach] since the lawsuit, that's clear in my mind." She next described her organization of Christian Research in 1958, with its "educational program" of alerting people about Communism in the United States. The principal means was the pamphlet *Facts for Action*, issued five times a year. Christian Research at first was only Gerda Koch, later a few friends were added and called a "committee"; in early 1963 it was incorporated and there was a formal "Board of Directors." But at all times Gerda Koch wrote *Facts for Action* and took full responsibility for its contents. In the fall of 1962, when the first attack on Rose was made in its pages, it had a regular mailed circulation of 350–400 copies. In addition, copies were sold for 25 cents each at her bookstore, at public meetings, and at the State Fair, and copies were given out or mailed to members of the state legislature.

Exhibits A, B, and D, the libelous documents against Rose written by Gerda Koch, were placed in evidence. (See Appendix I. Exhibit C was the letter written by Adolph Grinde to the Anoka County commissioners; it was introduced into evidence later in the trial. See Chapter 1, where it is quoted in full.) Miss Koch admitted writing and assembling all three, distributing A and B (issues of *Facts for Action*) herself, and supplying the material in D to one of Rose's opponents in the legislative race of 1962, who then had it printed. Whereas the first publication of Exhibit A was on October 28, 1962, *before* the election, Miss Koch admitted adding to Exhibit A *after* the election a request to the public to oppose the seating of Rose in the legislature and republishing it December 5, 1962. Newhall then got Miss Koch to reaffirm that she had been trying to prevent Rose from taking his seat in the legislature, after he had been certified as elected in a legal election.

> Newhall: Do you believe in the right of a person who runs for election in a legal election and gets more votes than his adversary, do you believe in the right of that person to have the seat for which he was running?
>
> Koch: That would have to be a qualified answer. I couldn't say "yes" or "no" on that.
>
> Newhall: In other words, you say it would depend on who it is, is that right?
>
> Koch: Will you repeat your original question, please?
>
> Newhall: All right. Do you believe in the proposition that under our American system, if a person runs for a public office in a public election and receives more votes from the qualified voters than his adversary does, that that person ought to be seated in the position for which he was running?
>
> Koch: We have the right to challenge it.
>
> Newhall: And on what basis — Were you challenging this on the basis of some illegality in the election?
>
> Koch: No.
>
> Newhall: It was a perfectly legal election, so far as you know?
>
> Daly: Well —
>
> Koch: Sure. I didn't challenge that.

Miss Koch estimated that a total of 1000 copies of Exhibit A were distributed, and that a special effort had been made to get it to each member of the state legislature. Newhall then went into Miss Koch's knowledge of Rose's public reaction to Exhibit A — his statement to the House of Representatives on March 23, 1963 (see Chapter 5):

Newhall: Now, do you remember that in March of 1963, Arnold Rose as a state legislator made a statement on the floor of the House of Representatives in which he stated, among other things, that he rejected completely Communism and what Communism stood for?

Koch: I read it in the papers.

Newhall: You read it in the papers about that time that he made such a statement?

Koch: Right.

Newhall: Did you also become aware that he pointed out in that statement that he had served the government on numerous occasions in positions of trust and positions which had required a security clearance?

Koch: I don't recall that specifically.

Newhall: You clipped out the newspaper account of this hearing?

Koch: Yes.

Newhall: And added it to your clipping file?

Koch: Yes.

Newhall then established by Miss Koch's statements that she distributed the second, and longer, attack on Rose (Exhibit B) about a month after his statement to the legislature denying that he was in any way pro-Communist, and that she distributed about 1300 copies of this issue.

Newhall went on to show the nature of the attack on Rose in Exhibit B:

Newhall: Now, if you will take a look at Exhibit B, you will find that the headline on the first page reads as follows, "ARNOLD ROSE, MINNESOTA UNIVERSITY PROFESSOR AND STATE LEGISLATOR, COLLABORATES WITH COMMUNISTS AND COMMUNIST FRONTERS." That is the headline, is it not?

Koch: That's right.

Newhall: And after that, down on the first page, you have a statement, "And today we have a 'collaborator' at the University who is at the same time a legislator at our state capitol! Will we learn before it is too late?" The person you were referring to there is Arnold Rose, is it not?

Koch: That is right.

Newhall: And then, followed by the headline "CLEAN OUT THE UNIVERSITY," right?

Koch: That is right.

Newhall: Now, your claim that Arnold Rose was a collaborator was based upon the fact that he had participated in writing the book *An American Dilemma*, no doubt about that?

Koch: That is right.

. . . .

Newhall: You didn't have any information regarding any collaboration by him with Communists or Communist fronters, other than the fact that he worked on this book?

Koch: Other than those that would be named in the book, I would say.

Newhall: Yes, and his collaboration, as you claim it to be, was based on the fact that he worked on the book, right? If he had not worked on the book, you would not have had anything with which to say he was a collaborator at that time?

Koch: Certainly if he had nothing to do with the book, he would not be a collaborator; that's natural, there's no doubt.

Newhall: All right; do you know when the book was written?

Koch: Yes.

Newhall: It was 1944, wasn't it, that it first came out, was first published?

Koch: Someone mentioned it yesterday and, of course, in writing the book, the work was done before. Wasn't it written in '41 and wasn't the copyright in 1944?

Newhall: That may be it. At any rate, it was early in the '40's?

Koch: Right, in 1941 Myrdal started with it.

Newhall: And Exhibit B was issued in 1963 and you used the present tense in Exhibit B and stated that Arnold Rose collaborates with Communists and Communist fronters; that is correct, is it not, on page 1 of Exhibit B?

Koch: That's right.

Newhall: And further down you say, "Today we have a 'collaborator' at the University who is at the same time a legislator at our state capitol," right?

Koch: That's right.

Newhall was here establishing that Miss Koch claimed that Rose was *currently* a Communist collaborator, whereas her evidence was his work of some twenty years earlier.

In the following cross-questioning, Newhall showed that Miss Koch took her material largely from the speech made on the floor of the United States Senate on May 26, 1955, by Senator James Eastland (D., Mississippi),[2] who stated that fifteen of the names listed in the "Author's Preface" of *An American Dilemma* were Communists or Communist fronters. Exhibit B also sought to establish that Ralph Bunche, mentioned in the "Author's Preface" to *An American Dilemma*, was a Communist, on the basis of a 1962 speech by Congressman James B. Utt (R., California) [3] and an article by H. L. Varney in the *American Mercury* of May 1956.

> Newhall: Your purpose in putting into *Facts for Action* these quotations from Congressman Utt and Varney was because Bunche worked on *An American Dilemma* and also Rose worked on *An American Dilemma*.
>
> Koch: Right.
>
> Newhall: And was that your purpose also in using the quotation from Senator Eastland, because of the fact that Arnold Rose worked on *An American Dilemma*, and Senator Eastland quotes to show that he believes some of the other people who worked on *An American Dilemma* had some Communist associations?
>
> Koch: You bring in the word "purpose" again. I think —
>
> Newhall: Well, you relate the Eastland quotation to Rose's work on *An American Dilemma*, do you not?
>
> Koch: Yes, yes.

Newhall next tried to find out if Miss Koch used any other sources besides Eastland, Utt, and Varney. She mentioned the writings of several right-wing extremists, and the statements of witnesses who had appeared before the House Committee on Un-American Activities, the Senate Subcommittee on Internal Security, and the Tenney committee of the California State Legislature.

Before closing the morning's session, Judge Barbeau ordered Newhall to provide all members of the jury with copies of Exhibits A, B, and D, and this was done at the opening of the afternoon session. Newhall next queried the witness about the sponsorship of an *An American Dilemma*. Miss Koch was mixed up concerning the various organizations founded by Andrew Carnegie, but reference to *An American Dilemma* showed that it was sponsored by the Carnegie Corporation of New York. Newhall introduced into evidence volume 5 of the *Encyclopedia Americana* to describe several of the Carnegie-established organizations, and to show that the Carnegie Corporation of New York, which sponsored *An American Dilemma*, was not the same as the Carnegie Foundation for International Peace, which was later headed by Alger Hiss.

> Newhall: And to the extent that Senator Eastland in his remarks there says that the group which sponsored *An American Dilemma* is the same one that Alger Hiss was associated with, he is mistaken, isn't that true?
>
> Koch: I would not say so.

Newhall: Well, the Carnegie Corporation is the one that sponsored
An American Dilemma, right?
Koch: Right.
Newhall: And the one that Alger Hiss was associated with was the
Carnegie Foundation or Endowment for International Peace, right?
Koch: Right. They are interrelated. It is still Carnegie.

Newhall next took up Gunnar Myrdal, the chief author of *An American
Dilemma.*

Newhall: And you called him a Swedish socialist, didn't you?
Koch: Right.
Newhall: And Senator Eastland called him a socialist or Swedish so-
cialist?
Koch: Right.
Newhall: And when you prepared Exhibit B, you thought of him as a
Swedish socialist?
Koch: Right.
Newhall: You didn't think of him at that time as a member of the Com-
munist party?
Koch: No.

Newhall now referred to page 2 of Exhibit B, in which Miss Koch implied
that Myrdal was a "notorious Swedish Communist," and that Arnold
Rose, by virtue of having collaborated with Myrdal in writing *An American Dilemma,* was a "Communist collaborator." The page in Exhibit B
which referred to Myrdal as a "notorious Swedish Communist" reproduced a document prepared by one "Col. Tom Hutton, SPX Research
Associates," and submitted to the Senate Subcommittee on Internal Security (Senator Eastland's committee). Hutton's report was entitled "The
Supreme Court as an Instrument of Global Conquest." It was not published by the subcommittee, although Gerda Koch's copy makes it appear
as though it were part of an official Senate document (Hutton himself
labeled it "The 'Suppressed' Report"); Gerda Koch admitted that she cut
out the portion which indicated that the Hutton report was *not* included in
any publication of the Senate Subcommittee on Internal Security. By
drawing an arrow to the statement in the Hutton report Gerda Koch implied that Myrdal was a "notorious Swedish Communist," while at the
same time she admitted she did not think of Myrdal as a Communist, but
as a socialist:

Koch: The arrow was drawn for that intention, but that is not to say
that I called him a Communist. We referred to the document.

136

Newhall: Yes. So down here you called him a "Communist" didn't you?
Koch: No.
Newhall: On the left-hand side?
Koch: I know my English; I studied that thoroughly. That is in quotes.
Newhall: You put it in quotes?
Koch: I put it in quotes.
Newhall: But you carried forth the capital "C"?
Koch: Another one's view.
Newhall: And at the time you did this, you didn't think that Gunnar Myrdal was a Communist, did you?
Koch: Because there were various opinions. That was the only one I read of that. Others said he was a socialist. Other researches said he was a socialist. We present all views.
Newhall: You yourself had called him a socialist, is that right?
Koch: I called him a socialist. Personally, I call him a socialist. Later on we identify other Communists, but I never identified Myrdal as a Communist.
Newhall: Senator Eastland didn't even call him a Communist, did he?
Koch: No.
Newhall: He called him a socialist?
Koch: Yes, right.

Newhall next took up the question of why Senator Eastland was criticizing Myrdal: It was to attack the Supreme Court for its Brown decision of 1954, which had declared that no state could segregate its citizens, and the decision had referred to Myrdal — among others — in a footnote.

Newhall: He made the statement that the Supreme Court relied upon the book *An American Dilemma* and then went on to say that *An American Dilemma* was contributed to by persons whom he considered to be Communists or Communist fronters and therefore, he was attacking the United States Supreme Court for its decision.
Koch: That's right.
Newhall: He was using that means to do it?
Koch: Yes.

Newhall then established that Eastland, Utt, and Varney had nowhere made any reference to Rose.

Ralph Bunche's biography from *Who's Who in America* was read into the record, as was Gunnar Myrdal's from the *International Who's Who*. Miss Koch said she had not gotten her information on Bunche and Myrdal from these sources. She admitted to having read "something less than thirty per cent" of *An American Dilemma*, and not having checked on Senator Eastland's statement that the book was adopted by the Communist party before reporting that as a fact in Exhibit B. She further admitted that she had not read any other of Rose's writings, attended any of his classes, heard any of his public lectures, or got in touch with him personally. Her attack on Rose was based solely on his work in *An American Dilemma* published over eighteen years earlier. She had but one contact with Arnold Rose before attacking him in *Facts for Action* in 1962. That was when she attended Myrdal's lecture in 1958 on "Nationalism and Internationalism in the Rich and Poor Countries," where Rose had been chairman, and had prevented her from fully asking her carefully prepared question about Ralph Bunche's alleged Communist affiliations.

Daly pursued this same point as he took over the questioning of Gerda Koch.

> Koch: [Rose] ruled the question out of order. I felt it was pertinent to the safety of our nation and concern for our welfare to put the question.
> Daly: And so the question remained unanswered, is that right?
> Koch: It remained unanswered.

Daly went over Miss Koch's background with her as an intermittent teacher in elementary schools, and then he had her read the paragraphs from pages 12–13 of *An American Dilemma* which she felt were indicative that the authors had held the United States Constitution in contempt. (These are quoted in full in Chapter 2.) During the rest of the trial Miss Koch never referred specifically to anything else in *An American Dilemma* as objectionable, although she said she felt the whole book was subversive.

Newhall took up his "re-cross examination" of Miss Koch. She testified that she thought, in April–May of 1963 when she published Exhibit B, that certain members of the United States government were "actually serving the Communist conspiracy," and she mentioned specifically Secretary of State Dean Rusk, Chief Justice Earl Warren, and a "number of others" on the Supreme Court. Newhall then had her read from her issue of *Facts for Action* of spring 1960, a time when Eisenhower was President, the following sentences quoting from a publication of the John Birch Society:

Dear Friends of our beloved country, did you know that according to the *American Opinion* (July–August, 1959): "The U.S. is 50% to 70% controlled by Communists?" *Very unpleasant* news, we agree — and frightening, is it not? We do believe *EACH* of you *WANT TO HELP* tip the scale the other way!

She said she had quite a bit of confidence in these reports of the John Birch Society. Another pamphlet prepared and distributed by Gerda Koch was entitled *A Moscow Directive and President Kennedy's Record.* After asking about an initial part of this, Newhall probed further about the meaning of the pamphlet:

> Newhall: And then it goes on and it says, "Which directive is the Kennedy administration following, that of the Constitution or that of Moscow? You decide — and Act." Now, which directive did you think the Kennedy administration was following?
>
> Koch: I think there are about twenty or twenty-one items listed here and every one of these is simply an historical fact that it helped the Communist party in all these moves. I'll just pick out one. "Granted a visa to Owen Lattimore for a 'study trip' to Outer Mongolia." Lattimore had been named by a Senate subcommittee as a "conscious, articulate instrument of Soviet conspiracy."
>
> The Court: Just a moment. Could you be a little more direct? He asked you a simple question and it is your answer then, if I understand you, and you're not answering directly, that the Kennedy administration was following the Moscow directive; is that your answer?
>
> Koch: It couldn't be interpreted any other way.
>
> The Court: All right, you've answered the question.

Daly then questioned Miss Koch further about this pamphlet. She read from the pamphlet twenty-one actions of President Kennedy which she said suggested that Kennedy was following the "Moscow directive." The judge intervened actively at this point to make sure he understood her meaning.

> The Court: One of the things that indicates that he was following the Moscow directive, if I understand her, is because he failed to call "Captive Nations Week" at a certain time, is that what you mean?
>
> Koch: That is one point —
>
> The Court: That's just one.
>
> Koch: — that the Communists liked, that it was postponed.
>
> The Court: All right. Now, let's have the next one.
>
> . . . .
>
> Koch: I am not saying and inferring the least that Kennedy was a Communist. In fact, in my heart I am convinced he was not; but I do believe he was used and manipulated to get these things across.

The next morning Newhall called Adolph Grinde to the witness stand, and established that he had sent a letter (see Chapter 1) to the Anoka County commissioners on November 30, 1963, in which he protested the library lecture series. The letter objected to Rose as a speaker because he "is co-author with Gunnar Myrdal (a notorious Swedish communist) of the book 'American Dilemma.'" He also enclosed a pamphlet by Miss Koch (Exhibit A, Appendix I) and the "Suppressed Report" of Col. Tom Hutton, which he had obtained from Miss Koch, as "material on the background of . . . Arnold Rose." In response to a question from attorney Daly, Mr. Grinde said he had looked on Christian Research as a reliable organization, and "I still do."

Newhall then called Arnold Rose to the stand. In response to questions, Rose said a few things about his background of training up to a Ph.D. at the University of Chicago, and his present position as professor of sociology at the University of Minnesota. Newhall asked him "what the science of sociology concerns itself with."

> Rose: It is one of the newest branches of scholarship. It is taught in all universities around the country. It is a study of human behavior in group settings. We deal with problems of population, crime, delinquency, housing, that is as a scholarly study. We deal with problems of racial group relations such as the Negro problem. We are concerned with institutions; the family, the church, the school, as social institutions. In other words, we try to study objectively the institutions, the organizations, the human behavior in groups in our society mainly and in other societies around the world.

Rose then went into his first contact with the Negro in America research project in the summer of 1940, when he worked with Professor Samuel Stouffer, Richard Sterner, and Paul Norgren, and then his later association with it, beginning in August 1941, when he worked with Gunnar Myrdal and Richard Sterner.

Following this, Newhall got Rose to list his subsequent employment as a statistician for the War Department, his induction into the Army, his receiving a Bronze Star medal for his service in the Army, his completion of the Ph.D. degree in 1946, his employment at Bennington College in late 1946 and 1947, his employment at Washington University from 1947 to 1949, his coming to the University of Minnesota in 1949, his receiving two Fulbright professorships for France and Italy. He mentioned that the State Department employed him to lecture in Europe in the summer of 1961, and in South Asia for six months in 1964–65.

Newhall then took Rose through his political activities:

> Newhall: Have you, Professor Rose, ever belonged to any Communist organizations or any Communist-front organizations?

Rose: Never.

Newhall: What is your political affiliation?

Rose: I'm a member of the DFL party.

Newhall: And you ran for office and were elected as a member of the DFL party, is that right?

Rose: Yes, I ran for office a couple of times. I was elected once to the state legislature.

Newhall: I see, yes. Have you ever voted outside your party?

Rose: Yes, I have, on occasion.

Newhall: And would that be for Republicans?

Rose: Yes, I voted a couple of times for Republicans, that I can recall.

Newhall: Now, have you ever belonged to any anti-Communist organizations?

Rose: Yes, the American Committee for Cultural Freedom was organized in the late 1940's; it was affiliated with the World Congress for Cultural Freedom and it was designed to combat the cultural attack, if you will, of the Russian government, which was being spread, particularly in Europe at that time. By cultural I mean matters of art, literature, scholarship, science. We were working on that level and I was a charter member of that group, American Committee for Cultural Freedom. It was also working to combat Communism in the United States, that is, the American Committee was, among artists, writers, scholars, scientists, in that area of life which I belong to. . . .

I might say that I consider the DFL party an anti-Communist organization, and I am a long-time member of that. It's a political party which is opposed to Communism. I would say both major parties are, the DFL and Republican parties. I also belonged to the Americans for Democratic Action for a brief period when I was in St. Louis; when I came to Minneapolis I found that there was no branch of the Americans for Democratic Action. I think it died out very shortly after I arrived, and I did not rejoin it here. It was a very active organization before that time, very much concerned with Communist activities in the United States at that period.

Newhall: Have you written a number of books and articles and papers of one kind or another?

Rose: I think you should not think in terms of anti-Communist activities when you refer to my publications — now we're shifting away from Communism completely. I'm a sociologist; I have written scholarly and scientific articles, approximately 150 of them.

Daly: Pardon me a minute. Reporter, will you please make a note of that, that last statement he made in the record, would you please make a copy of that during recess.

Rose: I did studies in sociology and published them, about 150 different articles, research articles, and a number of books, about a half

141

dozen books under my own name, and a half dozen books under my editorship — my name appears on the front cover as editor rather than as author.

The passage in Rose's remarks that Daly wanted was the statement that "we're shifting away from Communism completely." Daly later tried to use that to show that Rose was not anti-Communist, but Rose merely intended to say that his scholarly writings were not on the subject of Communism. Newhall later had Rose refer to short sections of his textbook on *Sociology: The Study of Human Relations* which indicated that he had no sympathy for Communism.

Newhall then asked Rose to describe the writing of *An American Dilemma*. The book was too long to describe adequately, but even the very short summary must have been tedious for the jury. A witness in a lawsuit has to forgo some of the usual standards of modesty:

> Newhall: Would you consider that the book constitutes a thorough and scholarly study of the problem?
> Rose: I do. I am partial, of course, but I am very proud of this book.
> Newhall: Were there some book reviews, or was it mentioned in magazines and in the press at the time that it came out?
> Rose: It was very widely reviewed.

Newhall now went into the persons mentioned by Myrdal in his "Author's Preface" — of which Gerda Koch claimed fifteen or so were Communists or Communist fronters.

> Newhall: And among all of those persons who are mentioned there in the preface, are you able to tell us whether there are any persons who are associated or were associated at any time with any organizations which may have been accused of being Communist fronts?
> Rose: Well, in the first place, I might mention that the preface was not written until September 1942, so I wouldn't be aware even of all of the people who Myrdal had met and asked information from. There are hundreds of names mentioned in this preface, well over a hundred, anyhow. I never counted them. I didn't know of the existence of what was in his mind until it was written in September 1942. I had heard of several of these people mentioned by name. I have since heard that some of them have been accused of Communism. I wouldn't know about that; it could be. A lot of people are accused of Communism or Communist-supporting, including in this case, which I don't think is true, and until there has been some responsible investigation, it seems to me that I have no way of knowing for sure.

142

Newhall: Now, in Exhibits A and B, reference is made to a man named W. E. B. Du Bois. Did you ever meet Du Bois?

Rose: I never met Du Bois.

Newhall: Did you quote him in some of the portions of the book?

Rose: I quoted him quite extensively, yes.

Newhall: Who was Du Bois?

Rose: This is very difficult to give you a complete answer without taking a few minutes.

Newhall: Well, at the time that you were working on the book in the early '40's, who was Du Bois? Let's start with it here.

Rose: Du Bois was a man about 75 years old at that time. He was one of the most distinguished scholars on different aspects of the Negro problem the United States has ever known.

Newhall: Was he a Negro himself?

Rose: He was a Negro. He was born in Massachusetts; not a southern Negro, but a northern Negro. He was the first Negro to get a Ph.D. from Harvard University, in history; 1895, I guess it was. He had been a professor at Atlanta University for many years, had written many scholarly works, also poetic works. He fancied himself to be a writer. He was certainly recognized generally among scholars to be a very distinguished scholar. His works in history particularly. He wrote a study called *The Philadelphia Negro Community*, which I believe was published in 1897 or 1899, which was one of the very best community studies ever to be written up to that time. At that time he was associated with the National Association for the Advancement of Colored People, which, incidentally, has had a long history of struggling with Communism within itself, and resisting Communism. Du Bois was at that time much identified with the anti-Communist position in the NAACP. Most of his career was spent as editor of their magazine, called *The Crisis*, which was the leading Negro magazine for many years. That was his job; he was editor of the magazine. He was co-founder of, and editor for, the NAACP.

Newhall: Can you tell us what happened to him in his old age?

Rose: He ran into trouble with the NAACP. Of course, he was now 75 years of age. He was retired, actually. There was an earlier period in which he ran into trouble with the NAACP, in the 1930's, because he came out accepting segregation. He felt that the situation in the South was so hopeless that there was nothing for the Negro to do but to accept segregation and try to make the best of it. That is, instead of asking for integrated schools, to accept segregated schools but better schools. That was his position. The NAACP, after arguing with him on this, didn't accept that position, and so he resigned.

He went back to Atlanta University, and then he had another altercation with the NAACP, somewhere in the late 1940's, for another

143

position that he took which was more leftist than the NAACP. But, anyhow, he was an old man at that time. Along about 1951, I read in a newspaper that he had married a Communist second wife. His first wife had died. He was then about 80 years old, somewhere around there; and I also later read in a newspaper that Du Bois — you know, he was really a very well-known person, and therefore, his actions got in the newspaper — at the age of 92, had joined the Communist party. Somewhere about that time, he left the United States to live in Ghana, and he died about the age of 95 or 96, in Ghana. This is a life story which I think is one of the greatest trage-dies in the United States, that a man with such ability and such dis-tinction, and with such brilliance, should end up as a Communist be-cause he felt that conditions in the United States were hopeless for the Negro. I think he was very pessimistic, but that is what he felt.

Rose gave a brief description of the career of Ralph Bunche also; Bunche had not moved toward Communist obscurity like Du Bois, but rose to great eminence as an American government official and interna-tional public figure. Gunnar Myrdal was then described: He had an equally brilliant, but not as well recognized, career as Bunche. Among other things, Rose described Myrdal as an "anti-Communist":

Rose: During World War II, the United States was an ally of the Soviet Union, and many American people were extremely friendly to the Russian government. We used to call Stalin "Uncle Joe" in those days; it was a kind of nickname for Joseph Stalin, the dictator of Russia. Myrdal used to say, "Americans are being foolish; they're being too friendly to the Communists; they are very dangerous." He said, "We Swedes have had a long history of contact with the Rus-sians and with the Soviet government and I think you ought to be a little more suspicious than you are of them."

Newhall asked for Myrdal's views in regard to the United States:

Rose: He was very pro-United States, although he didn't hesitate to be critical also. He wrote a number of books on the United States, one in Swedish to describe the United States for Swedes. It is called *Con-tact with America*. He has written a book recently called *Challenge to Affluence*. In *An American Dilemma* he makes a number of criti-cisms of the United States, but it is infused with admiration and sup-port and friendliness towards the United States.

Rose then explained the theme of *An American Dilemma*: "The whole thesis of this book . . . is that sometimes the American people don't be-have in accord with their ideals. But the ideals are nevertheless real for Americans — the ideals of liberty, equality, and the right of each man to pursue happiness — even though whites don't put them into practice when it comes to Negroes."

Newhall now went into Senator Eastland's statement, copied by Gerda Koch in her second attack on Rose, that *An American Dilemma* was officially adopted by the Communist party. Rose stated bluntly that the opposite was true: The Communist party on several occasions denounced *An American Dilemma*. He produced a small book written by one of the leading officials of the Communist party, Herbert Aptheker, which was a violent denunciation of *An American Dilemma*. Rose read from the summary of Aptheker's book: "In summary, we find Myrdal's philosophy to be superficial and erroneous, his historiography false, his ethics vicious and therefore, his analysis weak, mystical, and dangerous." [4] Rose noted that the preface to this Communist book, written by Doxey A. Wilkerson, who had been employed by Myrdal in 1939 and 1940 to write a memorandum on "The Negro in Education," was as strong a diatribe against *An American Dilemma* as Aptheker's book itself. (Statements from the preface have already been quoted, in Chapter 2.)

Rose testified that he had been introduced to Wilkerson in 1940, had shaken hands with him, but in no way had "worked with him." At that time, in the summer of 1940, there was no evidence, to Rose's knowledge, that Wilkerson was a Communist. Sometime in either late 1941, or 1942, Rose testified, he had heard that Wilkerson had become a Communist. Certainly Wilkerson was closely associated with the Communist party by 1946, when he wrote the preface for an official Communist denunciation of Myrdal and *An American Dilemma*. But this did not make Rose a "Communist collaborator" when he shook hands with Doxey Wilkerson in 1940. Wilkerson was cited several times in *An American Dilemma*, but for statistics he had compiled on Negro education in his earlier writings. Wilkerson, and all the others mentioned by Miss Koch and Daly, never "contributed to" *An American Dilemma*: This was solely the work of Gunnar Myrdal, Richard Sterner, and Arnold Rose, and they cited the work of nearly every scholar who had written on the Negro in the United States in their compendious book.

Newhall then shifted the questioning of Rose to his becoming aware of the attacks on him by Gerda Koch in the fall of 1962 and the winter of 1963. Rose testified that George Murk, one of Rose's opponents for the legislative seat in the 41st District, had used Gerda Koch's material against him in the campaign of 1962. Rose had prepared an extra campaign leaflet to combat this, at a cost of something over $300. Rose testified that he had become aware in March 1963 that Miss Koch had distributed Exhibit A to virtually all the members of the Minnesota State Legislature, and that Miss Koch and her friends were trying to influence legislation in the committee hearings at the state capitol. They had succeeded in killing several bills, notably the anti-genocide resolution (see Chapter 5). At that juncture, on March 23, 1963, he had made the speech on the floor of the House defending himself as an anti-Communist and denouncing the right-wing extremists as "just as subversive and just as revolutionary against American society" as the Communists (the whole speech is quoted in Chapter 5 and was now read in the courtroom). Rose had not mentioned anyone's name at that time, even when a newspaper reporter asked him, but on the witness stand, Rose acknowledged that he had had Gerda Koch in mind.

Rose pointed out the falsehoods in Exhibits A and B, and described the newspaper stories damaging to him that appeared when Grinde sent his letter and Exhibit A to the Anoka County commissioners in December 1963. He described the harassment he had been subject to when these newspaper stories appeared. Newhall put into the record and read to the jury one of the letters that Rose happened to have kept from that time.

Newhall: "A year ago when you knocked on my front door soliciting support for yourself as a Rep. of our district here, you had an awful sneaky look on your face and now that look is coming for everyone to see that you are playing hand in hand with the Commies and their teaching and are trying your best to poison the minds of our school kids with your Commie ideas. Don't forget that all this will be thrown in your face come the next election and I for one will do my best to prevent you in getting in office to continue your practice. Sincerely, John R. Ternes, 1934 Buchanan Street N.E., Minneapolis 18."
Did you know John R. Ternes?

Rose: I don't recall him, but he refers to the fact that I knocked on his door, which I undoubtedly did, because I knocked on many, many thousands of doors during that campaign of 1962. He was a constituent of mine; I've no doubt of that, that I knocked on his door, but I don't recall him. There were other phone calls then and letters to that effect, but that's one that I happened to have kept.

Newhall asked if this harassment contributed to Rose's decision not to run again for the legislature.

Rose: There were, of course, many reasons why I decided not to run.

My health, for example, was not in very good condition at that time, in December 1963, but certainly this is one of the factors that I knew would make it a very rough campaign, with this kind of garbage being spread about concerning me. It would make the campaign much more difficult than it might otherwise have been and I didn't feel that I wanted to go through a hectic experience like that at that time.

Newhall: Since that time, since the time that these libels have been circulated about you and since the publicity in connection with the Anoka lecture series, among your associates and the public generally, have you noticed any change in attitude towards you?

Rose: Well, I can't say so among any of my associates at the university, as far as I know. However, there have been some people that take the position that, you know, where there is smoke, there is fire, there might be something to it if all this continues, so that I have felt a little bit of suspicion that I might be a subversive character; yes.

That was the end of Newhall's direct examination of Rose.

Daly then began his cross-examination:

Daly: And what religion do you belong to?

Rose: I'm a Jew, a member of the Jewish faith.

Daly: You belong to the Jewish religion?

Rose: Uh-huh.

Daly: You have been brought up in the Jewish religion?

Rose: I have been.

Daly: Do you still attend the Jewish services?

Rose: I am not a religious person. I consider myself a Jew; I'm a member of the Jewish faith; it's not incumbent on a Jew to actually go to synagogue or temple. There are many different varieties of Jews.

Daly: In your childhood you went to the synagogue?

Rose: I went to the children's school; it would correspond to the Sunday School, the school for children.

Daly: And you completed high school in Chicago?

Rose: I did, yes, sir.

Daly: While you went to school, did you attend the Jewish services?

Rose: Yes. Occasionally, yes.

Daly: So in other words, you were brought up in the Jewish religion, is that right?

Rose: That's right.

Daly: And what did you do after high school?

Rose: I went to the University of Chicago.

Daly: Now, when did you quit going to the Jewish church?

Rose: I never quit going to the Jewish church; I have gone on occasion on high holidays. I have gone occasionally, now and then. I am not

147

a consistent churchgoer, or temple-goer; I have been in temple here in Minneapolis on a couple of occasions.

Daly: At what point in your life did you lose your consistency?

Rose: Consistency? I don't think I was ever any more consistent or less consistent concerning this matter. I have always considered myself a Jew. I have not consistently, even frequently, gone to the synagogue or temple.

. . . .

Daly: What training have you had with reference to the rest of the individual?

Rose: I've had ethical training. I've read the Bible several times, if that's what you're interested in. I have read other books —

Daly: Both the Old and the New Testaments?

Rose: Yes; although I would say I know more about the Old than the New, because the Hebrew Bible, of course, is the Old Testament only.

Daly: That is the one that you go by?

Rose: Yes, although I have read the New Testament some years ago, yes.

Daly: What other documents have you read?

Rose: Well, I have read many times the Declaration of Independence, the Constitution of the United States, the other documents which I think are ethical in character.

Daly: Well, give me a list of all the documents which you've read with reference to rights of the individual.

Rose: With reference to rights of individuals?

Daly: That's right.

Rose: Oh, I think I have read from some writings of John Locke, Thomas Jefferson, I mentioned already the Declaration of Independence, the Constitution of the United States, especially the Bill of Rights which is the first ten amendments to the Constitution and deals with the rights of the individual in American society. I've read a good chunk of the State Constitution of Minnesota.

The Court: I think we'll recess at this time. Spectators will remain in their seats until the jury has left the room. If I hear any more giggling or whispering in the courtroom, this courtroom will be cleared of everybody in it except the press. Now, remember that.

After the recess, Congressman Donald M. Fraser was allowed to go on the stand as a character witness for Rose, thus postponing for two hours further cross-examination of Rose.

Newhall: When did you first become acquainted with Arnold Rose, the plaintiff in this case?

Fraser: I think I first came to know him personally around the beginning of the 1950's; that would be ten to fifteen years ago.

Newhall: And in what connection did your acquaintance originate?

Fraser: Well, at that time or about that time, I was chairman of the Second Ward Democratic-Farmer-Labor party organization and Professor Rose became active in the club, and I came to know him in that capacity.

. . . .

Newhall: And did you then become quite thoroughly acquainted with him?

Fraser: Yes, from that time, really, up until the present, I have known him, both through association in public life and in political activities, and both my wife and I have come to know their family socially.

Newhall: Have you and he cooperated politically in any respects?

Fraser: Yes, sir, we — as fellow Democrats — work with each other in political activities. I supported him when he ran for the chairman of the Second Ward Club; I supported him when he ran for the legislature.

Newhall: Have you had discussions with him about political, economic, and social problems?

Fraser: Yes, both, I think, in personal conversations and in political meetings, I've talked with him, I've heard him, I've expressed my own views about a wide range of subjects, economic problems in the United States and around the world, social problems, and problems generally which are the subject of political discussions.

Newhall: Of your association with him, have you reached some conclusions as to his political and social viewpoint and opinions?

Fraser: Well, I always thought they were very good.

Newhall: And what had you thought them to be? What had you concluded them to be? In summary form.

Fraser: Well, in summary, I would say that I regard Professor Rose as an experienced, intelligent, and constructive sociologist, one who is dedicated to democratic ideals, one who's dedicated to the cause of freedom, and one who plays a very constructive role on the American scene, as, of course, many other people do.

Newhall: And have you at any time in your association with him observed or heard anything to indicate to you, to make you suspicious that he has any Communist leanings or sympathy of any kind?

Fraser: To my knowledge there is absolutely nothing in anything he's ever said, anything he's ever done; there's nothing, to my knowledge, of any kind whatsoever which would lead me to believe in the slightest that he had any sympathy for the Communist ideology.

Daly began his cross-examination of Fraser. He had him testify that he favored the Declaration of Independence, the Constitution, and the writings of Jefferson and Jackson; he had him testify about his philosophy of government and his understanding of the structure of the American government. Finally, after about twenty minutes of this, Newhall objected that this line of questioning was "incompetent, irrelevant, and immaterial, and improper cross-examination," and the judge sustained the objection. Daly got to the point he was aiming at:

> Daly: Let's take the banks for instance.
> Fraser: The banks?
> Daly: The Federal Reserve Banks. Are you acquainted with the Federal Reserve System?
> Fraser: I try to understand it.
> Daly: Are you acquainted with the national banking system?
> Fraser: In a general way, yes.
> Daly: And they are banking corporations incorporated under the laws of the United States, the national banks?
> Fraser: Yes.
> Daly: Now, if a banking organization were to deny the Declaration of Independence and the Constitution of the United States and the fact that sovereignty resides with the people, you would look upon that organization as being dangerous and subversive, would you not?
> Fraser: Well, I would. It's not the kind of view I would expect from our banks, but if that should come to pass, yes, I expect one could draw that conclusion.

Daly then brought into evidence a court record of a case he had earlier tried for a plaintiff against the Federal Reserve Banks in the United States Court of Appeals in St. Louis. Judge Barbeau said he did not see its relevance to the current case of *Rose v. Koch*, but admitted it into evidence because Newhall did not object. When Daly began to read at length from the document, Newhall did object, not only because the material was irrelevant, but also because the document was in evidence and hence available to the jury.

> Daly: I think this is something that should be aired. It is our position that there is a Communist conspiracy going on in these United States for the purpose of overthrowing the government of the United States, and this is at the root of it.
> The Court: This lawsuit you started down in St. Louis is going to tell us something about the Communist conspiracy aided by the banks?
> Daly: That is right, that is definitely right.
> The Court: Well, as far as I am concerned, it is irrelevant to the cross-examination of your witness. Objection sustained.

150

Daly tried in various ways to read aloud in the courtroom statements on the issues in the St. Louis case, but the judge regularly ruled him out of order.

Daly: The Commercial State Bank of St. Paul denies in their answer the Declaration of Independence, do they not?
Newhall: The same objection.
The Court: Same ruling.

. . . .

Daly: What do you think about these banks coming in and denying the Declaration of Independence and that sovereignty resides in the people?
Newhall: Same objection.
The Court: Objection sustained.
Daly: As I understand it, we had an understanding that he could answer the questions if he wished.
The Court: If you have a great desire to answer that particular question.
Fraser: I would just say I am sure the banks are adequately represented by counsel. I think that in general the banks are performing in important service for the American people. They are important institutions. By and large the people who run them are responsible citizens who are as dedicated as I am sure you are to the Constitution of the United States and to the cause of freedom but beyond that, I profess no knowledge about it.

. . . .

Daly: What do you know about the invisible government of the United States?
Newhall: Objected to as incompetent, irrelevant, and immaterial. There is no evidence whatsoever of any such invisible government of the United States.
The Court: Objection sustained.

. . . .

Daly: By the way, are you on the House Committee on Un-American Activities?
Fraser: No, my two committees are the Foreign Affairs Committee and the District of Columbia Committee.
Daly: You say you are not on the House Committee on Un-American Activities?
Fraser: No, sir, I am not.
Daly: You are in favor of that committee, though, are you not?
Fraser: Well, I'm critical of some of its style of operation, but as a duly

constituted committee of the Congress, of course, I support its role along with the other committees of the Congress.

Then there was much more questioning on Fraser's philosophy of government, including his opinion of Karl Marx.

Daly: Is this discussion beneficial to you?

Fraser: It's interesting.

Daly: Seems like you're enjoying it; I am.

Fraser: It's a new kind for a courtroom, but —

Daly: Well, now, in front of this book, *American Dilemma*, there's listed — showing you a copy of it — in the "Author's Preface" — Did you, before you came to court today, read the "Author's Preface" to determine who these people were in the front of the book who are listed as scholars and experts?

Fraser: No, I did not.

Daly: And so when in arriving — or in expressing an opinion in here today about the activity of Arnold Rose — you did not base your opinion on any knowledge as to who these people were or what their activity had been?

Fraser: As I tried to make clear, I base my opinion on my firsthand conversations with him, in which we talked about political philosophy, talked about the problems that faced this country and our community, that's what I did. And he is what I would regard as an extremely effective and responsible public servant.

. . . .

Daly: The defendant has called Arnold Rose a collaborator with Communists; are you aware of that?

Fraser: Only in the general sense.

Daly: And your understanding of the definition of a collaborator is one who cooperates in writing of a work?

Fraser: If you are asking me what I would interpret that to mean, I would say that anybody that would make that [court record garbled] — that is suggesting that a person has knowingly cooperated with the Communists in achieving a common goal.

Daly: Knowingly done that?

Fraser: Well, I assume that's the implication; otherwise, there is no point in making the statement.

Daly: And if it did turn out that Arnold Rose had knowingly done that, would that change your opinion?

Newhall: That's objected to as incompetent, irrelevant, and immaterial.

Daly: Had knowingly cooperated with Communists in the achieving a common goal, would that change your opinion?

Newhall: That's objected to as immaterial.

The Court: Well, I'm not quite sure I understand the question. Is what you mean, Mr. Daly, if Congressman Fraser had it proved to him by valid evidence — is this what you mean — that Arnold Rose was a Communist or a Communist collaborator, if that was proved to him by valid evidence, are you asking him then if that would change his opinion?

Daly: Yes.

The Court: Well, I'll let him answer that question if he wants to.

Fraser: I would answer in this way, that it would only change my opinion if the collaboration were knowingly to accomplish some non-democratic goal and you must understand why I say this. The United States cooperated with the Soviet Union all through World War II, the whole government and all of the people, and I was in World War II and I'm sure you were, at that time we were fighting Germany and Italy and Japan; so that a parallelism in activity doesn't change the political philosophy of a person. So I would say it would only change my opinion if it were proved that they were seeking to do something which I regarded as outside legitimate democratic values or legitimate democratic goals. But I think you would agree that our government itself and all of the 180 or 160 million people were not Communists because we collaborated with the Soviet Union in trying to win World War II.

Daly then went back to his attack on the Federal Reserve Banks:

Daly: Well, if the money supply was absolutely shut off, it would cause a general depression, would it not?

Fraser: Well, I know my wife would be unhappy.

Daly: Well, you would yourself, would you not?

Fraser: Yes.

Daly: And all the working people would be?

Fraser: Yes, sir.

Daly: And you are aware of the fact that the complete control of the money system rests in the hands of the federally owned Federal Reserve System?

Newhall: I would object to that. I thought we were —

Court: Well, it's immaterial. This has got nothing to do with the lawsuit. The objection is sustained.

Fraser: Your Honor, may I just respond to that question?

Court: Yes.

Fraser: I think, that to suggest that the control of the money supply of the United States government insofar as it's controlled by the Federal Reserve System, to suggest that this is a part of an enormous Communist conspiracy, to make that suggestion probably serves the Communist cause more than anything I can think of right at the moment.

Daly: To make that suggestion —

Fraser: To assert it as a fact, because what it does is mislead people, it confuses them, and to my knowledge it's not based on any evidence that I've heard in my 41 years of life.

Daly: That question —

Fraser: In other words — let me just put it this way. I think to make wrong statements of this kind, which tend to take people's attention away from where the real problems are, tends to be a disservice to the cause of freedom and the cause of the democratic way of life and that's my reaction to your inquiries about the Federal Reserve System. The people I know on it are dedicated, hundred per cent Americans and to start throwing up a dust storm about questioning their fundamental loyalty is — the implications are so enormous as to be staggering. Also I think that if you persuaded people to believe this, since there is no foundation for it, you would be hurting the cause of free government.

. . . .

Daly: The Federal Reserve Bank issues shares which are held by member banks?

Fraser: Yes, I think that is right.

Daly: There is not one person on civil service in a Federal Reserve Bank of New York or Minneapolis?

Fraser: Let me say one other thing.

Daly: Just answer the question. Is that right or wrong?

Newhall: I am going to object to that.

Court: Objection sustained. It is immaterial and irrelevant.

Daly: Well, you don't mind chewing the rag about that?

Court: We are not at a stage of whether it is a question whether you and Congressman Fraser mind chewing the rag. I have got a courtroom to run; I have got a job to do. I have got fourteen citizens away from their homes. When irrelevant matters are going to drag out the trial, I feel it my duty as a public servant to step in. It isn't a matter of whether you and Congressman Fraser are enjoying yourselves. It is a matter whether it has got to do with the lawsuit. It is a matter of when these people are going to go home, when they are going to finish.

Daly: I take exception to the court's remarks. He [Rose] is the one that brought the lawsuit.

Court: He is the one that brought the lawsuit, and Miss Koch is defending, that's fine. But when things go on in almost a deliberate waste of time in spite of their interests for twenty, thirty minutes, I must stop it. I have sustained an objection to your last question. If you have another question, ask the next question.

Because the judge cut Daly off, upon objections from Newhall, in his questioning about the Federal Reserve Banks, Daly now turned to an attack on Fraser personally. He introduced a new document into evidence.

Daly: You ran for election last when?

Fraser: 1964.

Daly: This shows your campaign signs posted in front of houses, does it not?

Fraser: That is what the picture purports to show, that's right.

Daly: Well, it is a reasonable portrayal of what it purports to show, is it not?

Fraser: Well, I mean all I can tell is what is on the picture.

Daly: I mean the pictures show a reasonable portrayal of what it purports to show? In other words, there is no distortion.

Fraser: All I can say is that there are the pictures.

Daly: What does it show?

Fraser: It shows a picture of a house and sign.

Daly: What does the sign say?

Fraser: It says "Fraser." It says, "Graham." There's a couple signs down here I can't read. There is one for Scott. I can't tell. There are a variety of political signs, but mine are shown in front of these houses, if that is what you are trying to demonstrate.

Daly: Did you know who lived at these addresses?

Fraser: No, sir.

Daly: Do you know a Mrs. F. L. Hanson, 3929 Clinton Avenue South?

Fraser: Yes, sir.

Daly: Do you know her personally?

Fraser: Yes, sir.

Daly: Do you know if any of the people who lived in these houses were Communists?

Fraser: No, sir.

Daly: Or Communist supporters?

Fraser: No, sir.

Daly: You did not. By the way, what has been your voting record with reference to appropriations for the House Committee on Un-American Activities?

Newhall: That is objected to as incompetent, irrelevant, and immaterial.

Court: Objection sustained.

Newhall: Unless the congressman cares to answer.

Daly: Would you care to answer that question?

Fraser: Well, it's on the record. I am happy to answer it, but I don't want to take up the time of the court. I just tell you, as I told you before, that some aspects of the work of that committee I have been critical of. I have demonstrated that in a variety of ways on the House floor.

155

Daly: It would have been easier to have answered the question than making a speech. What has been your voting record as to voting appropriations, for or against?

Fraser: Twice I have voted in opposition to the dollar amount that was on the floor.

Daly then tried to enter into evidence a report of the Committee on Un-American Activities, but Newhall objected that it was irrelevant, the judge sustained, and Daly asked to make an offer of proof which the judge permitted. Then Daly let Fraser leave the stand, and court was adjourned for the day.

Jerome Daly had begun what was to be his attack during the following two weeks: an effort to show that Rose was a "Communist supporter" and that his character witnesses had unwittingly also supported the Communist conspiracy. He was to develop the point that the Communist conspiracy was directed by the Federal Reserve Banks. He was beginning to attack Rose's witnesses in such a way as to make Rose miserable that he was asking his friends to submit to such indignities and harassment. Daly was attorney for the defendant, but his defense had become a kind of prosecution.

9

The Trial, II

The defense defeats
itself

COURT opened the next morning on time, and Rose was back on the stand for cross-examination by Daly. The spirit of the preceding day's interrogation of Fraser continued. Daly began by asking Rose his conception of the government of the United States and of Soviet Russia. He soon got back to his questions about the Federal Reserve Banks and their taking over the power of Congress to coin money. Newhall objected on the ground that the subject was irrelevant.

Daly: Your Honor, I take the position that the control of money and money manipulation is the common denominator of all Communistic activity at this time.

The Court: You have stated your position. I think the questions have gone too far afield.

Daly: Now, the banks to which Congress surrendered this power to coin money and regulate its value, these banks that they surrendered it to are privately owned, are they not?

The Court: Just a moment. I stopped this line of questioning yesterday, and I discussed this matter with you in chambers. I am not going to listen to your St. Louis lawsuit about the Federal Reserve Banks and the national banks in the case of Rose versus Koch and Christian Research. I am not going to try that St. Louis lawsuit, and had there been an objection earlier, none of these records or anything would have been in here. Starting right now, as I told you last night — you can put your exception in the record, but we are not going to sit here all day and hear you try the lawsuit of the Federal Reserve Bank in the case of Rose versus Koch. That is a matter for the federal courts. I understand they have disposed of it. The decision will be here for the jury to see. I am not going to listen to a long cross-examination like we listened to yesterday about the banking system. I don't care whether you are right or wrong in St. Louis, whether the court is right or wrong down there or not. But I do know it has nothing to do with the lawsuit of Rose versus Koch.

Daly: I take the position that I have a right to try my case on my own theory or our theory.

The Court: I know you take that position, but I am in charge of the lawsuit. Right or wrong, you can appeal, but I have made a ruling that we are not going ahead on this banking system case. You know what is going to happen to you if you persist in ignoring the court's ruling. You will have a chance to take this matter to the higher court if I am wrong, but my decision is final, right or wrong.

Daly: Let the record show an exception.

Daly then questioned Rose on the 125 names mentioned by Myrdal in his "Author's Preface" to *An American Dilemma*. He asked questions about each person named. Rose had no personal knowledge at the time, in the early 1940's, about the first fifty-one names since they were scholars and experts on the Negro problem who Myrdal had consulted when he first arrived in the United States in 1938 to start his research. But he responded about many of them in terms of their reputations as scholars, and he testified that he met several of them subsequently (these persons are discussed briefly in Chapter 1). Daly interspersed questions about their alleged Communist affiliations, which Rose said he had no knowledge about and strongly doubted. It was apparent that Daly, like Miss Koch, had got several persons mixed up because they had the same, or similar, names. The House Committee on Un-American Activities didn't come into existence until after *An American Dilemma* was published, but Daly asked Rose many times why he hadn't checked on the people quoted in *An American Dilemma* with the reports of the committee. Rose testified that, of the 125 persons mentioned in the "Author's Preface," the only ones he had read about becoming Communists were W. E. B. Du Bois and Doxey A. Wilkerson, and they had done so considerably after the time their works had been written that were referred to in *An American Dilemma*. Daly called Du Bois a lifelong Communist, which was absolutely false: Du Bois showed no signs of even being sympathetic to Communism until about 1955, when he was past eighty-five years of age, and he did not formally become a Communist until 1961, when he was over ninety years old.

Of the many people Daly said were Communist or pro-Communist, according to the reports of the House Committee on Un-American Activities, he was especially insistent about Frederick Osborn. This is the interchange, which will give the flavor of what went on in court that day:

Rose: Frederick Osborn, I have already identified him. He was in a leading public relations firm in New York and still is. I believe it is Batten, Barton, Durstine, and Osborn. It is a famous name in New York. He was a general in the United States Army in World War II. I think he was the president of the Population Council and is something of an expert on population generally. That is why he was written to; he is an expert on birth rates, death rates, migration, matters of that kind. He was also, I believe, the founder and first president of the Eugenics Society of America. He is on several boards of corporations. He also was — I don't think he is today any more, maybe he is, I couldn't swear to that — was for many years at least on the Board of the Carnegie Corporation of New York.

Daly: What is the connection between Osborn and Samuel Stouffer?

Rose: They knew each other very well. Stouffer has been dead for some years.

Daly: They were very friendly toward each other?

Rose: I believe so. Both of them were quite conservative. To my knowledge they were consistent Republicans throughout their lives. I used to have a fairly continuing friendly discussion with Stouffer about our differing political views. I met Osborn, but I can't say I knew him well. Stouffer I knew well.

Daly: Was Stouffer ever employed by Osborn?

Rose: Osborn was a general in the United States Army, and I believe at that time he employed Stouffer to head up a research operation in the United States Army. Stouffer may have been later directly under General Marshall. But I believe it was Osborn who initially hired him or recommended him to General Marshall in the Pentagon during World War II.

Daly: What was the name of this organization?

Rose: General Osborn's? Well, they changed the name of it from time to time, but as I recall it now, it was the Information and Education Division of the United States Army.

Daly: What various aliases did they go by?

Rose: These are branches, not aliases, of the United States War Department, now known as the Department of the Army. I think at one time it was called the Morale Division, later on it was called the Education and Information Division. I don't know if they changed it any more or not.

Daly: What is the name of the organization which Osborn belonged to that you are talking about?

Rose: The United States War Department.

Daly: What did they publish?

Rose: What did the Education and Information Division publish? It wasn't engaged in publishing. It made studies. It provided information to soldiers. It provided educational opportunities for soldiers. They could take courses while they were in the Army, and Stouffer was at one time the head of the research activities. He has published books on this. One of them is a four-volume work called *Studies of the American Soldier in World War Two* or *Study of Social Psychology of the American Soldier in World War Two.*

Daly: Do you know that he had his finger on our defeat in Korea in the Korean campaign?

Rose: I have no knowledge of it. I doubt it very much. You might be getting mixed up with people of similar names.

So the discussion continued about Osborn, whose only contact with Rose was a casual introduction once in 1943.

Daly then tried to show that Rose was favorable toward Karl Marx. He found a footnote in Appendix 2 of *An American Dilemma* which he had Rose read. Appendix 2 was a technical one, entitled "A Methodological Note on Valuations and Beliefs." The footnote turned out to be unfavorable to Karl Marx. Daly quickly switched back to Rose's political views and along the way he asked if Rose was a radical or conservative liberal. Newhall objected that the question was impossible to answer.

The Court: He told you he was a member of the Democratic-Farmer-Labor party. He told you he was a Liberal and that he caucused with the Liberals in the legislature. Now, I'm not going to sit here and go into a pedantic discussion as to the fine points of some spectrum that's all out in left field to start with. And by left field, I'm not referring to the right and the left, I'm referring to the baseball team.

Daly: Thank you for clearing that up, Your Honor.

The Court: By left field, I meant where Bob Allison plays.

So a bit of humor entered into this fantastic grueling. Daly then began to pick apart various phrases Myrdal used in the "Author's Preface." For example, in expressing appreciation to Sterner and Rose, Myrdal wrote, "I have felt more than I have ever experienced before the stimulation of an ideal cooperation where we not only added together the results of our labor but imagined that we in our concerted endeavors sometimes reached higher than an arithmetical sum." Daly asked Rose to explain this:

Rose: Discussing matters with each other we learned from each other something that we wouldn't each one of us independently have thought about. Out of the discussion arose something which was more than any one of us might have thought about.

Daly: Well, "higher than an arithmetical sum," is higher than infinity, is it not?

Rose: No, sir. You can have numbers one, two, and three, and they add up to six. That doesn't mean there are no numbers beyond six.

Daly: Do you know what an egomaniac is?

Rose: In a general way, yes.

Daly: It is a person who has grandiose delusions about his own importance?

Rose: Uh-hum.

After a recess, Newhall called on Richard H. White to testify, out of order. White was a member of the Minnesota House of Representatives who caucused with the Conservatives and usually voted on the opposite side of Rose on partisan issues. After establishing his background — which included a period of service with the FBI to investigate Communist subversion — Newhall asked him if he ever found anything in his association with Rose "to suggest any Communist leanings or sympathies of any kind." White answered with an emphatic "No." Daly then established that White's sole contact with Rose was during the five months in 1963 when they both served in the Minnesota State Legislature, and that he knew nothing of Rose's associations when he worked on *An American Dilemma.*

Daly further questioned Rose on the associates of Gerda Koch in Christian Research whom Rose had dismissed from the lawsuit. Rose explained that they had written him letters denying any responsibility for the libelous materials, indicating that they knew nothing of Rose and had had no intention of defaming or libeling him. He felt that these were apologies and he could not sue them. Daly then stopped his cross-examination, and Newhall took up a "redirect examination" of Rose.

Newhall: Dr. Rose, reference has been made to your remarks on the floor of the state legislature when you made a reference to certain persons as "dangerous revolutionaries, and no different from Communists in this respect," and somewhere in here I believe, "as dangerous as Communists." Will you explain to the jury why you feel that to be true?

Rose: Yes. I would like to explain that, why I considered these people subversive. I say here exactly — I do not say they are Communists — I say they are "just as subversive and just as revolutionary against American society." We have already entered in evidence a state-

ment in which Miss Koch testified, as I understand it, that President
Kennedy was acting in accord with the interests of the Communists,
at least in many significant respects. Mr. Newhall, we entered another
document in evidence. I don't know which exhibit it is, but it is the
Christian Research newsletter for spring 1960. I would like to quote
from that.

Newhall: Here it is.

Rose: This is Exhibit L, headed "Christian Research, Spring 1960." I
would like to point out that the spring of 1960 was a time when Eisenhower was President of the United States, and there was a Republican administration. The exhibit is in the form of a mimeographed letter presumably written by Gerda Koch, I believe it was
testified to the other day, and I saw this some years ago. I quote from
it:

"Did you know that according to the *American Opinion*," which
is a magazine, I guess, " 'The U.S. is 50% to 70% controlled by
Communists?' " And I believe she testified the other day that she
agreed with this statement. In other words, it was my interpretation
of this that in spring 1960 Gerda Koch thought that 50 to 70 per cent
of the United States was controlled by Communists. This would be
regarding the Eisenhower administration. In other words, her feeling
was — my understanding of her feeling was — that the United States
government, both in the Republican administration and in the Democratic administration, was a gigantic Communist conspiracy, and if
I believed what she did, which I do not, then I believe I would probably be a revolutionary myself.

Miss Koch says here later on, "We are in direct contact with at
least twelve national organizations," and she immediately refers right
after that to having sent her material to the "very effective and well
organized John Birch Society in Massachusetts, directed by the able
Robert Welch." Then her newsletter quotes a letter from the John
Birch Society to her: "Many members of the John Birch Society are
aware of *Facts for Action*. Our research department is also abreast
of your work, and, of course, such information is passed to our co-
ordinators in the field."

In other words, I judge from these two documents and other documents which have already been presented here that she regarded
both the Republican and the Democratic administrations as controlled by Communists, at least in large part. She has said in other
documents, and I have heard her personally say, that students — and
she has included herself among them — I believe this was a statement
made in court the other day, and the record will probably show this
— "do not accept the Supreme Court decision of 1954 as the law of
the land." Now, my understanding is that it is the law of the land un-

til it may at some time possibly be reversed, and a person who does not accept the law as the law I consider to be a revolutionary.

She was in earlier years at least — I don't know about now — admittedly by her own statement, a member of the John Birch Society. That was in her deposition. I believe it was also testified in court. Now, of course, she may not agree with everything that was stated by the president of the John Birch Society, Robert Welch, but Robert Welch was widely quoted many, many times, and it is a matter of record, as saying that Eisenhower was a conscious tool of the Communist conspiracy. I don't know if Miss Koch agrees with that statement, but she agrees in general with the man who made the statement, Robert Welch. She has attacked the university, attacked the public school system, attacked other institutions which I consider basically fundamental to the United States. I don't agree with them in all details, but her attack was far more than disagreeing with details. I hope later we will have some further evidence of this when the opportunity arises. I would like to make a general point here. That in addition to making these subversive and revolutionary statements, that in addition to that, by attacking people who are not Communists she camouflages the real Communists. It is like the old story of the boy who cried, "Wolf, wolf!" as a joke and thereby hid the danger when the real wolf arose. By calling people like Eisenhower, Kennedy, and if I may — I don't mean to put myself in the same company — but people like me, calling them Communists and Communist collaborators when we have worked against Communists in our own way, I consider that helping the Communists, the real Communists of the United States by camouflaging them.

Mr. Newhall, I would like to have Exhibit A.

Newhall: Yes. There is A and B.

Rose: A part of Exhibit A not previously referred to here — you remember pages 7 and 8 of Exhibit A were an attack on me, and incidentally, an attack on me in my professional capacity as a professor, the heading of it is, "ARNOLD ROSE, UNIVERSITY PROFESSOR," and as a scholar — but outside of that I am coming now to the next page. This page was a fictional letter addressed to "Dear Sleepy Joe," and signed "Lefty Louie." These were supposed to be fictional characters who are defining for the readers what "leftism" is because the letter is signed "Lefty Louie," and by leftism I understand Miss Koch to mean some kind of a Communist or pro-Communist. This "Lefty Louie," this fictional character says, "I am working to get control of every area of your life." He is talking to ordinary citizens. "I plan to do this through socialized medicine," and I assume this is a reference to the Medicare Bill before Congress — that was the only current bill at that time having reference to socialized medicine — "ur-

163

ban renewal, 'Fair Housing' laws, Metro government," by which reference is made to metropolitan government, I assume, "the trade expansion act, federal aid to education, disarmament."

I assume this is what Miss Koch meant by Communism or pro-Communism. That was my interpretation of it. If a person favored any of those things, then he favored Communism.

Now, since Congress has either passed prior to this letter or has since passed all but two of the laws referred to here, then I assume that Congress, the Congress of the United States, elected with the consent of the governed, representing all sections of the country, I assume from this statement that she is saying that the majority of the Congress who voted for this bill or these bills were supporting Communism. That was my interpretation of it.

I would like to make something more of a general statement.

Newhall: All right.

Rose: At first I didn't think that Miss Koch was very important, but I hope she will be pleased to learn that I now think she is quite important. Her statement from Exhibit L states that she was in direct contact with at least twelve national organizations. She is the Minnesota distributor, as I understand it, for the publications of these organizations — documents, pamphlets, leaflets for revolutionary groups around the United States. There is evidence that some of these organizations have armed forces at their disposal; at least I understand so from people who are investigating these things. Reports of training with weapons have appeared in the newspapers, and I know of some people who have received threatening letters from them. I have received, as I say, many threatening phone calls myself, although I don't know who made those phone calls, but they were stimulated — I don't say that Miss Koch made the phone calls; I am sure she didn't because I would recognize her voice; or that any of her direct associates did so. But she stimulated people to make those threatening phone calls, and I have other friends including Congressman Fraser, who testified here yesterday, who received similar kinds of threats, much more drastic than mine because I am not as important as he is. I can testify from my own direct experience that Miss Koch tried to and possibly succeeded in influencing some legislation in the state legislature. She appeared at several hearings. She appeared down at city hall and influenced some legislation. She has a perfect right to appear and testify, but the content of her testimony was subversive. I think the evidence will be presented next week on this, and I just want to give you my impression why I think she is important at this point. And finally, I think most important for this suit is that it is her material, which we call here Exhibit A, which, after being distributed by Mr. Grinde to the Anoka County Board, and further distributed through the newspapers to the public, re-sulted in a general attack on the University of Minnesota which I consider a very major institution in this state, one that I am per-sonally attached to. It created an attack on the university and was a threat to the university, which, insofar as I am concerned, there was no foundation for, and stimulated at one point an investigation of the university. I think the legislature has a perfect right to investigate the university, but the whole uproar was created by these three things started by Miss Koch: the preparation of this material, the circula-tion of the material (which I ignored for more than a year after it came out). But then when it got distributed, widely circulated, and became a foundation for an attack on the university, then I felt that Miss Koch was important, important enough to state what I thought about her publicly and to try to show what she stood for to the public. I believe I have other material along these lines, but it hasn't been introduced in evidence, Mr. Newhall.

In this lengthy answer to Newhall's question, Rose had a chance to express much of his opinion concerning Gerda Koch and Christian Research.

That was the end of one week of the trial. The second week opened with Newhall calling character witnesses for Rose. The first was C. A. (Gus) Johnson, who was the one Independent in the legislature, caucusing with neither the Conservatives nor the Liberals. He testified:

Johnson: I would say from the talks and conversations and what I saw and heard of Mr. Rose that he believes in the principle of democracy; that he certainly is no more a Communist than I am. He was inter-ested in the dignity of man; he was interested in education, that every-one should receive an education; he and I discussed the senior citi-zens, aging; we discussed welfare; we discussed assistance to the un-fortunate people. And I remember one thing that Mr. Rose stated, that everybody should not live on the dole or anything like that. The government should not be responsible to the full extent, but that each individual should, to the best of their ability, help themselves; that, for instance, the senior citizens, they should not be allowed to rust out, but that they should, if they can do any work, physically work, that the localities, the communities should take advantage of it so that these senior citizens could help and they should earn what they possibly could and then, if there is a deficiency, the state or the gov-ernment should assist. What I gathered from Mr. Rose was that it was not his idea that anybody should just sit back and let the gov-ernment feed them, but they should make reasonable effort, as far as they were concerned.

Newhall: From your association with Professor Rose at the legislature

was there anything that you observed about his actions or his statements or his positions that would lead you in any way to think that
he was sympathetic with the Communist point of view?

Johnson: Not one. And particularly after I read some literature that
was placed on my desk and on the desk of other representatives, I
paid particular attention to what Mr. Rose said. In fact, in my conversations with him at times I endeavored to bring out something to
see how he felt about it, and the more I talked to Mr. Rose the more
I learned in my judgment that, if anything, he was opposed to Communism and that he was an advocate of democracy as we understand
it.

Daly established that Mr. Johnson's opinion of Rose was based solely on
their association in the legislature in 1963.

Professor Harold Deutsch, chairman of the Department of History at
the university and chairman of the Faculty Legal Protection Committee,
was next called to the witness stand as a witness for Rose.

Newhall: What would you say that his [Rose's] general and political
and social philosophy is?

Deutsch: Well, of course, he is known to be a member of the Farmer-
Labor-Democratic party and essentially would, I think, share its basic approaches. With respect to his more general approach, I would
say that he is a dedicated American patriot and democrat with a small
"d" and an absolute supporter of democracy as the American way of
life, as it has been defined in the past.

Daly cross-examined Deutsch on his knowledge of the names listed in
the "Author's Preface" of *An American Dilemma*. Deutsch knew Ralph
Bunche well when they worked together in the Office of Strategic Services, the American intelligence service during World War II, and he testified at great length concerning Bunche's career. He was also asked by
Daly, "Tell us everything you know about Donald Young," another of
the 125 persons mentioned in Myrdal's "Author's Preface" whom Deutsch
said he knew, and how selections were made for Fulbright professorships
abroad, which took some time. But the big thing that Daly latched onto in
cross-examining Deutsch was the latter's membership in the local branch
of the Council on Foreign Relations.

Daly: Are you acquainted with the fact that it has been labeled as the
secret government of the United States?

Deutsch: I know it has been maligned in such a fashion, yes.

Daly: And is that not the fact?

Deutsch: No, I think it is the most preposterous thing imaginable. It consists at the top of virtually all of the most respected Americans interested in foreign relations. I think President Eisenhower is a member, for example. But then, of course, some people call President Eisenhower a dedicated servant of Communism.

Daly: What do you know about the Federal Reserve System?

Deutsch: Very little. I'm not an economist and I would say I know about as much as any American reads in the papers.

Daly then asked a number of detailed questions concerning the purposes, membership, address, programs, rules, etc., of the Council on Foreign Relations.

Daly: Who's the top dog?

Deutsch: We have — I'm trying to remember the name of the new national secretary. The last one was named Barber, but there's a new national secretary who is — came out here just a couple of weeks ago and I met him for the first time and had lunch with him, but at the moment I just can't — his name escapes me at the moment. I didn't know him before.

Daly: He is the head of the Council on Foreign Relations?

Deutsch: He is the executive secretary or has some such title.

Daly: Executive secretary, huh? And you say that you can't remember his name at the present time?

Deutsch: Not at the present time. I could easily get it. I have had correspondence with him since.

Daly: How could you learn — you've had correspondence with this man?

Deutsch: Well, just — he sent me a letter in which he thanked me for my hospitality and the lunch at the university and expressed the desire to meet again, so I had a letter from him.

Daly: How long ago was this?

Deutsch: About a month.

Daly: Where did you meet him?

Deutsch: At the university. Our local secretary of our local committee asked me whether I wouldn't want to talk to him. That man had come out for the purpose of becoming acquainted with our committee and attending one of our meetings and to find out any suggestion we might have for the way in which the Council would operate. As a member of the executive committee, he very naturally thought of me. I am a charter member, incidentally, going back to 1940. It was founded in connection with the situation that we faced after the war began.

. . . .

Daly: How did you find out that he was coming?

Deutsch: Our local secretary called me.

Daly: Who is your local secretary?

Deutsch: Robert Smith of the *Star* and *Tribune*.

Daly: Robert Smith?

Deutsch: Of the *Star* and *Tribune*.

Daly: What position does he hold there?

Deutsch: He is the secretary of our organization, of our local committee. At the *Star* and *Tribune* he is, I believe, chief of the editorial page. I forget which paper. The *Star*, I believe.

The Court: The *Minneapolis Star*.

Daly: Chief of the editorial page of the *Minneapolis Star*?

Deutsch: I believe he is chief at present. He has been there for some twenty years or more.

Daly: He is secretary of your organization here?

Deutsch: Yes.

Daly: Now, can you remember now who this man was who came from New York?

Deutsch: No, I can't, but I could easily get it for the record if I had a chance to look up his letter.

Deutsch could not remember the name of the new executive secretary of the Council on Foreign Relations, and several days later Daly subpoenaed him to bring the name, as well as his file on the local Council on Foreign Relations, into court. Three hours after the trial was over, some weeks later, Gerda Koch asked Judge Barbeau to let her see the file — she wanted to copy out the names of the members of the local committee. The judge refused to let her have it — the file itself not being in evidence — but Deutsch later said that Miss Koch or anyone else could get the names of the board members by simply writing a letter to the secretary and asking for them.

Daly: Now, did you know that John Kennedy was a member of the Council on Foreign Relations?

Deutsch: I believe all our Presidents have been. I don't know about President Johnson, but all of our Secretaries of State for the last few years have been, Mr. Acheson, Foster Dulles, Herter, and I think Mr. Rusk is a member, too.

Daly: Did you know a Miss Mary Davidson, 712 Summit Boulevard, West Palm Beach, Florida?

Deutsch: Never heard of her.

Daly: Did you know she wrote a pamphlet, *The Secret Government of the United States*?

Deutsch: I have heard about the pamphlet. I think I have seen some

168

parts. I have heard it mentioned on the radio program of Mr. Smoot, who makes a career of attacking the Council on Foreign Relations.

Daly: That is Dan Smoot?

Deutsch: Yes.

Daly: Where is he from?

Deutsch: I don't know where he makes his headquarters now, but he has been running a series of radio programs for many years. I have occasionally caught him by accident while on the road.

Daly: Do you know the extent of John Kennedy's activities in the Council on Foreign Relations while he was alive?

Deutsch: Not the extent, but I know he had some relation to it. It would be impossible, I would say, for any American leader not to know what the Council on Foreign Relations is because it has a great study organization which furthers research. They have a great research program, and they have continual discussion programs in New York and through these committees throughout the country in which we discussed every problem of American foreign affairs.

Daly: Are you acquainted with the fact that Mary Davidson asked him by letter what the extent of his activity on the Council on Foreign Relations was and that he answered her by letter?

Deutsch: No.

Daly: Did you ever see the letter that he wrote to her?

Deutsch: No.

Daly: You did not?

Deutsch: I don't know a thing about it.

Daly: Would that interest you?

Deutsch: Pardon me?

Daly: Would that interest you?

Deutsch: Yes, it would. I am very much interested in his answer particularly.

Daly: Well, I will quote it to you.

The Court: Just a moment. It may be interesting to both of you, but it isn't interesting enough to me to keep dragging this lawsuit on, and it is not material. I haven't any objection from you, Mr. Newhall, and there should be. I wish you would please object, Mr. Newhall.

Newhall: I object.

The Court: It is incompetent, irrelevant, what you two are interested in. You can take it up on your lunch hour or this evening.

Daly asked a series of questions about the Federal Reserve Banks and about President Kennedy, all of which were objected to by Newhall as "incompetent, irrelevant, and immaterial," and the judge sustained the objections. Daly next questioned Deutsch about a speech he gave in 1961 at the Minnesota Civil Liberties Union in which he criticized a movie, prepared by some right-wing extremist organization, called *Communism on the Map*. Daly then went back to banking and money:

Daly: Did you know that Benjamin Franklin stated that the real cause of the Revolutionary War in 1776 to 1781 was the taking away of the colonies' right to issue their own colonial money by the colonial governments?

Newhall: Immaterial.

The Court: Objection sustained.

Daly: Were you acquainted with the fact that Franklin stated that the Revolutionary War was precipitated by the London bankers?

Newhall: Immaterial.

The Court: Sustained.

Daly: Were you familiar with the fact that the London bankers at that time had King George III directly under their thumb?

Newhall: Immaterial.

The Court: Sustained.

Because Deutsch was a university professor like Rose and chairman of the Faculty Legal Protection Committee which raised the funds to help Rose pay for the lawsuit, Newhall asked him questions which provided evidence of damages to Rose and to other professors (see the first page of Exhibit B, Appendix I, for some of Miss Koch's attacks on other professors).

Newhall: The material which is the principal subject of this lawsuit is Exhibits A and B, two issues of *Facts for Action*. On page 7 of Exhibit A, Arnold Rose is attacked, and in Exhibit B he is attacked practically throughout the entire document. Have you seen those before?

Deutsch: Yes.

Newhall: Now, you in your position as head of the History Department at the university, your field is social science?

Deutsch: Right.

Newhall: And as professor of sociology, is Arnold Rose's field also social science?

Deutsch: That's right.

Newhall: Do you have an opinion as to what an accusation of that kind would do to a person in social science work?

Deutsch: Very much so. This in fact is a major moving factor in my own reaction to this whole situation.

Newhall: What is that?

Deutsch: Well, a social scientist is much more under the gun, you might say, with respect to any suspicions of extremism of any kind than a man who is in animal husbandry or mathematics.

170

The Defense Defeats Itself

Newhall: You are speaking now of persons in the educational world?

Deutsch: That's right. A man who is teaching those other subjects, fields removed from the social sciences, isn't expected to be an expert except in his own line, and he may or may not have any other work which qualifies him to form judgments. He may never have had any history course at all, or only one in his freshman year, or a sociology course or a political science course, so you can make allowances for people like that. They are just like ordinary citizens with respect to their folly or wisdom as they may show it in their life. But a social scientist is expected to have some basic understanding of the fundamentals of society, and so if he is accused of something like Communism, which is obviously a world conspiracy of the worst type, which involves a movement of extreme socialism tending toward totalitarian society of utmost intolerance in all respects and with no scruples with respect to methods, this is very serious indeed. Anyone who is tarred with that brush, if the tar is made to stick, is finished professionally; that is, he is obviously either a sinister conspirator or such a complete dupe that he is hopeless as a social scientist. And I don't believe that one social science department out of a hundred would employ anybody who is known to be a Communist, would hire such a person because it wouldn't have any respect for his competency. Not that we wouldn't allow him to have his own views and so on, but we wouldn't have any feeling of admiration for his professional ability under those circumstances. So this is really a fatal type of accusation to make against a social scientist. May I say I am very happy that in my more than 36 years now at the University of Minnesota, I haven't met a social science colleague who has even been seriously suspected of being a Communist. Now, there are people who suspect Eisenhower of Communism, but you throw up your hands and say, "they suspect anybody." As far as any serious consideration of Communist suspicion is concerned, I don't know of any colleague having this charge leveled against him for 36 years.

This statement of Professor Harold Deutsch deserves to be recorded in the history of social science and of academic life. Daly was not ready to let up on Deutsch: He took him through Judas Iscariot, General Edwin Walker, Robert Kennedy, Mao Tse-tung, Dean Rusk. Daly then got back to his favorite topic, the Federal Reserve Banks as the leaders of the Communist conspiracy in the United States:

Daly: In rendering us your opinions here today, have you made any study with reference to the history of money and its manipulation?

Newhall: That is objected to as immaterial.

The Court: Sustained.

171

Daly: Have you made any study with reference to the history of bankers and their precipitation and carrying on of wars?

Newhall: The same objection.

The Court: Sustained.

Daly: In your opinion since you came here today, have you made any study with reference to bankers and their precipitation of every depression which has occurred in the United States?

Newhall: Same objection.

The Court: Sustained.

Daly: In your study as a professor of history, have you made any study with reference to the purpose of their precipitating depressions?

Newhall: That's objected to, if I may make this statement to the court. There are three witnesses whom I have here waiting to testify this morning and they will be seriously inconvenienced if they have to come back another time. And I think these questions are wholly immaterial and it has been ruled over and over again that they are, and I do not see why you persist in asking them.

The Court: Well, they're immaterial in this lawsuit, Mr. Daly. Objection sustained.

Daly: Do you believe that the Communist takeover is going to come by a banker precipitating depression and throwing the people into chaos and then taking the country over?

Newhall: Objected to as immaterial.

The Court: Well, it is immaterial and it assumes that they are going to take over and I don't know —

Daly: Well, they told us they are going to take over. They told us they're going to bury us.

The Court: Well, you didn't say what they said they were going to do; you said what they were going to do; objection sustained.

Daly: Well, Khrushchev —

The Court: Objection sustained. Ask a question or be quiet.

Daly: You heard Khrushchev promise that he was going to pat us on the cheek with a spade and was going to bury us, did you not?

Newhall: Objected to as immaterial, assuming facts not in evidence.

The Court: Well, it is immaterial, but I'll let him answer if he heard or not, or read it.

Deutsch: Well, I'm sure that he and every Communist in the world have every intention to bury us politically.

Daly: How do you suppose they're going to carry this into effect in the United States?

Deutsch: They're not going to carry it into effect; we're not going to let them.

Daly: Do you agree that their plan is to precipitate a depression through the closing down of the money supply, throwing the country into chaos and then take over?

Newhall: Objected to as immaterial.

The Court: Objection sustained.

The cross-examination by Daly went on and on, with Newhall now objecting to nearly every question as "immaterial, irrelevant, and incompetent," and the judge sustaining the objection. Finally, Daly said, "I think that's all," and Professor Deutsch was excused.

Earlier in the trial, Newhall was hesitant about objecting to Daly's questions unless he tried to bring in irrelevant exhibits, for fear of giving the jury the impression that he was trying to hide something. But as it became apparent that most of Daly's questions were not relevant to the trial of *Rose v. Koch*, Newhall objected more frequently, although he never lost his initial concern. Daly's statements, usually added to a question directed at whoever was on the witness stand, established him as a right-wing extremist, with a similar political philosophy to that of Gerda Koch. The blatant irrelevancy and peculiarity of Daly's statements and questions, and his badgering of Congressman Fraser and Professor Deutsch, must have begun to lose him the sympathy of the jury — at least Rose and Newhall felt so.

Daly and Miss Koch were not unintelligent people, nor were they mentally disturbed in the usual psychiatric sense of that term. But Daly's questions and Miss Koch's answers were making it clear to everyone in the courtroom other than their own followers (who were present in considerable numbers) that they were living in a different mental world — a world of "Communist conspiracy." Daly had good grounds for believing that he was going to win the case on points of law, so he must have felt that he had considerable latitude in handling the "facts" of the case. Daly and Miss Koch were apparently using the trial as a device for public education — as was Rose also, as a matter of fact. Their goal, in Rose's opinion, was to educate the public to believe that there was a gigantic Communist conspiracy in the United States, led by the Federal Reserve Banks and the Council on Foreign Relations, with political leaders like Presidents Eisenhower and Kennedy (later on, Presidents Roosevelt, Truman, and Johnson were also thrown in) as their "conscious tools." How Arnold Rose was to be linked to these powerful personages and institutions came out later in the trial. But Daly and Miss Koch probably did not expect to win the trial in court on the basis of these "facts"; they expected to win because of the weak law of libel. Nevertheless, it was becoming apparent, even at this early stage of the trial, that they were hurting their position with the "average men and women" — the jury — who had to listen through hour after hour of their wild charges. Rose and Newhall began to feel that there was a hope of victory. The defense was beginning to defeat itself.

Newhall called to the witness stand additional character witnesses for Rose — Robert Latz, a young legislator of the DFL caucus; Salisbury Adams, a young legislator of the Conservative caucus (who identified himself as a Republican); York Langton, a businessman in Minneapolis who had once run for congressman as a Democrat. All were treated to the same kind of irrelevant questions, as well as some about Arnold Rose. Adams, who was establishing for himself a fine reputation in Minnesota as a leading Republican politician, testified:

> Adams: I felt that Arnold, being a Liberal, was the type of Liberal that I thought was a credit to his particular group. I thought he was sincere and very industrious and always made an effort to be fair and to understand the Conservative point of view, if there is such a thing, and to make his own evaluation of legislation, perhaps not always following his party line, so I developed, I would say, a high respect for Arnold as a legislator and as an individual.
>
> Newhall: And in your association with him and your observations of his actions and his statements there in the legislature, did you find anything that happened that would lead you in the slightest to think of him as a Communist sympathizer in any respect?
>
> Adams: Not at all.

Daly emphasized Salisbury Adams's upper-class background; he even elicited from him the fact that he was a descendant of Samuel Adams, one of the Founding Fathers of the United States.

York Langton was kept on the witness stand by Daly for over an hour and a half, mainly because he knew so much about the United Nations. During this whole time he was asked only four or five questions with regard to Arnold Rose; the rest of the time was spent on the nature of Communism, Ralph Bunche and the armistice between Israel and the Arab countries, the seventeen associations that Langton belonged to, the officers and directors of the National Association for the Advancement of Colored People, Karl Marx, the national debt, the structure of the United Nations, Alger Hiss, the Russian head of the military affairs section of the United Nations, the Gaza Strip and Congo operations of the United Nations, the war in Vietnam. Except toward the end, Newhall was still being cautious about raising objections to this irrelevant questioning, and the judge seemed to be getting impatient, although he specifically admitted some irrelevant testimony. The witness was anxious to explain the United Nations, and Daly egged him on. At the end of this long day, when the judge was delivering his usual caution to the jury not to discuss the trial with anyone, he interjected: "You have done a very good job, and from the last few days of this case — I don't know how long it will go on — but if we have the tragedy of a mistrial, I don't think we would want to put anybody else through this again." In chambers, the judge warned Daly about a possible contempt of court charge if he persisted in arguing with him in open court about his rulings concerning what was irrelevant.

The next day was not much better. The first witness was a professor of economics, John G. Turnbull, who testified briefly in response to Newhall's questions that in his associations with Rose over thirteen years he knew of nothing that would indicate any Communist sympathy, and that Myrdal was a world-famous economist. Daly took Turnbull in detail over his education, and then began to ask about money and banking. Newhall immediately objected, the judge sustained. Daly asked if Turnbull knew any of the names in the preface to *An American Dilemma*. It turned out that Turnbull knew Donald R. Young, former president of the Social Science Research Council, and then Daly took half an hour to have Turnbull describe the SSRC and Young (whom Daly characterized as belonging to Communist or Communist-front organizations).

The next witness was Stanley J. Wenberg, vice president of the University of Minnesota, who had known Rose since the latter first came to the university. It turned out that Wenberg was well-read: He had read works of Myrdal, Boas, Benedict, Herskovits, and so Daly had him testify concerning these leading social scientists, but he could not get Wenberg to agree they were Communists. Daly got onto political philosophies and tried unsuccessfully to trip Wenberg concerning Americanism and Communism.

Daly was relatively brief with the next witness — the Reverend Deane R. Postlethwaite, in whose neighborhood church Arnold Rose and his wife had participated in many civic and social events; the distinctive question to him concerned a Harry Ward who had been connected with the Methodist Church, and who was completely unconnected with the case of *Rose v. Koch*.

Arthur L. Johnson, the next witness, was a professor of sociology at the university — in the same department as Rose. He testified that he was an active Lutheran, a lieutenant colonel in military intelligence (in the Army Reserve Corps), and an independent voter. Unlike many of the other character witnesses, he had read *An American Dilemma* through: He characterized it as "one of the more significant documents in trying to give us an encyclopedia view of race relations in America" and said it would be "subversive only to Communists; that is, they would find it threatening because it speaks of orderly change, of a society trying to solve problems." Rose wondered if Johnson had not thus put his finger on why *An American Dilemma* was considered subversive by the right-wing extremists. Johnson said that "Rose is an opponent of the whole Communist ideology." Following the pattern of questioning he had used with other witnesses, Daly had Johnson go over his background after he had — only a few minutes earlier in response to Newhall's question — already given it in court. In several questions, Daly tried to get Johnson to agree with him that the civil rights movement was linked up with Communism, but Johnson said such a position was "naive." Then, as he did several times during the trial, Daly read a paragraph out of Appendix 2 of *An American Dilemma*, and implied that it was an example of Communist thinking. It happened to be a quotation not from Myrdal or Rose but from William Graham Sumner, a conservative Yale sociologist who lived at the end of the nineteenth century, and was certainly the antithesis of a Communist. Daly misquoted many times during the trial; he surely knew that this quotation was from Sumner, not from Myrdal (incidentally, Myrdal quoted the paragraph to disagree with it):

> Daly: "The great stream of time and earthly things will sweep on just the same in spite of us. . . . Every one of us is a child of his age and cannot get out of it. He is in the stream and is swept along with it. All his science and philosophy come to him out of it. Therefore the tide will not be changed by us. It will swallow up both us and our experiments. That is why it is the greatest folly of which a man can be capable, to sit down with a slate and pencil to plan out a new social world."
>
> Doesn't what I read to you shoot Socrates, Jesus Christ, Thomas Jefferson, Thomas Paine, and Benjamin Franklin right out of the saddle?

Daly had obviously misunderstood Sumner, but this sentence was quoted in the newspaper the next day — it made good copy. Daly next showed Johnson a list of names selected from the "Author's Preface" of *An American Dilemma*, a list which Gerda Koch had titled "A Tabulation of Communists, Communist Fronters and Others (who collaborated with Communists)," and asked him if he could identify the names.

Johnson: Having looked at it and from prior testimony here, I can say that the list is a kind of collection of some of the most distinguished minds at that time who had something to contribute to the study of race relations in America.

Johnson then identified the names, one by one, as those of distinguished scholars. Daly wanted to know if Johnson had ever examined the files of the House Committee on Un-American Activities or the report of the Senate Subcommittee on Internal Security. Johnson had not, but said that his work in Army Intelligence had to do with foreign Communist subversion. Daly commented: "Well, you could be working with several Communist agents and not know it."

After lunch, Newhall called to the stand Henry E. Allen, coordinator of students' religious activities at the University of Minnesota. Allen had known Rose since he had come to the university in 1949, and praised Rose for a survey he had made of students' interest in the campus religious foundations. He also took the view that "everything that he [Rose] has done and said would be definitely of a kind to be anti-Communist in its impact." Following a statement by Allen that Rose had worked for human equality, Daly had a lengthy interchange with him concerning the nature of human equality. Allen said Exhibits A and B were untrue about Rose and "if it was said about me, I would be fighting mad." Allen said he had regularly read the reports of the House Committee on Un-American Activities, but the judge would not allow him to testify about them (after Newhall objected on grounds of materiality).

Arne Schoeller, a Republican who in 1961 had defeated Rose in an election for the Minneapolis School Board, was then called to the witness stand. He testified that Rose was active in trying to improve school facilities, both as president of a high school PTA and later as a state legislator. He made the following characterization of Rose:

Schoeller: Mr. Rose is an extremely active citizen and believes in active participation for people in governmental affairs and I believe he has been very active in a constructive way in local and state problems, particularly in this state and in addition to having been, I believe, very active and constructive in connection with his own party's affairs. It happens to be not my party, but I think he has been a very constructive member of the DFL party.

177

Newhall: And in your associations with him, as you have described them to us, has there ever been anything in his conduct or in his speeches or what he has said or done that would indicate to you any sympathy on his part for the Communist point of view?

Schoeller: None whatsoever; on the contrary.

Daly went over the nature of Communism and atheism with Schoeller. He took him through the names in the "Author's Preface" to *An American Dilemma*. He asked him a dozen irrelevant things, to which Newhall objected, and the judge sustained.

The trial was proceeding very slowly. In fact, Daly was making it a kind of filibuster.

Newhall closed the afternoon by putting on the stand Mrs. Adina Rahm, a cousin of Gunnar Myrdal who lived in Minneapolis. She had tape recordings of two talks Myrdal had given in Minneapolis when he visited the city in 1958. Newhall played the shorter one for the jury (the judge required that the recording be played for him privately, before he would allow it to be played before the jury) — so they could have some direct contact with the man about whom they were hearing so much. Myrdal certainly didn't sound like a Communist, in fact he poked a little fun at the Communists at one point. Daly asked for the longer recording so that he could have it played in court if he wished. This longer recording was of the speech which Myrdal gave at the university in 1958 on "Nationalism and Internationalism among the Rich and Poor Nations," at which Gerda Koch had asked her irrelevant question concerning the "Communism of Ralph Bunche." He never fulfilled his promise to play it in the court. Daly also got Mrs. Rahm to deliver to the court a file of letters which her father and Myrdal (who were first cousins) had written to each other over a period of some twenty years. The letters were full of personal matters, and Daly graciously did not question Mrs. Rahm much about them.

When, before the trial, Newhall had asked Rose to suggest persons who might best serve as character witnesses for him, he indicated that he wanted persons prominent in government, at the university, and in civic life, who had a sufficient acquaintance with him to testify to his character and political beliefs. Newhall had sent letters to the forty or so persons listed by Rose, telling them about the forthcoming trial and asking them if they would be willing to be character witnesses. Thirty responded that they were able and willing to do so. Newhall said this was too many, and pared the list to sixteen. He then arranged a time schedule for these, so

178

that they would not have to wait long for their turn at the witness stand. Newhall never kept a witness on the stand for longer than ten minutes, but Daly had kept most of them on for more than an hour. So Newhall was obliged to rearrange and rearrange the schedule, and as the time was taken up more and more by Daly, he reduced the list still further. The jury must have been getting restless, and both Newhall and Rose felt the press of other duties. The trial was already in the middle of the second week, and Daly had not even begun his case yet. So Newhall said that one more witness would be sufficient; Rose agreed. They decided to call the lieutenant governor of the state as the last witness for Rose. Daly kept him in the courtroom for three-quarters of a day.

Alexander MacDonald Keith — Sandy was his nickname, of course — was a possible candidate for governor at the next election, and at the time of the trial, his political opponents were needling him about his affiliation (Keith was a lawyer by profession) with an insurance company which had gone bankrupt because of illegal financial manipulations. So it took a lot of courage for Keith to submit himself to Daly's cross-examination at that time. Newhall gave warning in chambers that he was going to object to any irrelevant questions concerning Keith's affiliations with the insurance company, but the judge said he was going to allow Keith to answer if he wished to (as was the practice for all prominent persons, regarding whom an unanswered question might be damaging).

Keith had known Rose fairly well since 1959, and now he answered Newhall's question about Rose's political philosophy:

Keith: He has the political philosophy of what I would call a person who fundamentally understands the American system of government, who has a deep feeling for it, who has a deep feeling for human beings and that each one of them has a right to develop his capacities. He understands that you have to use certain means to achieve certain ends, that you can't simply use any means to justify any ends. He is a man of reason and persuasion. He is not emotional. He lacks much of the emotion that most politicians have, for that matter. I think he deeply loves this country. I think he is dedicated to its future, and I think he has made a real contribution to state government in the short time he was in. He certainly made a contribution to the Democratic-Farmer-Labor party, trying to get it oriented to the issues, to contribute something, to help people, and fundamentally I think he is a fine person, and I have been very privileged to know him.

Daly went over Keith's background, his employment as associate counsel for the Mayo Clinic at Rochester, his activity in politics, and he added a few questions about his relationship with the governor, which as everyone knew was not good at the moment. Daly then asked Keith if he knew about a federal law on "Control of Subversive Activities" and proceeded to read the act; Newhall objected but the judge said he was going to let him read it. The reading of the act (including all the boring definitions) consumed forty-five minutes, and it established that there was a Communist conspiracy in the United States. It was never made explicit in the courtroom that the Communist conspiracy which Congress had reference to — one that owed its primary loyalty to the Soviet Union — was not the same "Communist conspiracy" that Daly had in mind — one led by Eisenhower, Kennedy, and the Federal Reserve Banks. Daly then went into the law of treason, the nature of Communism, the origins of the jury, King George the Third, and the Declaration of Independence. He finally got back to Rose, asking Keith about Exhibits A and B, the libelous material prepared by Miss Koch: "It is outrageous," said Keith, and made a magnificent statement about the damage done to a person falsely libeled a Communist or fascist. Daly then asked Keith about his relationship with the defunct insurance company, and the judge let him answer over Newhall's objection. Daly berated Keith for not sending Miss Koch's material to the House Committee on Un-American Activities; he said it was part of his duty as lieutenant governor to inform the congressional investigating committee whenever any accusations were made that any individual was a Communist or Communist collaborator. Daly questioned Keith about *An American Dilemma* (Keith had read it in college), his knowledge of the names in the "Author's Preface," the philosophy of Jefferson and Jackson, Keith's belief in the Hereafter, his attitude toward the Council on Foreign Relations, all of Keith's memberships (he pulled the cards out of his wallet, one after the other). Finally he was finished with Keith.

Newhall had told Daly the day before that he would finish his side of the case with Keith. But now Daly was not ready to start his own case, so he said: "I was under the impression that counsel was going to call more witnesses." The judge recessed the court until the next day. In chambers, Daly moved to raise the counterclaim from $75,000 for his three clients to $750,000. This was at the end of the second week of the trial! Judge Barbeau pointed out that there had been two pre-trial hearings and the proper time to raise a counterclaim was before the trial began; he denied the motion.

Daly's "opening statement" to the jury presented the case as he saw it: "This is apparently an argument between the forces of Communism and the forces of Americanism, of our Constitutional form of government and the forces of God and the forces of atheism." He then proceeded to read Exhibit A in its entirety with a few side comments, which consumed about three-quarters of an hour. It is not customary for one lawyer to object to the opening statement of the opposing lawyer, but when Daly began to read Exhibit B, Newhall objected on the ground that the exhibit was already in evidence and that the jury had had individual copies for over a week. Further, this was not a proper opening statement, in which the attorney was supposed to set forth what he intended to prove. The judge sustained the objection. Daly pursued his basic argument:

> Daly: We are taking the unqualified position that this man Arnold Rose is a part of this Communist conspiracy. . . . this man is one of the most resourceful Communists in the whole United States with reference to the Communist conspiracy as it exists in this country today.
>
> We are further going to show that they are the character assassins, that Arnold Rose and the people he is acting in concert with are the actual assassins of John Kennedy.

To put it mildly, this was an extreme statement. It was, in fact, more extreme than the one earlier made by Gerda Koch — her belief that Arnold Rose was a collaborator with Communists or Communist fronters and a security risk. In the course of his amazing opening statement, Daly made these additional remarks:

> [Chief Justice Earl Warren] became a dupe in their [the Communists'] hands.
>
> [To Newhall] I am hot on the trail now, and you know it.
>
> A Supreme Court decision is not the law of the land, but merely of a particular case.
>
> We are going to get Senator Eastland of Mississippi here, Mr. [Kenneth] Goff and Colonel Tom Hutton, and anyone else who may shed some light on the charges which are leveled in this lawsuit.
>
> We are going to show that Ralph Bunche, who is high in the U.N., is a part and parcel of the Communist conspiracy in the United States.
>
> We are going to show that these big money corporations and foundations [reference is to the Federal Reserve Banks and the Carnegie Corporation of New York] are the men who are behind this and that the American Negro is being prostituted for their unlawful and immoral purposes.
>
> The Declaration of Independence is incorporated into the Constitution of the United States through the Ninth Amendment.

181

Compulsory education laws are involuntary servitude. They can't compel a child or a parent to send their child to any public institution for school purposes, that the parent has a natural right to educate that child as the parent sees fit and at home, if necessary.

He [Rose] apparently has a direct pipe into the *Minneapolis Star* in this community and has been able to visit these statements on the general public through the *Minneapolis Star.*

Rose had publicly stated that Gerda Koch and her associates were "subversives, revolutionaries, and just as dangerous as the Communists in this respect." He had been somewhat worried about proving the truth of this statement — for which he was being sued on the counterclaim. But now he was no longer worried; Daly was proving it for him in court.

The defense was defeating itself.

10

The Trial, III

The jury renders
judgment

THE reader may think the author biased for devoting two chapters to the plaintiff's case, and less than one chapter to the defendant's case. But there wasn't much of a case presented for the defendant — it consisted mainly of trying to get into the record more than two hundred books and articles, nearly all written by right-wing extremists and none of them having to do with Arnold Rose or the other authors of *An American Dilemma*. They dealt with the Communist conspiracy, with the Federal Reserve Banks, with the Council on Foreign Relations, with Presidents Eisenhower and Kennedy, with Chief Justice Warren's and President Johnson's "treason," and so on. Judge Barbeau ruled about half of them inadmissible, but he allowed the others to go into evidence because they met two tests: (1) They mentioned the name of some person whose name was also in *An American Dilemma* (there were thousands of social scientists and others mentioned in that book). (2) They were stated by Gerda Koch to have influenced her "frame of mind" before she prepared the libelous Exhibits A and B. These books and pamphlets were admitted, the judge explained to the jury, not for the truth of the statements made in them, but to establish the defendant's frame of mind when she prepared the libelous exhibits. They could be used by the jury in their determination of whether she had "malice" toward Rose, not on the more basic question of whether what she said about Rose was true. If she had no malice, even though she committed libel, the jury could not (1) require her to pay punitive damages to the plaintiff in his capacity as citizen, (2) require her to pay compensatory damages to the plaintiff in his capacity as public official. In other words, Rose would lose the suit if Gerda Koch had published her statements without malice — that is, if she had based her opinions solely on the documents, reliable or unreliable, which she had read.

Miss Koch was a voracious reader of right-wing literature: She brought into the courtroom literally hundreds of books and over a hundred neatly marked files containing "documentation" about the alleged "Communist activity" of over a hundred people. She was so diligent, precise, and orderly that Rose wished he could find a research assistant as able in these respects as she. She had two persons assisting her, and the three of them were able to furnish Daly with "documents" within a minute or two whenever Daly wanted something or Miss Koch thought he should have something.

While the space devoted to the plaintiff's case in this book is greater than that devoted to the defendant's case, Daly had dominated the plaintiff's case through his cross-examination, as we have seen. He also dominated the defendant's case, as we shall now see. Newhall's role was almost limited to raising objections to Daly's questions or attempted introduction of documents as "immaterial, irrelevant, and incompetent" or "hearsay." He also put questions on cross-examination to Miss Koch's witnesses which led most of them to indicate that they believed in the same "Communist conspiracy" that she did — with Eisenhower and Kennedy as the leading "Communists." These witnesses were not at all hesitant to indicate this; in fact they often volunteered the information without Newhall's specifically asking them. This did not mean that Newhall had an easy task: He had to be alert to object as often as he did.

In the opening examination of Miss Koch by Daly, she mainly repeated what she had said before about her own life, work, and attitudes, but she brought out one or two more facts also:

Daly: Have you ever had any tendencies toward atheism?
Koch: No, I remember there was a time in my life that I thought I would either throw the Bible in the garbage can or stand by it entirely; I remember that in my young life. It was a struggle with myself.
Daly: You decided to stand by it entirely?
Koch: That's right; that's right.

Miss Koch then presented the names of those persons from the "Author's Preface" of *An American Dilemma* who she averred were Communists or Communist fronters. These were, she testified:

The Jury Renders Judgment

W. W. Alexander	Thomas Jesse Jones	L. Hollingsworth Wood
Ruth Benedict	Otto Klineberg	J. G. St. Clair Drake
Franz Boas	Ralph Linton	G. James Fleming
Midian O. Bousfield	Alain Locke	Lyonel C. Florant
Sterling Brown	Frank Lorimer	T. Arnold Hill
W. O. Brown	Howard W. Odum	Bernhard J. Stern
Ralph J. Bunche	Frederick Osborn	Walter Chivers
Eveline Burns	Robert E. Park	Edmonia Grant
W. E. B. Du Bois	Arthur Raper	Louis O. Harper
Edwin Embree	Ira De A. Reid	James E. Jackson, Jr.
Clark Foreman	Charles H. Thompson	Wilhelmina Jackson
E. Franklin Frazier	Jacob Viner	Lewis W. Jones
Abram L. Harris	Walter White	Rose K. Nelson
Melville J. Herskovits	Doxey A. Wilkerson	George C. Stoney
Charles S. Johnson	Faith Williams	Joseph Taylor
Guy B. Johnson	Louis Wirth	Richard B. Whitten

The judge explained to the jury that the unusual procedure he intended to follow was not the best one, but one that would save time since Miss Koch wanted to introduce into evidence many hundreds of books and pamphlets.

> The Court: I am a strong believer in the jury system and that the juries know what they are doing. It is not considered good practice to let certain conclusions go to a jury. Witnesses are to testify as to facts. But I am going to let Miss Koch go on the stand and take up the names of these people that she claims to know certain things about, and I'm going to let her, over objection, make her statement that so-and-so is a Communist or Communist fronter or works with Communists, and then whatever documentary or other evidence she has to back her up. It is a decision for me to make whether it is valid evidence or whether it is proper evidence or whether it isn't. I am then going to let counsel, both of them, look at the documents, and I will look at them myself and decide whether they are objectionable as to hearsay or immateriality or something else. If in my judgment I feel that the documents or other evidence that she produces are unable to support her conclusion that so-and-so is a Communist, then the evidence will be ruled out, and her conclusion will be ruled out that so-and-so is a Communist or Communist fronter.
>
> Now, the danger of that and the reason some judges wouldn't like that is that I am letting her call someone a Communist and then later might tell them to disregard it. I have a lot of faith in the jury system. If I tell you that such-and-such is now let in and later on that I am striking it out, I am satisfied it won't confuse you, and you will understand what I am doing and go along with me. So in effect I will let her make the statement about any given party that she wants, and

185

then if she has evidence to substantiate it. If she has no evidence to substantiate it, in my judgment, that is my decision — if I am wrong, there is a higher court to look over what I do — it will be stricken, and you can disregard it. On the other hand, if I let the testimony in, that doesn't mean that a given person she is talking about is a Communist. It means that you may consider the evidence, and you may decide whether or not that given person is a Communist or a Communist fronter.

Rose was nervous about the procedure adopted by the judge. Its effect on the jury would depend on their understanding of the statement quoted above. Could the jury be expected to distinguish between Miss Koch's sincerely expressed slanderous statements and proved fact? The judge, as he admitted, could have held a session in his chambers over the weekend, out of hearing of the jury and the spectators, and asked Miss Koch to present her evidence that the above-mentioned people were Communists or Communist fronters. Then the judge could have ruled out the improper and slanderous testimony so that it would never appear in open court. Judge Barbeau said this could have been a better procedure, and at the time Rose strongly thought so too. But the judge said he didn't think of it on Friday, and now it was Monday (of the third week of the trial), and he didn't want to waste the jury's time.

The procedure adopted worked out just fine for Rose. Miss Koch made her slanderous accusations and then presented such flimsy evidence, from such unreliable sources, that soon it appeared that no reasonable person could rely on what she was saying. Even though most of her documents were unreliable, she showed in court that she went beyond what they said in her attack on Rose. This was one of several crucial instances in the trial where the judge allowed Miss Koch and Daly to go through certain legal barriers, and they rushed right through to impale themselves on the facts. Another crucial instance of this was the judge's decision not to allow a distinction between Rose as a public official and Rose as a professor, scholar, or private citizen: Even though Miss Koch libeled Rose as a professor and scholar, not for his legislative actions, the judge required the jury to treat Rose as a legislator. This meant that the plaintiff Rose had to prove malice as well as libel in the defendant Koch, and again the defendant personally helped the plaintiff to show the jury that she had malice by displaying reckless disregard for truth. The end result of the judge's legal rulings, which ordinarily would have aided Miss Koch and Daly, was to give Rose and Newhall a tighter case on any appeal from the jury's decision to the higher courts. With the jury the facts were so strong on Rose's side that it was better for Rose to have the judge make legal decisions on Miss Koch's side. Then the higher courts, who decide only on law and not on facts, would have little basis for overturning a jury decision favorable to Rose.

This does not mean that the judge was personally favorable to the Koch-Daly position. It was obvious to everyone that the judge was upset by Daly's turning courtroom procedures into a shambles, and he reprimanded Daly many times for these tactics. While he showed no sign of being favorable or unfavorable in attitude toward Miss Koch, he had to rule many of her statements out of order as "hearsay," "irrelevant," or "not responsive to the question." But the judge did not allow the performance of the defense to affect his decisions on the law. He decided most legal doubts in favor of the defense, and this worked out in the final analysis to the benefit of the plaintiff, for it allowed many facts to be presented in the courtroom which might otherwise have not been allowed. The defense showed — right in the courtroom — that it was unreliable on facts, slanderous as well as libelous, willing to make subversive and revolutionary statements in regard to the Constitution and democratically elected government of the United States, and — finally — that it had malice in regard to Rose. In not one of the many hundreds of books and pamphlets that Miss Koch brought into the courtroom to document that there was a Communist conspiracy — a fact which in itself Rose did not dispute — was there a single reference to Rose. The only "evidence" Miss Koch had was that Rose collaborated in writing *An American Dilemma*. By the time the defense rested, the plaintiff need not have put on a case at all.

So the days wore on. Gerda Koch was allowed to testify that each of the persons listed a few pages back was a "Communist or Communist fronter," and to present her "documents" to back up the statement. If the "document" mentioned the alleged "Communist or Communist fronter" by name, the judge allowed it into evidence, even though it might be completely unreliable and false. But Gerda Koch tried to get into evidence a great number of other "documents" — which had no reference to any name mentioned in the case — to show what she claimed to be the background of the Communist conspiracy. The judge ruled such "documents" out of order unless she could cite specific page numbers which supported her case. Since she often refused to cite specific page numbers, Gerda Koch wrecked any credit she may have had with the jury concerning her reliability. When she did cite specific page numbers, her evidence turned out to be so flimsy that it became increasingly evident through the days that she herself was now, right in the courtroom, engaged in slander.

Part of Miss Koch's and Daly's problem was that they assumed — as do so many people — that everything in print is true. At one point, they showed full credence in the Communist newspaper the *Daily Worker*.

> Koch: Your Honor, I couldn't bring the *Daily Worker* along, but in the *Daily Worker* — and I'd have to check this one again —
> The Court: It wouldn't make any difference if you brought the *Daily Worker* along or not, because that's not admissible testimony either.
> Daly: The Communist *Daily Worker*?
> The Court: No.
> Daly: Well, there's — it's common knowledge, and everybody throughout the whole territorial jurisdiction of the —
> The Court: So what if the Communist *Daily Worker* last week said Jerry Daly is a Communist; does that make you a Communist?
> Koch: Well, don't be silly.
> Daly: Well, I don't think that they are ever going to come out in the *Daily Worker* and say I'm a Communist.

At best, Miss Koch and Daly relied on reports of the House Committee on Un-American Activities and of the Senate Subcommittee on Internal Security. But the reports they relied on were clearly labeled "not findings of the Committee." They consisted simply of testimony provided by witnesses: Anyone could go before the House or Senate committee and testify that so-and-so was a Communist or Communist fronter. There was no proof necessary, no opportunity for counter-testimony, no judicial determination, not even a committee finding. This is why Judge Barbeau pointed out to the jury that these committee reports did not constitute evidence that the persons referred to were Communists or Communist fronters.

The jury could not have been expected to have ever heard of most of the persons named by Miss Koch as "Communists or Communist fronters," even though most of them were eminent social scientists. The one name they possibly had heard of, and the one name that received general recognition and acclaim from Rose's distinguished character witnesses, was that of Ralph Bunche. It didn't help Miss Koch's case when she insisted he was a "Communist." But it was Miss Koch's and Daly's attacks on the Presidents and the other members of the government of the United States that established Miss Koch as unreliable and subversive. Daly at one point became threatening:

Daly: I might as well say for the record right now that the next one [the next issue of *Facts for Action*] is going to advocate the organization of a Citizens' Militia. We will take care of this Communist conspiracy.

There was so much that was irrelevant, and very revealing, in Gerda Koch's testimony that occasionally the judge let some of the irrelevancies into testimony.

Koch: [The United States government leaders] were getting under a foreign government outside of our Constitution.
Daly: Under control of a foreign government?
Koch: That's right.
Newhall: I move that be stricken.
The Court: What you mean is that the United Nations is a foreign government; is that what you mean?
Koch: It is.
Daly: Well, there is no question that it is foreign with reference to ours.
Koch: A Trojan horse brought in here to capture our own government, I believe, yes.
The Court: She has made her answer. I don't know that it is material, but I am going to let the answer stand.

As mentioned, the judge permitted Miss Koch to bring into evidence any document referring to any person listed in the "Author's Preface" of *An American Dilemma*, or to any organization said — by Senator Eastland — to be one to which any of these persons belonged and to be subversive, which contributed to her state of mind when she prepared Exhibits A, B, and D, without showing that it contained reliable and true statements. But when it came to producing such documents, she actually had very few. Instead, she tried to bring into evidence almost her whole library of right-wing extremist documents. For example, Miss Koch tried to bring into evidence a book attacking the United Nations; Newhall asked her if it had anything in it on Ralph Bunche or anyone else listed in *An American Dilemma*; she said no; Newhall objected; and the judge sustained the objection. Miss Koch could not see what was relevant to the trial; the fact that there was a Communist conspiracy seemed to her by itself to prove that Arnold Rose was a "Communist collaborator." This was not merely "guilt by association" but "guilt by association in Gerda Koch's mind."

There was an air of tragedy about Gerda Koch as, one after another, her carefully read books and pamphlets were rejected by the court. "I am lost if I cannot bring in this government report. It is a report prepared by the United States government!" she exclaimed at one point. The report in question did not have a single reference to any of the 125 persons listed in the "Author's Preface" to *An American Dilemma,* or to any of the organizations alleged to be subversive in the speech by Senator Eastland, and so the judge ruled it out as irrelevant to the case. At another point Miss Koch was almost in tears when a book written by a well-known right-wing extremist was also ruled out as immaterial, because it was published in 1964 and therefore could not possibly have contributed to her state of mind when she prepared the libelous exhibits in 1962 and 1963. Here was Gerda Koch, surrounded by library materials describing a dangerous, atheistic Communist conspiracy, getting only a hundred of them into evidence, and not being allowed to testify about their contents; the judge said that the admitted exhibits would be available to the jury and that the jury would have to decide on their meaning, not Gerda Koch or anyone else. "I feel hampered," she said at one point. But she had no standard of relevance: "I deal with so many facts that I cannot keep them all straight," she apologized at one time for a misstatement about whether Ralph Bunche was named in a pamphlet under discussion.

Part of her problem was that the right-wing extremist literature was so poor. It contained a lot of exciting general statements, but few specific references or allegations. Even regarding Doxey Wilkerson, there were only one or two references in all of Miss Koch's hundreds of books and pamphlets. As mentioned, in not one of the exhibits was there any reference to Rose; nor could she refer to anything that she used – or that influenced her mind – in preparing her libelous attacks on Rose in which he was even mentioned.

In the middle of Miss Koch's testimony, Newhall got permission from the judge to put Rose back on the stand for Daly's further cross-examination because Rose had been invited to a conference out of town for a few days. This time Daly tried to get Rose pinned as a "Communist collaborator" in terms of the real facts of the case. He had Rose testify again that he had heard, sometime between late 1941 and 1943, that Doxey Wilkerson had become a Communist. But Rose had no contact with Wilkerson at that time; it had been in 1940 that Rose had been introduced to Wilkerson. Daly had Rose testify again that he had seen in the newspapers that W. E. B. Du Bois was giving signs of being pro-Communist in the 1950's and had finally joined the Communist party in 1961. But, pointed out Daly, when you (Rose) wrote a new preface for the twentieth anniversary edition of *An American Dilemma* in 1962, you did not mention that Du Bois and Wilkerson had become Communists.

Rose: I did not refer to that fact. I mentioned no names. . . .

Daly: Did you relate anywhere in the book anything about the Communist activity of these people?

Rose: This is a book about the Negro problem. "The Postscript 20 Years Later" [which Rose wrote] refers to social change in the Negro problem, as it is entitled. It is not an evaluation of the book. It doesn't refer to any of the people quoted. The people who are cited in the first edition were cited because they were believed to have been reliable sources. This is neither an evaluation of the references — of which there were many, many thousands in the first edition — nor an attempt to evaluate the book itself. It was, as I have said here several times, a summary of the events affecting the Negro problem in the United States during the intervening 19 years. A little bit over-condensed, because it had to be gotten into brief form, but it is a summary of the main events. There is no mention of people made in here.

Daly wandered off after this, to Ralph Bunche, to Rose's understanding of Communism, to Gunnar Myrdal's recent book *Beyond the Welfare State*, to the suite of offices in the Chrysler Building where Rose worked in the summer of 1940. He swung more and more wildly:

Daly: Well, didn't you have a party celebrating the completion of this book?

Rose: We had no party celebrating the completion of this book, because the book was finished in 1943, in January as I have testified, and I was the only one, at that time, working on it. I might have had a party for myself —

Daly: What Communists were you in contact with at the time that you were writing this book?

Rose: I knew of no Communists that I was working with at that time or any other time.

Daly: How old were —

Rose: I don't work with Communists, to my knowledge.

Daly: How about Sibley?

Newhall: Objected to as immaterial.

The Court: Objection sustained.

. . . .

Daly: As a matter of fact, since 1940, you have been in the company of, from time to time, and the whole course of your conduct has either been with Communists or Communist-front members, has it not?

Rose: That is slander. I have never, to my knowledge, been in any sympathetic company with Communists.

Daly: Are you in sympathy with Gunnar Myrdal?

Rose: I am very much in sympathy with Gunnar Myrdal and I do not regard him as a Communist. I regard him as an anti-Communist.

Daly: Are you in sympathy with the welfare state?

Newhall: That's objected to —

Rose: Is that a title of a book or — [Myrdal wrote a book titled *Beyond the Welfare State.*]

Daly: Just — do you know what the welfare state is?

Newhall: Objected to as immaterial.

The Court: Well, I would say the question is a little bit difficult to answer. I don't know what you mean by the welfare state either. Objection sustained.

Daly: Well, do you understand that the welfare state is that everybody is on welfare and the state is at the whim and caprice of the welfare agent and commissioner?

Newhall: Objected to as immaterial.

The Court: Well, you've got a definition now, Professor Rose; he just said, "Do you understand that welfare state is where everybody is on welfare." Are you for that kind of a state?

Rose: I am very much opposed to that kind of a state.

Daly: Would it shock you to find out that Gunnar Myrdal is not opposed to it?

Rose: It would certainly shock me, because I don't believe it.

On redirect examination, Newhall got Rose to explain his article "Marx's Influence on American Thinking," which was published in the *American Journal of Economics and Sociology* in January 1951 — which Rose brought to Daly's attention at the time of his deposition on May 6, 1964, as an example of his anti-Communist writings, and which Daly had referred to several times during the trial as a pro-Communist statement. Since Daly refused to object to the reading of portions of a document already in evidence, the court permitted Rose to quote from the article:

Rose: [quoting] "Marx's theories . . . are also used by Communists in non-Communist countries as a Trojan horse, a way of getting inside the defenses of these countries to weaken those defenses. . . .

"Actually, people in Communist countries have had little evidence of the government acting for their economic benefit. . . .

"When the Communists gain control of a labor union or a voluntary association, they do not try to use it as an instrument of social reform or betterment of condition for their members, but primarily to make a big noise, promote resentments and hatreds, and to manipulate the group toward revolution . . .

"This is, incidentally, a reason why communism can never be democratic, even if — by some miracle — the dictatorship should disappear. The Communist conception of man is that he is an economic being, concerned with the satisfaction of his wants. Marxist theory ignores man as a creative ego, striving to create a better society. . . ."

There were other statements in the article which Rose thought pertinent, but the judge objected to further reading except for one last quotation which Newhall wanted to get into the record since it contained the word "eulogy," which Daly kept referring to as evidence of Rose's pro-Communist sympathy.

Rose: "The points we have covered add up to a eulogy of a great thinker — Karl Marx. Few men have had ideas with such great influence, especially on those who believe they abhor the man and his ideas. We have singled out those of his ideas which have had the greatest influence on Americans, and have found that the influence has been harmful to democratic action, capitalist economy, and clear political thinking . . . One of the strengths of a democracy over a dictatorship is that it can rise above the errors of even the greatest philosophic and political geniuses."

Thus, one more of Daly's misinterpretations of Rose's writings was cleared up.

Newhall then brought out something which had the effect of a bombshell on Daly.

Newhall: It has been indicated that you will not be here tomorrow and the next day, Professor Rose. Will you explain why that is?
Rose: Yes. I have been invited by the President of the United States to attend a conference in Washington to plan for a larger conference in the spring on the race problems of the United States.

Two telegrams were introduced into evidence, one inviting Rose to the conference, the other inviting Rose to a reception at the White House — the first Rose had ever received. It came at an interesting time; Daly later claimed that it proved that Rose was a high-placed Communist who used United States government officials as his conscious tools.

While Rose was in Washington, Daly put Daniel Slater on the stand — the right-wing extremist legislator mentioned in Chapter 5. Slater was very fair concerning Rose:

Slater: I think he [Rose] was sincere and a very conscientious and hard-working legislator, but I believe that his philosophy was considerably different from mine.

Slater testified about the anti-genocide resolution on which he and Rose had crossed swords, and said he thought Rose was in favor of too much federal government control, in favor of "the total welfare state." He praised Gerda Koch and her organization:

> Slater: I have found that Christian Research is a source of information and material that is important in evaluating world conditions and local conditions and knowing more about particular issues. . . . I believe when she [Gerda Koch] speaks and when she writes, she does it as honestly and as intelligently and factually as possible. . . . Gerda Koch has served a real purpose in alerting the American public to a position that too often today has been totally or nearly totally concealed by the usual means of communicating — communications. And we might even carry that to the point to some degree in not only government but to some degree in other areas, whether it be education, unions, churches; there is always the tendency to protect and preserve that which we have today because of our vested interest, be it good or bad.

Slater did not think Rose was a Communist, but believed he, perhaps unconsciously, served the Communist cause:

> Slater: His [Rose's] philosophies in these areas of vital importance to the future of the country as a free nation closely parallel many times the programs that will bring us to, in my opinion, eventually a Communist state. Now, this does not make him a Communist.
>
> Newhall: Closely parallel the policies of the President of the United States, Lyndon Johnson, too, don't they?
>
> Slater: I would say in answer to this, the charge against Mr. Rose that he is a collaborator, aren't we now collaborating with Communism to make sure that the Communist nations will not crumble, are we not carrying out in one part of the world programs of collaboration, in the other part, war with the Communists.
>
> Newhall: You feel that the American government at the present time is collaborating with the Communists?
>
> Slater: It's been stated that we must support the Communist economy in many areas.

On redirect examination Daly took up the case of a man named A. J. Porth in Topeka, Kansas, who refused to pay his income tax (whom Daly was defending in court). Slater answered in terms of statements made in a pamphlet distributed by Gerda Koch.

194

Newhall: That is what it says in the pamphlet. That is where you got your information, isn't it?

Slater: Apparently the papers don't put anything in about it for some reason.

Newhall: Perhaps they don't think it is important.

Daly: You understand he has passed all this information to the news media, and they will not print it?

Slater: That's right.

Daly: That shows control of the news media by the Jewish Shylock moneylenders.

Daly shifted back to his earlier case against the Federal Reserve Banks.

Newhall: Objected to as incompetent, irrelevant, and immaterial.

The Court: Objection sustained.

Daly: Well, Your Honor, this goes to the question —

The Court: Mr. Daly, you are back trying the Federal Reserve Bank case. That was tried in some other court.

Daly: I am trying the question of who was subversive here, going to whether the Jewish Shylock, the usury element, which I am satisfied Arnold Rose is a part of, is subversive, or whether my client is subversive.

The Court: Objection sustained.

Newhall: I move that the remarks of counsel be stricken and that the jury be directed to disregard them.

The Court: Well, I think I will let them stay in the record. Even though they are highly improper and constitute the most flagrant misconduct, I think they should stay in the record.

Up to this time, the Minneapolis newspapers had reported the trial cautiously, balancing off the arguments against Miss Koch and Rose about equally. But the next morning, the *Tribune* headlined its news story with "DEFENSE: ROSE PART OF SHYLOCK ELEMENT IN U.S." and the afternoon *Star* made the statement "Jerome Daly said he was 'satisfied' that Rose is part of the 'Jewish, Shylock usury element' in America. The remark was called a 'gross impropriety' by Judge Donald T. Barbeau." These newspaper stories elicited many personal expressions of sympathy to Rose, of which the following telegram was typical: "Good luck in your case. Our democratic system can survive only if men like yourself arise to fight for its principles. A well-wishing Metallurgy student."

Daly had hinted at anti-Semitism earlier in the trial, but this first of several open expressions of it possibly damaged his case in the minds of the jury and of the public.

Daly then asked Slater a number of questions which were all ruled out as immaterial to the trial. The questions were lengthy and so framed as to get Daly's beliefs across to the jury, even though they were later ruled out. Some of Daly's statements were the following: "The income tax statutes as they exist on the books are unconstitutional." "The fraud [was] committed on the American people by the Federal Reserve Banks and the international bankers." "These income tax officials usually take after or go after somebody on the grounds of income tax evasion that they want to get out of the way." "The income tax amounts to involuntary servitude." "The Federal Reserve Banks are the prime plunderers of the American people." Slater agreed with Daly on these matters, with some qualifications: "The Federal Reserve System has been authorized as a private body to carry out the monetary policies of our government. To the extent that they carry out the practices of the controlling administration, they can be used to do this, if that's what the controlling administration desires." Continuing, Daly said: "The Carnegie Foundations are behind the Council on Foreign Relations." "The Council on Foreign Relations is a club of millionaires." "They took care of the American people in short order here, through the Federal Reserve Banks." "Every depression has been created by the bankers." "Every time we have ever been drawn into a foreign controversy or foreign war, it has been by the international bankers." "The Jewish people are still worshiping the golden calf today." Slater was on the stand all this time, for two and a half hours.

The next witness was Norman Boehnke, a crew dispatcher for the Great Northern Railroad, who testified that he belonged to the Communist party in Minneapolis from 1960 to 1963, with the approval of the FBI. He said the Communist party had him write reports on labor conditions and technical operations of the Great Northern Railroad. Daly said this was brought into the trial to indicate the resourcefulness of the Communist party, and Newhall agreed resourcefulness was demonstrated. The witness testified that he did not know Arnold Rose, did not know anything about him, had not read any of Rose's writings, was never instructed to support Rose for election, and could not tie any Communist activity to Rose.

Gerda Koch returned to the witness stand and brought the Bible into evidence: "I believe it is God's word for me." She repeated that she believed Rose to be a "socialist and a Marxist."

Three character witnesses for Adolph Grinde were brought to the stand out of order. They testified that Grinde was a sincere, Christian gentleman who had no malice against Rose, but was concerned about the Communist conspiracy. One of these witnesses was the Reverend Mr. Oman.

Oman: He has been patriotic and defends the principles upon which this country was established as set forth in the Constitution.

Daly: That he believes in the form of government we have?

Oman: That's right.

Daly: And your — what have been your observations with reference to truth, veracity, and integrity, so far as Mr. Grinde is concerned?

Oman: Well, he has always been truthful and honest in any dealings I have had with him.

It turned out that Grinde was a member of a Hebrew-Christian Mission church that was trying to convert Jews to a fundamentalist form of Christianity.

The lawyer who incorporated Christian Research and was a member of Gerda Koch's group testified as a character witness for her:

Daly: Approximately how many meetings have you attended there where she has been in attendance?

Bergsten: I wouldn't be able to say, but probably close to a dozen, thereabouts, between ten and fifteen somewheres.

Daly: What is your opinion of her as a person with reference to truth, integrity, veracity, and stability?

Bergsten: I would trust her anywheres.

Daly: You would?

Bergsten: I have the highest regard for her character, yes.

Gerda Koch was permitted to read into the record the page numbers in *An American Dilemma* where works of Doxey Wilkerson on Negro education were referred to. Daly then elicited from Miss Koch the information that Rose's counterattack on her damaged her sale of extremist literature and other forms of support:

Daly: How have these slanderous attacks instigated by Rose through the *Minneapolis Star* affected your business of Christian Research?

Koch: Well, it has taken a terrific amount of my time and money of Christian Research and it has scared quite a few — some friends away from us.

Daly: What effect has it had on your standing in the community?

Koch: Through the papers it has damaged us terrifically.

Daly: Well, how has it damaged you; will you go ahead and explain how it has damaged you?

Koch: Well, it's not only by what is printed, but what is not printed. Our side has never been presented or very, very seldom. We're called

197

revolutionaries; we're made to appear as though we're just crackpots and goofs and that's the general impression people get. Even the reports now that come out —

The Court: Are you referring now to the *Minneapolis Star* and the morning paper when you say they make you appear like a crackpot?

Koch: Well, the general impression is — the general impression is —

The Court: He referred to the press, your lawyer did. I just wanted to be more specific. Do you mean the Minneapolis papers?

Koch: I think that includes the St. Paul press.

The Court: All right.

Daly: And how has this affected your ability to reach other news media, including radio and television?

Koch: We just are not able to reach them. May I enlarge on that?

Daly: Well, I wish you would.

Koch: Well, for instance, on the T.V., when Dr. Rose spoke about his *An American Dilemma*, I made as many efforts as I possibly could to get on T.V. and present another view on *An American Dilemma*, but we were never successful. Whether it's because we haven't got the big corporations behind us or what, I don't know.

Newhall: Well, I move that that be stricken as a conclusion.

The Court: The last sentence, "whether or not it's because," will be disregarded. The fact that she didn't get on or that they wouldn't let her on, I'll let that stand.

Koch: I tried to get on radio. In fact, we was told us over Bill Diehl over the radio, "Open Mike," that I had been able to talk over quite frequently, I was cut off; I was told you have a lawsuit against you and some friends say, "Well, we don't hear your voice any more, what happened?" They think we collapsed. [There is garbling of words in the original record; Miss Koch's speech was quite coherent.]

Daly: Has your subscription rate fallen off or increased?

Koch: It has fallen off considerably. That is, perhaps, due to the fact that we don't have the time to devote to the publication.

Daly: You mean, preparing the defense of this lawsuit has been quite a chore to you, is that right? What reference do other people make to these articles — newspaper articles?

Koch: Well, it's perhaps that we do not get quite as few calls regarding — some people call up and want to know about it. Again new ones are getting interested, but some of them, in general, perhaps in general I would say as far as speakers or public speakers, which we have received quite a few calls before, which — for information, for speeches and for papers, which we have not received since. [Again, garbling of record.]

Daly: By the way, has an effort been made to get you to stop publishing Christian Research?

Koch: Well, I think that's what the whole lawsuit is about.

Daly: You say that the *Minneapolis Star* doesn't call you up for your side of the controversy, is that right?

Koch: I cannot say that they do not call up at all; I was approached once during the session here, a kind, friendly approach. I think it was sincere. They want — but you told me that I should not and I felt the judge told us not to talk and I felt just out of obedience that I was not to talk.

Clearly, Miss Koch and Christian Research were set back by Rose's lawsuit, although Miss Koch got quite a bit of additional newspaper publicity.

With Miss Koch's consent, Newhall had sent his assistant, Jack Strothman, to her bookstore, and he bought a number of the pamphlets sold there which had the label "Christian Research" stamped on them. Newhall began to substantiate Rose's charge that Gerda Koch was "subversive and dangerous" by introducing these pamphlets into evidence. Miss Koch was very pleased to have the pamphlets placed in evidence; in fact she made copies available free for each of the jurors. The pamphlets bore the following titles: *The Eisenhower Myth*, which purported to show that Eisenhower worked with the Communists; *The Kennedy Boys and Our Invisible Government* and *Why Kennedy Must be Impeached*; *Wanted, Earl Warren for Impeachment* and *Impeach Earl Warren*; *Red Star's Tract, the Reds Are Back in Hollywood*; *Why Congress Must Thoroughly Investigate the State Department: How Did Reds Get Secret U.S. Defense Details*. Miss Koch testified she was one of seventy persons to whom Robert Welch of the John Birch Society sent a manuscript copy of his *The Politician*, before it was published. That book analyzed Eisenhower as a "conscious tool of the Communist conspiracy." Miss Koch said that either this was true or Eisenhower was a dupe of the Communists to further his personal ambitions. Among these "Communists," according to Miss Koch, were the Council on Foreign Relations "who are still working with this hidden force called X." This was not, however, the same X that Colonel Tom Hutton wrote about in his pamphlet on SPX.

Koch: SPX is Soviet Principle No. 10, to get us and our government in a state of paralysis to carry the people away without them knowing where they are going. . . .

She then went on to describe what she meant by the hidden force called X.

Koch: Various organizations. Now, the British Intelligence Digest calls it Organization "X." Some other group — I don't know which it is — they call it "The Establishment." Someone else calls it — I simply identify it as — they think it is the Council on Foreign Relations. It is simply just like algebra, "x" is the unknown number. That is the way the British Intelligence Digest uses the "X," and they say how they infiltrated into the different organizations, planning, urban renewal and so forth.

Newhall introduced another pamphlet distributed by Miss Koch.

Newhall: Would you agree that the burden of this piece is to take the position that President Kennedy followed the Communist line during his administration?

Koch: To a great extent, and as I said, I do believe he was killed because he stopped. I think he said "no" finally. I think he knew where they were taking him to.

Newhall: I see. But up until that time he had been following the line?

Koch: I would not say consistently. In general.

. . . .

After much more on Kennedy:

Newhall: So you believe, Miss Koch, that Kennedy was guilty of treason?

Koch: According to the Constitution and the Declaration of Independence, to surrender us to a foreign government, which this is, to the United Nations, to the best of my thinking, responsible to God alone and my country, I would have to say yes.

The Court: All right, the question's answered. Now, get on to something else.

Newhall saved his prize exhibit from Miss Koch's collection to the end, *Communism, Hypnotism and the Beatles.*

Newhall: That last one, about the Beatles, where do they come into the picture? What's the burden of that pamphlet? Are they a part of the Communist conspiracy?

Koch: It was about three, four years ago and we got some material from a Don Riggins, who had done some research as to the guild records, the records that were used in the public schools to destroy a certain part of the nervous system of the children and in creating mental disorders and to destroy what they call the inhibition system, which would make them fall easily into delinquency and facts which are immoral and illegal and unlawful.

Newhall: Is this a program which has been going on in our public schools?

Koch: I've checked with our own Minneapolis public school system and one of the best things in a public school system is the music. I talked with the director at length and I checked and double-checked; it's not in the Minneapolis school system.

Newhall: No. Is it in some schools in the United States, in your opinion?

Koch: It is, according to the pamphlet, it is music that is widely sold and it is destructive. I believe that I know the young man who wrote it, David Noebel; I've quite a bit of confidence in him. I think he has an exact mind as to doing that specific research and recalling it. I can't recall the various specific things; but the people's records at a number of phases of those is directly connected. Pete Seeger is connected with some of these records and this music and he is identified as a Communist. The Communists use trade, music, art, they use everything to destroy the civilization. That is their first purpose, to destroy us morally.

Newhall: And they're using the Beatles, right? Is that your position?

Koch: Well, read the booklet yourself. Let it stand for itself. I trust the jury to have minds and make their own decisions.

Daly got Miss Koch to tie up the Communist conspiracy to the Federal Reserve Banks and the Council on Foreign Relations.

Koch: In the last two years the money question has come up. We've been getting criticisms too, from other patriotic groups and from people who are trying to help this nation, that we're not spotting the right degree of danger, so the last two years I have been working somewhat on the money question and we do find that the Foreign Policy Association — I'm sorry, the Council on Foreign Relations, which is the mother, I think, of the Foreign Policy Associations — that that is tied up with the Federal Reserve, with the Social Science Research Council, with the —

The Court: You've answered the question.

Daly asked Miss Koch to characterize the literature from her bookstore that Newhall had earlier introduced:

Daly: With reference to the literature that Mr. Newhall offered today, is this typical of your literature in general?

Koch: No. He picked out certain elements that were perhaps hard for uninitiated persons to accept. It is for the more advanced student. It would seem radical to the inexperienced person, to, what shall I say, the layman, of the whole Communist cause. We don't start people with that type of literature. We have many other types of literature, and we offer this to people who have read for several years. We don't give this other literature to the beginners, so to say.

Daly: Well, it is available there if anybody wants to take it, is that right?

Koch: Right.

201

Daly: In other words, people can come into your bookstore, look around and take what they want?

Koch: That's right.

At the end of the third week of the trial, Daly called Sheldon Emry, the vice chairman of Christian Research, to the witness stand. Emry made a fine appearance. He testified that he spoke before "several student groups, including Young Republicans and other of the student groups at the University of Minnesota." In describing Communism, Emry used the word "dialectic," and Daly asked him what he meant by that:

Emry: When they [the Communists] speak and write, they speak in what we call a dialectic. They use our words with different meanings. They can talk to each other in speeches, newspaper articles and so on, knowing what they mean, and the American people accept it as another meaning and do not understand it. "Peace" in Communist dialectic means victory. When they say "peace," in Communism they mean victory. . . . The words "thesis, antithesis and synthesis" are Communist words, and U Thant of United Nations used those words and would indicate to the Communists he was a Communist. At the same time, we thought he was working toward some nice future society. The American people misunderstand. They do not understand what they are talking about. . . .

Daly: What knowledge do you have with reference to the use of the income tax as a tool in the Communist conspiracy within the United States?

Emry: It is one of Marx's ten points for Communist conquest.

Daly: One of Marx's ten points?

Emry: One of his ten major points for conquest of a non-Communist country.

Daly: Well, now, can you elaborate on that?

Emry: Yes. It is a method of taking money from people, moving it to a central government from a source where it can be used to further Communist conquest. In fact, the very feature of withholding is outlined by Communists themselves as a means of taking the money from the people without them realizing it is being taken in large amounts, billions of dollars.

Daly: In other words, it is taken from the people to a central place in the government?

Emry: Right, where it can be used in large and massive amounts.

Daly: So that at the end of the year the working man is left flat broke?

Emry: He gets a little bit back to make him think his government is doing him a favor, and that was by design, too.

Emry and Daly took an odd position with regard to United States foreign policy — close to that of the American left.

> Daly: And the engagement by armed forces of the United States beyond territorial jurisdiction is an act of aggression against another international foreign power, isn't that right?
>
> Newhall: Objected to as immaterial and calling for a conclusion of the witness and incompetent.
>
> The Court: Well, do you want him to say what we're doing in Vietnam is an act of aggression by us, is that what you're asking?
>
> Daly: Yes.
>
> The Court: I'll let him answer.
>
> Emry: Yes, it is.
>
> Daly: And it's without a formal declaration of war?
>
> Emry: No legality as far as the American people are concerned whatsoever.
>
> Daly: And how about the Bay of Pigs invasion by Kennedy?
>
> Emry: Same situation.
>
> Daly: And the same situation exists in the partial blockade of Cuba in the Cuban crisis?
>
> Emry: Yes, and more recently in the Dominican Republic.
>
> Daly: There has been an invasion by United States troops into the Dominican Republic without a declaration of war?
>
> Emry: Yes.

Emry followed the earlier line developed by Miss Koch and Daly that all recent Presidents of the United States were traitors.

> Daly: You accept the definition of treason in the Constitution of the United States?
>
> Emry: Yes, I do.
>
> Daly: And treason against the United States shall consist only in levying war against them or in adhering to their enemies, giving them aid and comfort?
>
> Emry: Yes.
>
> Daly: And you recognize that this is giving aid and comfort to the Communist conspiracy?
>
> Emry: Giving control by them, partial control by them of our own military forces.
>
> Daly: And this activity has been perpetrated and carried out by Truman, Eisenhower, Kennedy, and the present President Johnson?
>
> Emry: Yes, it has.
>
> Daly: Now, with reference to the power to coin money and regulate its value, that, you recognize, has been surrendered to private persons completely?

Emry: Yes, it has. . . .

Daly: Do you believe that the United States is 50 to 75 per cent Communist-controlled as alleged by Robert Welch?

Emry: About 50 per cent is my personal opinion.

Daly: With reference to foreign policy what is your opinion?

Emry: About 90 per cent.

Daly. With reference to labor unions?

Emry: This 50 per cent figure, it is high in some quarters, low in others and nil in other parts of the United States. Labor unions perhaps less than 25 per cent actual Communist control.

Daly: What about education?

Emry: It is high in large cities; practically nil in the small towns.

Daly: How about higher education?

Emry: It is pretty high in universities and colleges. . . .

Daly: Do the Communists actually use these sociologists as tools?

Emry: Yes.

Daly: What has been the Communist infiltration into churches and church groups?

Emry: Similar to the schools. It is very high in some church groups, very low in others.

Daly: What about the military, the lower echelon of the military?

Emry: Very little.

Daly: How about the higher echelon of the military?

Emry: Practically 100 per cent.

Daly: Can you elaborate on that?

Newhall: Objected to as immaterial, and it would be hearsay.

The Court: Objection sustained. A hundred per cent, I don't think that has to be elaborated on.

Daly: What about defense communications?

Emry: All the defense lines out of the Pentagon and entire northeast United States are handled by the American Communications Union, which is a Communist-controlled union. They have access to every message sent out of our Defense Department.

Adolph Grinde was called to the witness stand by Daly. He testified that he was not a member of Christian Research, but was a subscriber to *Facts for Action*. He admitted distributing some copies of the libelous issues of *Facts for Action*, but only during the time Rose was a state legislator. Grinde testified that he had lost two-thirds of his customers at his business of rug and furniture cleaning during the past year, probably as a result of the lawsuit. He believed the libelous information he distributed about Rose, Exhibit A prepared by Miss Koch, was factual and true.

Daly called to the witness stand several additional character witnesses for Miss Koch. The first was the pastor of her church, who testified that she was a faithful attender of the church, a loyal citizen, and superior in honesty, integrity, and veracity. The second was Kenneth J. McDonald, the Americanism chairman of the local American Legion, who had first called for a legislative investigation of possible Communist activity at the University of Minnesota in the summer of 1963. He testified that he had known Gerda Koch for four years and had found her reliable. He further said that Du Bois was a lifelong Communist, Bunche was an "international socialist," and "Eisenhower did, in many cases, whether knowingly or unknowingly, give aid to the Communists in some manner or other and did collaborate with one, at least, who was known to be a Communist," and that "Communists have an influence over the decisions of our government in many areas." After McDonald, three other character witnesses testified that Gerda Koch was a patriotic, truthful, thoughtful, and careful woman. One of them, Paul K. Helm, confused Christian Research in Minneapolis with the Christian Crusade in Florida. He agreed with her and with Robert Welch that the United States is 50 to 70 per cent controlled by Communists; he stated: "One of our top government officials tried to get Alger Hiss back in the government service." He held that rock-and-roll music was based on principles discovered in Russia, and used to break down resistance to morality.

There was more. But finally the defense "rested." The plaintiff was happy to "rest" also. Newhall and Rose had expected the trial would last a maximum of seven days, and now it was three and a half weeks since the trial began. Newhall had another case pending in which a contract for $1,600,000 was involved, and Rose was missing his classes (in which Mrs. Rose was substituting for him) as well as some writing obligations for which there were deadlines. Now there were only the final "summaries" of the two lawyers to the jury. These are not legal evidence, since the attorneys are not under oath, but they can be influential with a jury.

Daly was true to form: He took approximately five hours for his presentation, and produced quite a statement. He started by saying that it was a case of atheism versus God, tyranny versus freedom, dictatorship versus free enterprise. He evoked the principles of Socrates, Jesus, Montesquieu, Locke, Paine, Franklin, Jefferson, and J. Edgar Hoover. He explained his theory of strictly constitutional government, and used as an example his belief that, when Kennedy died, Johnson had no right to take the oath of office as President, but merely as Acting President. Finally he came to Arnold Rose, whom he described as a "communist with a small *c*." But the distinction between that and a card-carrying Communist is only hypocrisy. Not coming out openly as a Communist permitted Rose to infiltrate the university.

Rose was dictatorial, he said; this was "one of the sins of Jews." He shut Gerda Koch up at the Myrdal lecture in 1958, and now by this lawsuit was trying to do it again. But Rose is intelligent; he has a seventh sense — he won't push ideas any further than he can. He wants to make some money out of this lawsuit: "Jews are interested in filling their coffers with gold."

Daly began to misquote from Rose's writings to prove that he was a "Marxian socialist." Then he read from the transcript of an early day in the trial: "Rose: I am a socialist." Newhall interrupted him for the first time during the summation: "Counsel, it says: "I am a sociologist." Daly quoted William Graham Sumner again (from page 1048 of *An American Dilemma*) and attributed the statement to Rose. He quoted some early poetry of Langston Hughes, which he claimed that Rose praised, to show he was atheistic. He attributed the recent Negro violence in the Watts area of Los Angeles to the instigation of people like Rose. He attributed the war in Vietnam to the decision of the Council on Foreign Relations, in which Rose played a central, if secret, role. But "they won't do anything about Castro in Cuba." He reviewed his theories about the Federal Reserve Banks having unconstitutional control over American money, and how they decided to assassinate Kennedy when he would no longer cooperate with the Communist conspiracy. Rose played a central role in that decision: Rose, you can see, he said, is not a minor Communist; he advises at the very center of power. His call to the White House right during this trial proves that. There is no malice in Exhibits A and B, no reckless disregard of the truth.

Daly described other "Communist traitors": Julius and Ethel Rosenberg, Morton Sobel, Ruth Benedict, Earl B. Dickerson, A. Philip Randolph, Ralph Bunche, Bernhard Stern, Langston Hughes, Paul Robeson, Mary McLeod Bethune, and others — some of whom were mentioned in *An American Dilemma*, and others not. Frederick Osborn, as a major general, was responsible for our surrender in Korea, along with General George C. Marshall and Professor Samuel A. Stouffer. Myrdal was merely a front for Rose in writing *An American Dilemma*. The Communist Aptheker's book was written solely for the purpose of lulling the public regarding *An American Dilemma*.

Rose is a part of the Jewish-Shylock-usury element, Daly continued. There are two kinds of Jews: those who "worship the Golden Calf" like Rose and Shylock, and those who were farmers and laborers, like Jesus. Gerda Koch was a part of the Judaeo-Christian tradition herself: witness the friendly Christmas note she wrote Rose in December 1962, when she personally sent him a copy of Exhibit A (the first libelous attack on him). Daly closed by declaring Miss Koch and Grinde innocent of any malice — they had written the strict truth in Exhibits A, B, C, and D.

Newhall gave his summary for the plaintiff in less than forty-five minutes. He started by calling into question the veracity of the defense attorney by noting his misquotations. He said the basic issues of the case were clear: Miss Koch had prepared and distributed pamphlets which were libelous per se, which meant that the words "tend to injure a person in his reputation or to bring him into public contempt," and it had been proved in court that there was no truth to them. The basic issue for the jury was to ascertain whether there was "malice," in the legal sense of publishing the accusations "with knowledge that it was false or with reckless disregard of whether it was false or not." Malice was not to be confused with sincerity; the plaintiff was not saying that Gerda Koch was lacking in sincerity. But she had engaged in malice, as shown by the following facts: (1) She had put into the pamphlets statements which she had admitted she knew were false. (a) She had used the present tense in stating that Arnold Rose "collaborates" with Communists, whereas she admitted that the only evidence she had of Arnold Rose's "collaboration" referred to events occurring almost nineteen years earlier during the writing of *An American Dilemma*. (b) She agreed with Senator Eastland's characterization of Myrdal as a socialist who favored the Communist cause, but by drawing an arrow to a photographed page of the SPX document, she had given her readers a clear implication that Myrdal was a "notorious Swedish Communist." Grinde, for one, had used this phrase even without quotation marks. (2) She had shown a reckless disregard of the truth, as shown by (a) the exaggerated nature of the libelous material itself (for example, she said in court she had used the word "collaborate" in its literal sense, meaning "to work with," on *An American Dilemma*, those who were later said to be Communists or Communist fronters, but the exhibits made frequent reference to Rose as a "Communist collaborator" as though he deliberately aided the Communists in all sorts of ways; (b) the appeal to stop the seating in the legislature of Rose, who had been duly elected by the voters even after she had made public charges against him; (c) the continuing attack on Rose after he had publicly denied the charges — in fact the attack had continued up to the present day; (d) Miss Koch's going beyond even her own extremist and unreliable documents in attacking Rose, who was not referred to in any of her documents. Miss Koch generally exhibited a "reckless disregard for the truth" as evidenced by her distribution of pamphlets accusing Eisenhower, Kennedy, and other American leaders of collaborating with Communists.

Why should Miss Koch have malice against Rose? He had shut her up publicly when, at Myrdal's lecture in 1958, she asked her question about Myrdal hiring "a well-known Communist, Ralph Bunche." She had actually referred to this incident four years later when she published her first accusations against Rose; it must have rankled all this time. There was another reason, said Newhall (and this point had *not* been suggested by Rose): Miss Koch lost one job when she publicly attacked Carl Rowan — a Negro — as a Communist supporter; she lost another job when she similarly attacked Max Lerner — a Jew. When she heard that Arnold Rose — a Jew who was known to be pro-Negro — was running successfully for the legislature, she was at least unconsciously motivated to find something wrong with him. Miss Koch's malice against Rose was evident right in the courtroom — nothing said by him, or for him by leading citizens, had changed her mind one bit; she still regarded him as a "Communist collaborator and a security risk."

The judge followed Newhall's summation with a statement to the jury. He read, and commented on, a statement of the law in the case which he had written out. The statements made by Miss Koch against Rose, and by Rose against Miss Koch, were "libelous per se." But truth is an absolute defense against libel charges, and the jury would have to ascertain the truth of both sets of accusations. The burden of proof depended on a "fair preponderance of evidence." After the jury decided what accusations were or were not true, they would have to decide the question of malice, and he read the legal definition of malice. At the request of both attorneys, the judge also listed briefly the specific kinds of behavior that could be considered by the jury in deciding whether there had been malice; these were all taken directly from previous Minnesota cases. Because Rose had been a public official from 1962 through 1964, the jury could not accord any damages to Rose for this period unless Miss Koch had shown malice. Since January 1, 1965, Rose had been a private citizen, and false libelous statements made about him since then would not have to have been made with malice for Rose to be given compensatory damages. (The judge emphasized this last point, which distinguished between Miss Koch and Grinde, since there was no evidence that Grinde had libeled Rose after January 1, 1965.)

The judge distinguished the two kinds of damages which the jury could accord: (1) general or compensatory damages, which are intended to compensate a person for the damage he has actually suffered because of the false libel against him (the damages awarded could be based on injury to reputation as well as specific financial losses); (2) punitive damages, which are intended to protect the community and to vindicate public decency — to punish the libeler regardless of any specific harm done to the persons libeled — and which could be awarded only if there was malice, even if the person libeled were a private citizen. The judge explained again why he had ruled out certain testimony and exhibits — they were irrelevant or based on hearsay. He had allowed in certain exhibits which were nothing more than hearsay, but the jury should read them not for their truth or falsity, but solely to understand the state of mind of the defendant when the libelous statements were made. This went to the question of malice again: If the defendant believed certain hearsay statements, he or she could not be said to be malicious, and punitive damages would be ruled out. Judge Barbeau closed by praising the jury for their carefulness in not talking to outsiders and in sitting through an unusually long trial. He felt certain, he said, that they would render a fair verdict on the basis of evidence presented from the witness stand, and not on the basis of what they may have read in the newspapers or heard from the lawyers in their opening or closing statements.

The jury went out to deliberate at about 3 P.M., and Rose rushed over to the university to catch the tail end of a seminar he was supposed to be teaching. At about 9:45 P.M. he received a phone call from a friend who happened to be at the courthouse that evening: The jury had rendered its verdict in favor of Rose against Miss Koch and against Christian Research, but denied all damages, either way, in relation to Grinde. There were both compensatory and punitive damages, for $5000 each, against both Gerda Koch and Christian Research — for a total of $20,000. The jury had arrived at its decision immediately by an 11 to 1 vote, but could not — under

Minnesota law — report its decision until six hours had passed, unless the decision were unanimous. The twelfth juror simply said, according to the foreman, that he was " 'concerned about Communism in this country.' We could not dissuade him." Rose, who had been trying to get the trial out of his mind, was elated by the decision. Newhall phoned a minute later to repeat the good news. The 10 P.M. news broadcast on television started with a flash announcement on the outcome of the trial. Three minutes later the phone rang again; this time it was an anonymous person who said Rose was a Communist and would still get what was coming to him. Rose disconnected the phone and went to bed.

The next morning the *Minneapolis Tribune* and the *Minnesota Daily* (the student newspaper) carried full stories on the outcome of the trial. The *Daily* also published a very gratifying editorial, linking up the case with the fact that the following day was Thanksgiving:

The entire University community should add last night's decision in favor of Prof. Arnold Rose to its list of things to be thankful for.

The 11 to 1 decision represents not only a victory for Rose, but a victory for free inquiry and freedom of speech in general. It diminishes the danger that others will be falsely labeled Communists by warning those who would so label individuals with whom they disagree, that their zeal may prove expensive.

When and if the Christian Research mimeograph machines are cranked again, we hope Gerda Koch will have had time to reflect on how she will modify her comment to meet the minimal restrictions on ideas allowed in the American marketplace.

While it is unfortunate that such a fight is necessary at all in a free society, we can be proud of Rose for making it. No small demand is made on a man's time, money, patience and fortitude when he undertakes to disprove an unfair charge. All those whose business is the examination of controversial ideas owe him a debt of gratitude.

Other newspapers throughout Minnesota carried a United Press report on the case, and there were news stories in the *New York Times* and the *Washington Post. Time* magazine carried the longest report on the case, since the magazine's editors apparently felt that if it were appealed to the United States Supreme Court, it would give the Court a chance to modify the *New York Times* decision.

When local right-wing extremists attacked him as a "Communist collaborator" during his campaign for the Minnesota state legislature in 1962, Sociologist Arnold M. Rose paid little attention. Neither did the voters who elected him. But when the attacks continued in a newsletter put out by Christian Research Inc., a Minneapolis outfit run by ex-Schoolteacher Gerda Koch, who says she belongs to the John Birch Society, Rose was deluged with bitter letters, unordered merchandise and anonymous, late-night phone calls. After he decided not to run for re-election and returned to teaching at the University of Minnesota in 1964, Miss Koch attacked him so often that the state legislature was moved to probe "Communists" on the campus — and Rose was moved to sue for libel.

Organization X. Although the "proof" of his Communism consisted of nothing more than that he had helped Swedish Economist Gunnar Myrdal write *An American Dilemma* — the famous study of U.S. Negroes that was cited by the Supreme Court in its 1954 school segregation decision — Rose had a tough legal precedent to contend with. Last year, in *New York Times Co. v. Sullivan,* the Supreme Court ruled that false criticism of a public official is not libelous unless the official proves actual malice. And since the court did not define "public official," lower courts have been moving toward an inclusive definition that would cover just about anyone in any capacity who becomes a figure in "public debate."

For the defense, Lawyer Jerome Daly argued that under the *Times* decision, Rose was a public figure both as legislator and professor. Daly declared that Rose was a member of "the Jewish usury element" which is "part of the Communist conspiracy" that is taking over Federal Reserve Banks. In her testimony, Miss Koch accused President Kennedy of "treason" for investigating disarmament and said that President Eisenhower was "engineered" into office by "them" — not Communists, exactly, but something more sinister called "Organization X."

Exaggerated Language. After 3½ weeks of such rambling, which was countered by a dozen eminent witnesses who testified that Rose had no Communist connection whatever, District Court Judge Donald T. Barbeau instructed the jury that actual malice may be inferred from "exaggerated language" as well as from repeated publication after the victim's denial. More important, he ruled out the need to find actual malice after Rose left the legislature: Rose's professorship at the state university did not make him a public official. Thus advised, the jury awarded Rose $20,-000 from Gerda Koch and Christian Research Inc. "I told my friends I would stand by the truth and sing praises to the Lord no matter what," said the defendant as she promised to appeal. If she keeps her promise, she may give the Supreme Court a chance to set some needed limits on libel by clarifying what the *Times* decision meant by "public official." [1]

When a *Daily* reporter got in touch with Rose over the phone, and asked what he thought of Gerda Koch's plans for an appeal, Rose — having in mind how carefully Newhall and Barbeau had followed the *New York Times* decision and other existing points of law, as well as being aware of the heavy costs of an appeal — said that this was probably an effort to save

211

face, which she had not considered thoroughly. Miss Koch wrote the following letter to the editor, which was duly published in the *Daily*.

In your Nov. 30 article, you state that "Rose said last week he thought Miss Koch's statement Tuesday night that she will 'very definitely' appeal the case was 'an effort to save face' which she had not really considered thoroughly." This is to let Arnold Rose, the university, the press, and all men, good and bad, know that I, Gerda Koch, did not "lose face" before God and His Christ, my Supreme Judge and Savior. This is what will count in Eternity. In the eyes of the world I "lost face" for the time being, and I am not insensitive to the deep sting, but I am not ashamed to say that I am a Christian and believe if we "suffer with Him (or for the truth) we shall also reign with Him." This of course is "foolishness" to the unbeliever.

". . . the natural man receiveth not the things of the Spirit of God; for they are foolishness unto him; neither can he know them, they are spiritually discerned." — I Cor. 2:14

"For the wisdom of this world is foolishness with God. For it is written, He taketh the wise in their own craftiness." — I Cor. 3:19

I have prayed and do pray for my opponent, Arnold Rose. The "Supreme Judge" who not only "sprinkles gentle snow," but whom I also fear as "a consuming fire," will award each and every one according to the deeds done in his body on this earth. We told the truth BEFORE the trial, and we tried to present it during the trial. The present verdict will be appealed to a higher court. I am not concerned to "save face" before university professors, before the public, and, IF need be, before any court, my ONE concern is to "save face" before my God and Maker, the "Supreme Judge," and to do so we shall print the truth also in the future and "nothing but the whole truth," despite 100,000 libel suits! "So help me, God!"

In her next issue of *Facts for Action* (November–December 1965) Miss Koch quoted Louis Budenz — an admitted ex-Communist who testified to a Senate committee — as saying that the Communist party decided that "all concealed Communists should sue anyone who accused them of being Communist, sue them for libel." So Gerda Koch was not withholding any further attack on Rose, and was coming closer to calling him an outright Communist. She also announced that she was writing a book on the case, and "We believe God can use all this to get a movement started; a fire, if you please, that can sweep the nation." It has never ceased to amaze Rose how people like Gerda Koch believe that they can manipulate God.

212

Epilogue
Lessons from a lawsuit

ONE of the prominent politicians of Minnesota — one of those who could not testify at the trial because he was away at the time — wrote a letter of congratulations to Rose after the trial, which said in part:

I want to join with all the others in warmly congratulating you on your victory. I know that this was a victory for you personally but, in a far more important and broader sense, for rationality in public affairs, and a well-deserved slap at the irresponsible rightists who picked you as one of their many targets. Congratulations! You've done a great deal for our state in that victory alone.

One might hope so, but one must also remain realistically skeptical. Rose at no time expected that he would be able to "shut up" Gerda Koch or her friends — as Daly so inelegantly put it during the trial. In fact, studies in social psychology convinced him that her failure in the courtroom would add strength to her conviction. Gerda Koch and her followers are so convinced of their monopoly on God and the Truth that they will not permit anyone from the outside to share them. So the verdict was only a little more than a month old when Gerda Koch published a new blast at Rose, coming closer than ever before to calling him an outright Communist. It may be predicted that she will lose all her little niceties and come completely to Daly's position, as stated in court, that Rose is one of the leading secret Communists in the United States, who directs all the others, and he does this from his "racial" heritage in the "Jewish-Shylock-usury element." Gerda Koch needs an "explanation" of why the world is not with her.

Gerda Koch appealed the jury's verdict. Daly first submitted to Judge Barbeau a lengthy brief calling for a new trial. This did not add anything that had not already been said at the trial, but it laid "particular emphasis on alleged biased misconduct by the Court, counsel for the plaintiff and, indirectly, the jury itself," according to the memorandum issued by Judge Barbeau denying the defendant's plea. Judge Barbeau rejected this charge, and went on to state what he considered to be the major issue in the case:

It is apparent to even the average student of justice that a case such as the case at bar provides a vehicle for a collision between the right of free- dom of speech and freedom of the press and the right of an individual to have redress for false defamation. This Court yields to no one in its deep commitment to the untrammeled right to criticize. This Court yields to no one in its commitment that debate on public issues should be uninhibited, robust and wide open and may well include vehement, caustic and some- times unpleasantly sharp attacks. This right of expression extends not only to public issues but, as well, to public leaders. Criticism of govern- ment is at the very center of this protected area.

However, this does not mean that the First and Fourteenth Amend- ments have stripped private citizens of all means of redress for injuries inflicted upon them by careless or reckless liars. The destruction that de- famatory falsehood may bring to an individual is often beyond the capacity of the law to redeem, but imperfect though the system may be, an action for damages is the only hope for vindication or redress the law gives to a man whose reputation has been falsely dishonored. After all, our fore- fathers adopted civil actions for slander and libel as a substitute for the duel and as a deterrent to murder.

Moreover, the preventative effect of liability for malicious defamation serves an important public purpose. Certainly if the 1950's taught us any- thing, they taught us that the poisonous atmosphere of the easy lie can affect and degrade a whole society.[1]

A portion of this memorandum was quoted in the Minneapolis news- papers, and there was at least one letter commending Judge Barbeau for his statement. It came from the executive director of the Minnesota Coun- cil of Churches, and said of the judge's decision: "It was one of the clear- est and finest expressions in support of the fundamental principles of American democracy that I have read in a long time."

Even though she is the chief distributor, for the state of Minnesota, of right-wing extremist literature published by many of the revolutionary groups in the United States, and she has a subscribers' list of 200–300 persons who presumably pay $10 a year to read what now has become the main feature of *Facts for Action* — the attack on Arnold Rose — Gerda Koch probably does not have much income or wealth. If legal judgment

214

could be entered against her, it is doubtful that anything more than a bookstore of right-wing literature could be collected. Of course, Daly did not work without compensation during the years he was employed on the lawsuit, and Gerda Koch was able to pay $1700 for the transcript of the trial within two weeks after the verdict, plus about $1000 in appeal costs and a large fee for the appeal attorney. Obviously, some persons of a like mind are supporting her cause, but they stay in the background, and some even publicly disassociated themselves from Miss Koch's activities, to avoid getting sued themselves. Miss Koch publicly vowed to fight the verdict all the way up to the United States Supreme Court if necessary, and she seems to be able to raise the necessary funds to do so.

Does this all mean that the lawsuit was to no avail from Rose's standpoint? Did he go to all the trouble without being able to accomplish anything — no stopping of the libel and no effective judgment to penalize Gerda Koch and her supporters? And if so, is not the American legal system hopeless? During the period between the end of the trial in November 1965 and the Minnesota Supreme Court reversal on October 20, 1967, Rose would have answered these questions in the negative. The following pages reflect Rose's thinking during that period. It seemed to him that he had actually accomplished the goals he set out to accomplish when he started the lawsuit. First, a good number of Miss Koch's supporters fell off. The clergymen who formerly passed around a collection basket for her at their church services considerably diminished in numbers. And many other misguided persons who genuinely fear Communism acquired some inkling of the difference between genuine anti-Communism and verbal "anti-Communism," which is in fact an attack on both liberalism and conservatism. For the while, it seemed doubtful that the right-wing extremist leaders around the country could make of Minnesota the haven and contributory fief they have made of California, Texas, Alabama, and certain other states. The only way to keep these people from preying on the very real fears of a large section of the American populace today is to expose them for what they are, before they consolidate their power in politics. The hard core will not be changed, but the recruits can be kept away. The trial outcome demonstrated at least that much.

As shown in Chapter 3, the United States has always had its small group of right-wing revolutionaries, but only at a few periods have they been a threat to the stability of our democratic-republican form of government, to the integrity of our legal system, or to the maintenance of our free public educational system. We are living in one of those periods. In 1964, Gerda Koch's fellow extremists seized control of the national Republican party away from the hands of the true conservatives. And while Senators Everett Dirksen and Thruston Morton, Governors George Romney and William Scranton, and other conservatives and "moderates" have finally come to the point of publicly denouncing the right-wing revolutionaries, they have not yet effectively re-established their control of the Republican party. Of course, they never lost control in New England, the Middle Atlantic States, Michigan, Oregon, or Minnesota — but these are still a minority of all the states. They are in graver danger than ever in most of the South, in California, and in South Dakota (where the hard-bitten conservative Karl Mundt had to face vigorous opposition from a John Birchite to retain his Senate seat in 1966). The international difficulties of the United States will enhance the fears of the well-intentioned but unsophisticated average American — fears on which the revolutionaries of both extremes always play. The "kooks," as former Vice President Richard Nixon labeled them, are out in full force these days. A college student from California telephoned Rose long distance in January 1966 to accuse him of being anti-Negro! But at least the numbers of such persons were no longer being significantly augmented in Minnesota during 1964 through 1967.

This great accomplishment, of course, was not solely the direct result of Rose's lawsuit and its outcome. But, in a sense, it was an indirect result. By his efforts, Rose did start a movement toward recognition by the Conservatives in the state legislature that they were not the same political species as the right-wing revolutionaries. No extremist politician stands much of a chance today in either of the leading political parties of Minnesota. And, equally important, Rose finally got across to the directors of the *Minneapolis Star* that their falsehoods against him were ultimately damaging to the public. Since the spring of 1964, the *Star* has no longer given favorable publicity to the extremist cause. At least between 1965 and 1967, the *Star* was circumspect about attacking the university and publishing false statements about its professors. The new caution of the *Minneapolis Star*, the state's leading newspaper in circulation, inhibits the build-up of the right-wing extremists as does no other single influence. Whereas in 1963 and early 1964, the *Star* did more to build up the extremist movement in Minnesota, and did more damage to the university, than any other single force, it has also proved more open to the message of a libel suit than Gerda Koch is. This effective commu-

216

nication to the responsible conservatives of Minnesota was the second major achievement, at least temporarily, of Rose's efforts.

There were other effects of the lawsuit, and of the change of the "political climate" that ensued partly because of it. The faculty of the university, in a state of considerable anxiety in the winter and spring of 1964, was again able to go about its business of teaching and research in its normal obliviousness to the outside winds of political fortune. In fact, it was so happily oblivious that many quickly forgot the events of 1963–64. All the potential candidates for governor in 1966, and almost all the candidates for the legislature, were "pro-university." While one or two professors and some students still occasionally make their puristic demands for "absolute academic freedom," and at the same time denounce the "stingy legislature," [2] the great majority on the campus have learned that there are more effective ways of maintaining academic freedom.

There is one aspect of the trial which the spectators find it hard to understand and presumably that will also be true for the readers of this book. This is that right-wing extremists like Gerda Koch and Jerome Daly are scarcely opposed to Communism. At one point Miss Koch stated that she was opposed to American military operations overseas such as that in Vietnam. There are obviously good reasons for opposing the Vietnam war, but a strong desire to attack Communism militarily is not one of them. When Daly vehemently stated his opposition to the income tax, and claimed it to be unconstitutional, Newhall triumphantly asked him how — without revenues from the income tax — the United States could resist an aggressive international Communism. Daly was not impressed. It is worth repeating the most revealing statement made by Miss Koch in her deposition, in response to a question about the Council on Foreign Relations, which she had attacked in *Facts for Action*:

> Newhall: You consider this to be a Communist-front or Communist-collaborating organization?
> Daly: That is the effect of it.
> Koch: The effect of it; my studies within the last two years point out the fact that Communism — now, this is a big statement — *Communism itself is a front really for the ones that are causing the trouble.*

Throughout the trial, Miss Koch and Daly made it abundantly clear that the "enemy" was the Council on Foreign Relations, the Federal Reserve Banks, the "international bankers," the Jews, Presidents Eisenhower and Kennedy, Chief Justice Warren, Congressman Fraser, and Arnold Rose.

The "Communists" were merely a "front" for these enemies of what Miss Koch and Daly held dear. Another original defendant to the suit put it another way in his deposition: "The ecumenical movement, Communism, one-worldism, liberalism — they're all one and the same thing." As the historian Richard Hofstadter [3] points out, and as was briefly discussed in Chapter 3, the contemporary right-wing extremists are carrying on an old American tradition, which can be traced back to the Populists and the Know-Nothings of the nineteenth century. They simply find it popular and expedient to call these enemies "Communists" in these days of the Cold War. As Rose stated on the witness stand, the right-wing extremists provide camouflage for the real Communists, and do not mind that they do. Most Americans will continue to be fooled by the right-wing extremist diatribes against the "Communists." It is difficult to realize that the same word — "Communist" — can mean something quite different to Gerda Koch and Jerome Daly, on the one hand, and to Judge Barbeau, 11 out of 12 jurors, Norman Newhall, and Arnold Rose, on the other hand. The right-wing extremists are primarily revolutionaries and subversives against the established order in the United States — against the democratic-republican political system, the modified free-enterprise economy, the large measure of civil liberties and civil rights, the freedom of the educational system — just as the true Communists are. The lawsuit brought out significant evidence on this point, which is important for all Americans to understand, but it cannot yet be said that the point has gotten across. [4]

The whole series of incidents, stretching from 1962 through 1965, led to a reaffirmation of the strength of the American political process and the American legal system. Despite its inevitable delays and its not-insignificant costs, the law did seem to come through for a while. The judge, the jury (that is, 11 out of the 12 of them), the majority of the casual spectators in the courtroom, the newspapers, the majority of the newspaper readers, were — in large measure — able to learn what this libel suit was all about. The filing of the suit, and, even more, the trial itself, was an educational experience in civic affairs for the state of Minnesota. The defendant's attorney provided even more of this education than did Newhall and Rose, to their great appreciation. It is the function of democratic legal systems to expose and to clarify, and the trial of *Rose v. Koch* did this admirably for Minnesota. The decision of one juror should provide some check on this optimistic statement, of course, and if there was one such person in twelve under the conditions existing in late 1965 there could be more than one if the political atmosphere were to become more confused or more poisoned than it was then.

On the whole, the trial verdict was a victory for Minnesota even more than it was for Rose or even the university. But Minnesota is only a small part of the United States, and Minnesota can readily be affected by what happens in the rest of the country. Senator Thomas Kuchel of California, Senator George McGovern of South Dakota, Quentin Reynolds and John Henry Faulk of New York,[5] and several others in other states have used the libel suit as a means of helping to restore civic sanity. Much more important is the struggle outside the courtroom — in the churches, in the educational system, in the voluntary associations, and above all in the political parties — particularly in the Republican party today, which is in danger of fission. At least not since 1895, perhaps not since 1864, has the United States been in such danger of revolution by extremists. Rose is aware that his little lawsuit was only a local battle in the larger struggle for civil liberties, academic freedom, and political democracy in the United States. But each such battle makes its contribution toward the common goal.

The situation as of 1965–67 described above may be reversed because of United States Supreme Court decisions during 1967. The implications of these decisions are broad, but let us look first at their impact in the narrow context of the *Rose v. Koch* lawsuit.

As mentioned, Miss Koch decided to appeal to the Minnesota Supreme Court after the trial judge turned down her petition for dismissal of the jury's decision. While retaining Jerome Daly as an attorney, she also hired Harry Peterson — a retired Minnesota Supreme Court judge — as appeal attorney, and his fee must have been pretty high. She held a public fund-raising dinner, but this could not have netted more than $500. The bulk of the thousands of dollars she needed to pursue the appeal must have been raised from a few well-to-do right-wing extremists.

After obtaining two extensions of time, Miss Koch's attorneys produced their appeal to the Minnesota Supreme Court. In sum, its arguments were as follows: (1) that trial judge Barbeau was prejudiced in favor of Rose and had used incorrect procedure throughout the trial (the Minnesota Supreme Court rejected this); (2) that Miss Koch's published statements about Rose were true and not defamatory (the Minnesota Supreme Court rejected this); (3) that what Miss Koch published about Rose was privileged because Rose was a public official and a public figure (the Minnesota Supreme Court accepted this, on the basis of United States Supreme Court decisions handed down subsequent to the trial and even subsequent to the appeal). Newhall's written response for purposes of the appeal made the following arguments: (1) that the Daly-Peterson brief on appeal had a considerable number of procedural defects and factual errors (the Minnesota Supreme Court ignored this and went directly to the heart of the facts and the law); (2) that Rose had ceased to be a public official on May 1, 1965, and therefore the Supreme Court rule of malice was not required when Miss Koch continued to defame him after that date (the Minnesota Supreme Court rejected this, on the basis of United States Supreme Court decisions after 1965 saying that public figures as well as public officials must conform to the rule of malice; the Minnesota Court held that Rose inevitably continued to be a "public figure" even though he avoided publicity in Minnesota after 1965); (3) that the plaintiff had proved that Miss Koch had shown malice toward Rose to the jury's satisfaction as evidenced by the fact that they awarded punitive damages as well as general damages (the Minnesota Supreme Court rejected this on the ground that trial judge Barbeau issued wrong instructions to the jury when, in addition to quoting the *New York Times* definition of malice, he acceded to the request of both Daly and Newhall that he list types of statements — from previous decisions — that might constitute examples of malice in this case; [6] the Minnesota Court here followed the United States Supreme Court decisions in the cases of *Associated Press v. Walker* and of *Curtis Publishing Company v. Butts*, handed down June 20, 1967 [7] — three months after it heard the appeal).

The Minnesota Supreme Court heard the appeal on March 19, 1967, but did not hand down its decision until October 20, 1967 — an unusual lapse of time. The unanimous 38-page decision, written by Justice C. Donald Peterson (no relation to attorney Harry Peterson), was carefully documented. Newhall, in his appeal to the Minnesota Supreme Court for a rehearing, objected to it on the ground that Peterson had not given any weight to Newhall's argument that the Daly appeal was full of procedural defects, such as presenting to the Court only selected excerpts from the trial court proceedings instead of the full transcript. Justice Peterson had ignored this argument of Newhall's, except to mention in a footnote that he had nevertheless read the full transcript of the trial. Newhall also objected to Justice Peterson's interpretation of Judge Barbeau's definition of malice for the jury. Newhall pointed out that Barbeau had cited the *New*

York Times definition and then had merely gone on to give examples from previous Minnesota cases which the jury *might or might not* consider as relevant to that definition and applicable to the present case. Newhall further objected to Justice Peterson's decision on the ground that it ignored the fact that Daly as well as Newhall had asked Judge Barbeau to instruct the jury with examples from previous decisions on what specifically might constitute "malice" in the Rose-Koch case under the *New York Times* definition. In other words, there had been a kind of lawyers' stipulation on this, although Newhall recognized that lawyers cannot stipulate on matters contrary to the United States Constitution, *if in fact* what Barbeau did was contrary to the United States Supreme Court definition of malice under the 1967 decisions. The United States Court in effect had changed its definition of malice three times in three years, even though these definitions were all considered as legally implicit in the First Amendment to the United States Constitution; it could change its definition again.

Rose raised two objections to the Peterson decision, which also went into Newhall's request for a rehearing before the Minnesota Supreme Court. First, although Peterson cited the *New York Times* definition of malice as ruling, he nowhere took cognizance of the fact that "reckless disregard of truth" was part of that definition. For example, on page 31 of the decision, Peterson wrote, "Malice is not proved merely by the existence of ill will or intent to cause harm. What must be proved is an intent to cause harm *through falsehood*." Newhall had presented evidence in the Rose-Koch trial that Miss Koch had shown "reckless disregard of truth": (1) She repeatedly used the present tense in saying and writing that "Rose *is* a Communist collaborator," whereas she admitted on the witness stand that the only evidence she was presenting about the truth of Rose's being a Communist collaborator was his work on *An American Dilemma* over twenty years earlier. (2) Miss Koch persistently repeated her accusation against Rose, even in the courtroom, despite Rose's presentation of evidence to the contrary. (3) Miss Koch admitted on the witness stand that she had never sought an independent check on Rose's alleged collaboration with Communists; she had never read any of Rose's other writings, checked with his colleagues or the university, spoken to Rose himself. As in the Butts case, to be described below, the defendant had plenty of time to make such an independent check but had not done so, and the United States Supreme Court had ruled in favor of plaintiff Butts for that reason. Justice Peterson did not take into account the fact that this evidence had been presented to the jury and that the jury might well have decided that Miss Koch had malice in the *New York Times* sense because of it. (4) In the libelous document Exhibit B (see Appendix I), Miss Koch had linked Rose to Communism by the device of presenting side by side the title page of *An American Dilemma* and the front page of the testimony of Col. Tom Hutton, of SPX Research Associates (a right-wing extremist organization), before the Senate Subcommittee on Internal Security. She deleted from the latter page a statement that it was *not* an official document but merely a presentation before the subcommittee (actually it was never accepted by the subcommittee, although it had been tentatively accepted by its chairman, Senator Eastland). She then drew arrows from this document to Gunnar Myrdal's name on the title page of *An American Dilemma* to show that Col. Hutton had testified that Myrdal was a "notorious Swedish Communist" and "a conscious and effective instrument of the Communist global conquest." She then drew another arrow from Myrdal's name to Rose's name, and still another arrow from Rose's name to a statement she wrote: "Do Minnesotans want a teacher at its University and a lawmaker at its capitol who collaborate with a 'Communist' and with Communist fronters?" The whole exhibit is based on falsehood, innuendo, and illogical implications indicated by the arrows, and may be said to show "reckless disregard of the truth."

Rose's second objection to Justice Peterson's decision was his statement in that decision (pages 20–21) that "The exoneration of defendant Grinde . . . argues to us the real possibility that the jury . . . found malice by implication and not actual malice in the constitutional sense." There is not, in Rose's opinion, the slightest ground for this interpretation; the reason why the jury exonerated Grinde has been explained at length in previous chapters.

The Minnesota Supreme Court routinely denied Rose's appeal for a rehearing.

Rose believes that Peterson's decision will be appalling in its social and political consequences, for Minnesota and for the country rather than for himself. But he also believes that Peterson went straight to the issues of fact and law, and tried to follow the confusing changes in the United States Supreme Court's definition of malice and libel. He believes, too, that Peterson tried to be fair to Rose himself: Peterson went out of his way to say that "the jury gave Dr. Rose total vindication of his reputation," and to praise Rose for the candor of his testimony and the quality of his achievements. Rose believes that, considering the character and language of United States Supreme Court decisions on libel since 1964, lower courts will tend to seek reasons to rule against plaintiffs in libel suits, in order not to be overruled, while they express their unhappiness in having to do so.

In assessing the final outcome of the case, Rose believes that Newhall cannot be criticized, because the United States Supreme Court changed the law several times between the commencement of the lawsuit and the Minnesota Supreme Court decision, and there was nothing significant that Newhall could have done at any point that — in Rose's opinion — would have changed the outcome. Judge Barbeau cannot be blamed because his "erroneous" instructions to the jury — which killed the decision for Rose — did not become erroneous until a year and a half after he gave them out. If we can say that there is a fault, and that dangers now confront the country which were not present under the law before 1964, the blame must be laid at the door of the United States Supreme Court.

Let us now briefly consider the relevant United States Supreme Court cases decided *after* the trial of *Rose v. Koch* which shifted the legal ground from under the feet of Rose and Newhall both before and after the appeal hearing in the Minnesota Supreme Court. The *New York Times* concept of "public official" was broadened in *Rosenblatt v. Baer* [8] to include a former and "nonelected" public official, a man who had been a supervisor of a county recreation area and whose conduct while in that position was criticized by a newspaper in defamatory terms. *Time, Inc., v. Hill* [9] extended the *New York Times* principle to nongovernmental issues and nongovernmental persons. It required proof of malice even when the false and defamatory statements were about the purely personal lives of the plaintiffs. The application of the *New York Times* rule on malice to defamation of nonofficial "public figures" was squarely reached in the aforementioned cases of *Curtis Publishing Company v. Butts* and *Associated Press v. Walker*. The persons claiming to be libeled were Wallace Butts and Edwin W. Walker. Butts was the athletic director of the state-supported University of Georgia and a respected figure in his coaching profession. Even though he had over-all responsibility for the school's athletic program, he was actually solely and continuously employed by the Georgia Athletic Association, a private organization and not a state agency. Walker, as the Court stated, was a private citizen at the time of the libel against him, although he had previously pursued a long career in the

223

United States Army. Seven members of the United States Supreme Court agreed that both Butts and Walker were public figures for First Amendment purposes.

That malice can be defined in libel suits in *no other words* than those found in the *New York Times* decision is made clear in *Garrison v. Louisiana.*[10] In that decision, a state criminal libel statute which defined "actual malice" to include a false statement not made "with reasonable belief of its truth" was held constitutionally deficient. A "calculated falsehood," the Court held, means "false statements made with the high degree of awareness of their probable falsity";[11] and the "reckless-disregard-of-truth standard" was held to require substantially more than the absence of reasonable belief of truth. In the aforementioned cases of *Time, Inc., v. Hill* and *Rosenblatt v. Baer*, the United States Supreme Court was equally adamant in requiring the *New York Times* definition of malice, *nothing less and nothing more*. In *Rosenblatt v. Baer*, the trial court's defining malice to *include* "ill will, evil motive, [or] intention to injure" was held constitutionally insufficient.[12] Until these cases, decided after the Rose-Koch trial, the *New York Times* definition of malice did not preclude a trial judge from explaining to the jury what the *New York Times* definition of malice meant — at least Judge Peterson so held.

However, in the cases of *Curtis Publishing Company v. Butts* and *Associated Press v. Walker*, the United States Supreme Court set up a weaker definition of malice than that found in the *New York Times* decision which might apply to "public figures" although not to "public officials." In the Minnesota Supreme Court decision in the case of *Rose v. Koch*, Justice Peterson seemed to disagree with the United States Supreme Court on this matter: "Attempting to apply two different rules to this case, framing one set of instructions for so much of the libel as occurred prior to December 31, 1964, and another set for the libel occurring thereafter, would tax the ingenuity of the trial court and hopelessly confuse the jury. We hold, therefore, that only the *New York Times* rule is applicable to a libel of a person who is for part of the time a public official and for another part of the time a public figure without being a public official."[13] Whether or not one agrees with this, the mere fact that Justice Peterson finds it necessary to take issue with the United States Supreme Court on the definition of malice, plus the rapidly shifting definitions of malice emitted by the United States Supreme Court itself, points up the hopeless situation of a plaintiff who is a public official or public figure, even if he can clearly prove that

224

he has been the victim of defamatory falsehood, and that the defendant showed malice under *some* strong definition.

To understand the full hopelessness of Rose's legal case under present conditions, we must also look at the following facts. In reversing the trial jury's decision, Justice Peterson was generous in "remanding" the case for a new trial. That is, he offered Rose the chance to start the lawsuit all over again. But this is legally and practically meaningless for the following reasons: (1) Financial and moral support for a new trial could never be raised again. (2) Justice Peterson – following United States Supreme Court decisions – stated, "Malice is not proved merely by the existence of ill will or intent to cause harm. What must be proved is an intent to cause harm *through falsehood*" (italics are Peterson's). Rose believes that this is logically and psychologically virtually *unprovable*, so he could not possibly win a new trial, although he recognizes that the United States Supreme Court can and probably will modify this statement, as it is already beginning to do in the Butts case by saying that the Curtis Publishing Company had an obligation to check on its false statements before rushing into print. (3) It would be next to impossible to find a jury of intelligent and reasonable men who have never heard or read anything about the first Rose-Koch trial, and are considered unbiased thereby. (4) Miss Koch's lawyer could win the case on minor technical issues, such as Rose-Newhall's failure to regard *Facts for Action* as a "newspaper" and to ask it for a retraction before commencing a lawsuit. (5) Rose could not once again impose on the outstanding witnesses he was able to call for the first trial. (6) The United States Supreme Court could change the libel law and its definition of malice again in midstream, just as it has three times since the lawsuit began, and any such changes would apply retroactively because a constitutional issue is involved. (7) No matter how retiring from public life Rose might become, he can never cease to be a "public figure" according to Justice Peterson; the latter even left open the possibility that Rose was a "public official" merely by virtue of the fact that he is employed by the University of Minnesota. (8) The lower courts of the country are paying less and less attention to the confusing and illogical remnant of the law of libel left by the majority of the United States Supreme Court, and are in fact paying more attention to the spirit of the minority opinions stated by Justices Black and Douglas that there is no law of libel left for public officials and public figures. The lower courts are recognizing that it is virtually impossible for a plaintiff to *prove* that a

225

defendant's libelous statement was made "with knowledge that it was false" or "with reckless disregard of the truth," because knowledge and recklessness are only in the mind of the defendant. Only the defendant can provide statements in court that he acted with knowledge of falsity or with reckless disregard, and if he does there is no reason for a lawsuit, since such statements constitute a retraction and implicit apology, which are what the plaintiffs are seeking.

There might be more hope for Rose to try to appeal to the United States Supreme Court, since there is always the possibility that that Court might recognize it has gone too far in wiping out the law of libel. But such a course is also expensive and risky — risky because a mere denial of certiorari (that is, denial of willingness to review the case) or a negative decision would further undo the beneficial effects of the original jury decision and of Justice Peterson's generous statement that Rose is vindicated by all the facts in the case. If the United States Supreme Court has not yet seen the potential danger it has created for the nation, it is not likely to be brought to recognition of that danger by the now-academic case of *Rose v. Koch*. It will take a powerful and dramatic case in which an incumbent senator or governor is defeated by an unscrupulous challenger who invents falsehoods to undermine the personal reputation of that senator or governor, or an equally powerful and dramatic case in which a famous scientist is denied funds for research because of false charges. Rose believes that a future Supreme Court will eventually be forced to change some of its reasoning in the *New York Times*, the *Rosenblatt v. Baer*, and the Walker-Butts cases.

It remains to be seen what effect Justice Peterson's decision will have on Minnesota particularly. Will Gerda Koch and her associates be able to attract back their following lost by disillusionment due to the Rose-Koch lawsuit? Many people cannot make the distinction that Justice Peterson made so carefully between Rose's vindication on the facts of the case and Miss Koch's winning the lawsuit on the legal ground that Judge Barbeau inadvertently gave "wrong" instructions to the jury. They simply know who "won" the lawsuit. Will there be another attack on the University of Minnesota, or some other socially important public or private institution, without this time the possibility of one of its directly accused members having recourse to a libel suit, which would have the indirect effect of protecting the institution? Will the *Minneapolis Star* and other newspapers (including *Facts for Action*) now consider that they have unlimited license to publish any falsehoods their reporters or editorial writers might present, deliberately or inadvertently, about any public figure? Will the many decent and responsible citizens of Minnesota who were appalled by the events of 1963–64 reported in this book, and who saw the Rose-Koch lawsuit as a rational, dignified, and nonviolent way of reacting to those events, now be disillusioned with the law? The alternative to a libel suit — as was true before libel suits were possible under European law — is some sort of violent or emotional behavior destructive of social order. Only time can tell if these effects will take place.

APPENDIX I. *Documents written by Gerda Koch and introduced as plaintiff's exhibits*

FACTS FOR ACTION

To Preserve Our Christian Heritage

NOVEMBER-DECEMBER-1962   VOL. I, NO. 22

"There Was no room for HIM in the inn." Luke 2:7
There IS no room for HIM in the U.N.
The Supreme Court leaves no room for HIM in the schools! - WHY?
Because HE is not KING of our hearts!
"ARISE, SHINE, FOR THY LIGHT IS COME"! Isaiah 60:1 - a - CHRISTMAS GREETINGS!

We encourage reading this entire issue before Christmas and following up with no
less than three points in HOW YOU CAN HELP - UNLESS you want to give your country,
your church, your children to Khrushchev for a Christmas present!!

CONTENTS:

THE KENNEDY'S INVADE U.S. MISSISSIPPI BUT MISS TO INVADE CUBA ---WHY??

WHY the Mississippi Invasion and none in Cuba? Are we already controlled by a foreign and invisible government? (See bibliography, The Invisible Government, p.10)
Our first deadly mistake was to have recognized the gangster government of Moscow
in 1933. Then followed the Trojan Horse of the United Nations.

The late Senator McCarran stated publicly: "I made an error which I shall regret
all the days of my life when I voted for the United Nations Charter before I had
even read it." How many Congressmen would be honest enough to admit the same mistake
and honestly and courageously get behind Congressman Utt's (Calif.) Bill H.R. 9567
"to rescind and revoke membership of the U.S. in the United Nations and the specialized agencies..." and help deliver us from this evil? (See HOW YOU CAN HELP p. 10)

In her testimony before a Textbook Committee of the Texas House of Representatives,
a Mrs. T.C. Wentworth asked the question: "Are We Already Occupied?" She brought
out what most of us know, that the head of the U.N. Military Staff always was a
Communist and that Hiss and Molotov planned it so that he always will be a Communist. "Gentlemen, that is why General MacArthur was not permitted to win the war,"
Mrs. Wentworth continued. Aren't the Communists now giving orders through the
United Nations to our State Department as to Cuba?

And what informed person can doubt that the Communists and the one-Worlders are behind the Mississippi and the Walker case? Recently we received a map of the goal of
the "World Government Plan" showing the world divided into sections under the proposed World Government. The map was adopted by the "World Association of Parliamen-
tarians for World Government," in 1952 according to the National Economic Council of
New York, through whom the map became available. This map shows the southern part
of the U.S.A. occupied by Russian troops!!! - Is the Mississippi invasion the beginning of this?

* * * * * * * * * *

ORDER FACTS FOR ACTION AS A CHRISTMAS GIFT FOR YOUR FRIENDS TODAY!

NOTICE: If your envelope is not marked '62, your subscription is overdue. In the
future we shall mark the month, as 3-63 meaning your subscription is paid up to
that date and is due then. An O means we have been sending you the paper gratis.
We believe you NEED the paper, but we also need your subscription. - $1.00 a year.

FACTS AND VIEWS ON THE MISSISSIPPI SITUATION FROM VARIOUS SOURCES

'The most dangerous weapon being used against us today is the conspiracy of Silence which utterly controls the Press." A former communist gave this statement to this writer ten years ago. Thanks to numerous new and loyal publications - the actual stories are available! We shall include excerpts from various sources in an effort to present some pertinent facts and opinions about the Mississippi situation. See bibliography p. 10.

The tragedy of the University of Mississippi ...was precipitated by the un-willingness of Attorney General Robert F. Kennedy and President John F. Kennedy to await the completion of judicial processes which they have evoked, and which, if permitted to continue would have resulted in a final determi-nation of the Meredith case and...("OXFORD- A Warning to Americans" by the Mississippi State Junior Chamber of Commerce -(Jaycees of Mississippi)

WHAT LAW?

Like Eisenhower before him, (Little Rock) Kennedy said he was enforcing the law of the land -- What law? - -

Only Congress can constitutionally make laws for the nation, and Congress has never made a law concerning integration in schools or colleges. In fact, the Constitution of the United States prohibits the Congress from making any such law. The Tenth Amendment says:

> The powers not delegated to the United States by the Constitution, nor prohibited by it to the States, are reserved to the States re-spectively, or to the people."

The Constitution does not delegate any power to the federal government to interfere, in any way, with the operation of schools and colleges in the individual states. - Obviously, then, when the Supreme Court, or any other federal court, tells the state governments how to operate schools or col-leges, that court is usurping power not delegated by the Constitution...
...DAN SMOOT REPORT. Oct. 8, '62.

The little town called Oxford in Mississippi, U.S.A. lies crushed and tattered by American military order, with two dead, and seventy-eight wounded. Over 200 arrested including a heroic general and a governor under citation for "contempt of court" while nearly 16,000 American troops kept a little American town under military control, and set an example for what may yet happen in every village, town and hamlet in the U.S.A.

The President, who could wait on Castro in Cuba, and could wait on Mr. Khrushchev in the Berlin, Laos...crisis, could not now wait for any chan-nels of legality to be followed through, in regard to the sovereign right of a governor who was a member of his own political party...why did they not use the same force against Fidel Castro and the Red troops entrenched in Cuba in violation of the Monroe Doctrine? - AMERICA'S TRAGIC HOUR by Kenneth Goff.

There is nothing in the Constitution of the United States or in the laws passed by Congress which authorizes the use of Federal troops to compel any public educational institution to admit a certain student ... The 1954 decision cited the 14th amendment as the basis for its ruling, but the amendment was never legally adopted by the necessary number of states.

Governor Barnett...has been threatened with jail-without due process of law. ...But the main point of criticism made by Senator Stennis was that the State of Mississippi was being denied a hearing by the Supreme Court of the U.S.. (DUE PROCESS OF LAW IGNORED- ROOT OF MISSISSIPPI CONFLICT SEEN IN ILLEGAL ADOPTED 14th AMENDMENT by David Lawrence (OXFORD - See Bibliography, p.10)

James Meredith, a 29 year-old negro, had been enrolled in Jackson State College, a Mississippi school for negroes, after a nine-year service in the U.S. Air Force.

The National Association for Advancement of Colored People (NAACP) according to several sources, encouraged and financed Meredith to secure entry into the all-white University. Mississippi has a law prohibiting negroes to enter the all-white school. It seems strange that the Kennedy's should encourage such defiance of the state laws. If he thinks they are wrong, he can encourage and recommend changes in the law.

Kenneth Goff, himself had been ordered to work in the NAACP when he was a Communist W.E.B. DU BOIS, a negro, was the founder of this organization. When Du Bois was a student at Harvard (around 1890. He is now 94 years old), he worked in the Minneapolis suburbs during the summers. Later he had his agent, Martin Brown, at that time at 909 Marquette Ave., Mpls., spread his books and literature in the area to sow his seeds of race cleavage and hatred. (Example: his DARK WATERS published by Harcourt & Brace).

On April 30, 1959 over the 10:00 o'clock T.V. news (WCCO) it was announced that Du Bois had received the $35,000 Lenin Peace Award. Just last week the Communist Party announced that Du Bois had become a Communist. He had done their work for years and so do many others. Ten Directors of the NAACP (According to the Georgia Commission on Education Publication of 1957) had a total of 141 "Associations with Communist Fronts," averaging over 40 apiece. Eleanore Roosevelt, much lauded "First Lady", was far above "average."!

W.E.B. Du Bois was also a contributor to the DAILY WORKER, the national Communist publication as well as to the book AMERICAN DILEMMA written by Arnold Rose (Professor at U. of Minn. and newly elected legislator for Minn.) and Gunnar Myrdal. The latter was named "a notorious Communist" in the SPX RESEARCH STUDY. (See p. 7 & 8)

February 5, 1962: The U.S. District Judge Sidney C. Mize, who heard the Meredith case, ruled that Meredith failed to meet the requirements for admission to the University of Mississippi and further found as a matter of fact that he had not been denied admission because of his race...

OXFORD ...MISSISSIPPI STATE JUNIOR CHAMBER OF COMMERCE

The NAACP lost in this first court decision, but the U.S. Circuit Court of Appeals in New Orleans reversed the decision 2-1. Judge Dozier De Vane gave his dissenting opinion as follows:

"In my opinion, Judge Mize was correct in finding and holding that the appellant bore all the characteristics of becoming a troublemaker if permitted to enter the University of Mississippi, and his entry therein may be nothing short of a catastrophe."   Jaycees - Miss.

On September 20, 1962 James Meredith was tried in a Mississippi State Court on the misdemeanor charge of falsifying official records, when he registered to vote. Meredith was convicted and sentenced to serve one year in jail and to pay a fine of five-hundred dollars. State officials also obtained a criminal indictment against Meredith for perjury in connection with his alleged falsification of official records.

Attorney General Robert Kennedy got a court order prohibiting state officials arresting Meredith.   DAN SMOOT REPORT. Oct. 8, 1962

Note: We deeply regret that DAN SMOOT is no longer on T.V. We would like to see him come up to Minneapolis. IF you are interested, drop us a line and let us know what you could and would do to help - work, service, money-wise.

TRAGEDY PRECIPITATED BY FEDERAL VIOLATION OF THE CONSTITUTION

A number of sources point out the illegality of the use of the troops, referring especially to Article IV of the Constitution, which says:

The United States shall guarantee to every State in this Union a Republican Form of Government, and shall protect each of them against invasion; and on Application of the Legislature, or of the Executive (when the Legislature cannot be convened) against domestic violence.

There had not been any disturbances, property damage, injuries, or deaths while Governor Barnett was allowed to be responsible for law and order in Mississippi. Neither had there been a clash between law enforcement officers of Mississippi and armed officers of the Federal Government. Mississippi officers were unarmed until after they were fired upon with tear gas. Governor Barnett (whose total force of State Highway Safety Patrolmen available for duty as traffic officers throughout the entire State numbers less than 225 officers) maintained peace and order at the University of Mississippi so long as he was permitted. The tragedy was not precipitated by Mississippi or its public officials. (Underscoring added)

The use of Federal troops in Mississippi or in any other state is an exercise of power of a police state at its worst. I believe such action is illegal.

So, ...think, at all levels of the Federal Government, among all authorities, this is a time to stop, look, and listen, with calmness, and to have a prayerful consideration of the major points involved...not just for my State, but for all States and all people of our great United States. We should calmly weigh the consequences. How many red lights are we running by?
                    Senator Stennis, Miss.- in "OXFORD- A Warning for Americans".

Governor Barnett invoked a Declaration of State Sovereignty. It is impossible to give a complete picture in these few pages. The chapter "The CONDUCT OF THE FEDERAL MARSHALLS" is most shocking. Let us no longer shy away from realities and the truth and say "It makes me sick" or "I cannot sleep if I read about all that." We should get sick of ourselves who have allowed all this to come upon us and then straighten up and face the ugly problem and trust God and fight for CONSTITUTIONAL GOVERNMENT, the heritage given to a God-fearing people.

WHO ARE THE REAL LAWBREAKERS - GOVERNOR BARNETT & GENERAL WALKER OR THE KENNEDY'S?

Did Walker riot, as was reported? We quote:

The highlight of it all occurred on the second day when General Walker who held a distinguished combat record in the Aleutians, Italy, France and Korea was arrested by bayonet point while traveling through the streets of the city in his own automobile.   AMERICA'S TRAGIC HOUR - Kenneth Goff

General Walker did not go to Oxford to lead a mob against the armed forces of the U.S. He sought, by his presence there, to encourage massive, peaceful protest against federal tyranny. This Report's experienced investigator, on the scene, emphasizes that press accounts of Walker's action in Oxford are erroneous, if not designed distortions. Walker actually advised the students against violence; and he took no part in the violence which Kennedy's marshals touched off. Nonetheless, on Monday, October 1, 1962, General Walker was arrested on charges of seditious conspiracy and insurrection against the U.S. He was incarcerated in a federal mental hospital at Springfield ...   .DAN SMOOT REPORT

The LAW requires Communists to register as agents of a foreign government or pay a fine or be imprisoned. Who has or who will inform the American people that they have registered? How many have been fined? How many imprisoned? We want to know!

Where was the Attorney General's court order prohibiting Benjamin Davis, National Secretary of the Communist Party, from speaking at the University? We saw ONLY policemen PROTECTING - not even protesting, let alone ARRESTING, the Communist, Benjamin Davis! General Walker was made out to be the criminal, the fit subject for arrest, NOT THE COMMUNISTS! WHO IS running our government?? We better find out - Soon! See Bibliography p. 10. And where are the Attorney General's court orders regarding all the other Communists in the U.S.A.

Just recently another Communist, Daniel Rubin, Editor of the new COMMUNIST VIEWPOINT spoke at the University of Minnesota. Students from the Peace Union, the Young Socialistic League, including the National Secretary of the Young Socialist Alliance joined in a panel with the "distinguished guest."

Say a miracle should happen - and some of us still believe in miracles- say, Minnesotans might gather enough moral courage to demand of their governor to take a stand and order this traffic with Communist speakers in the University to cease, would the Attorney General send troops to protect the Communist and perhaps enforce his "freedom of speech" OR, would he support the governor and the people of Minnesota? We can be grateful to Mississippi for their integrity and resistance to totalitarianism and Minnesota ought to follow her example to make a test case with the Communist speakers at the University and every other state should take a stand for their constitutional rights and RESPONSIBILITIES, especially those whose rights and liberties have been prostituted by some federal agency, the Supreme Court, the Agricultural Department, or others.

> When we slavishly obey a court decision that we know to be in error, we destroy our government of liberty-protecting laws and substitute a government by arbitrary decree. - A court decision is not the law of the land; it is merely the law of the particular case ...
> "MUST GOD GET OUT OF OUR GOVERNMENT?"- MANION FORUM - Dean Manion

??? "SIBERIA U.S.A." ???

Contrary to controlled news released, bail bond of $100,000.00 was offered immediately to release Walker; however, U.S. Marshals refused to accept it...They insisted Walker was ill and should be taken immediately (via helicopter) to Springfield, Missouri, "WHEN WE DARED TO SAY-SIBERIA U.S.A."
by CONGRESS OF FREEDOM

General Walker has been denied even basic rights. Without the consent of his family or being judged in a sanity hearing before a jury and without any evidence that he was in need of psychiatric care, this great military hero was whisked away to an asylum, apparently at the order of Bob Kennedy and it was only because of tremendous public opinion that General Walker was released from the asylum October 7. Although a U.S. Judge originally affixed his bail bond at $100,000, the Justice Department announced they were holding the General for sixty to ninety days for psychiatric treatment, denying Walker's friends the right to put up his bail for his release. Thank God they didn't get by with it! If the President and his brother can commit a political opponent today, what will happen tomorrow to those who may disagree with them? This action smacks of a dictatorship. You might expect this in a Nazi Germany or a Communist Russia, but it is unbelievable that it is happening in the United States.

Dr. Billy James Hargis

When Ben Bella arrived in the United States enroute to see Fidel Castro, we gave him a twenty-one-gun salute and promised him more money and financial assistance...
Robert Morris in THE WANDERER.

235

While a heroic General was in a mental prison and is under constant fire by
certain segments of the press; the Algerian Red, Ben Bella was on a mission here
to participate in the fight to seat Red China in the United Nations, we enter-
tained at our White House; and now in Cuba has slurred the United States, and
was royally treated by Castro. At the same time permission was given to the
administration to give foreign aid to our Red enemies in Yugoslavia, Czecho-...

...a political prisoner...While his attorneys made ready to rush to Springfield
and while an all-night vigil on the part of patriots throughout the nation,
arousing many ministers out of their sleep, to gather together groups to pray
for God's intervention that Walker might not be given the "Brain-washing" treatment during the night...Thank God for patriots who stood in the gap when needed!
                                        AMERICA'S TRAGIC HOUR by Kenneth Goff.

Mr. Goff goes on to describe "the tremendous power that was being exerted to destroy
this great American hero." Mr. Goff, once a communist himself, took the course in
Psychopolitics. He has given us a "Synthesis of the Russian textbook on Psychopolitics" in his booklet BRAINWASHING. (See Bibliography, p.10)

                                IMPEACHMENT?

It is because of his testimony before the SASA (Senate Armed Services Committee - Special Preparedness Subcommittee) that he is a special target of the
Administration. On April 4, 1962, General Walker said:

> My experience and observation indicate that control has been taken
> from the hands of those legally responsible for it and placed in
> hands not fully identifiable, but which operate through the media
> of mass communication, the U.S. Department of State, and the infor-
> mation Offices of the Services. In soldier language, The "PIO'S"
> run the Army. What the average soldier does not realize is the extent
> to which outside media run the PIO'S, and unidentified forces run
> the media.

WHO CAN PROVE THAT WHAT HE SAID ISN'T TRUE!
        CONGRESS OF FREEDOM - Publisher of The Secret Government of the U.S.
                                        See Bibliography, p.10.

Dan Smoot justly states: "Kennedy violated the Constitution. It is possible that he
committed a felony under the laws of the United States." Many agree that the only
solution is to get a Congress at Washington that will honor the constitution and
have the courage to uphold it. We close in quoting Dan Smoot, because he expresses
so clearly what we so deeply feel.:

> Such a Congress could bring a bill of impeachment against John F. Kennedy,
> and also could impeach Robert F. Kennedy so that he could be removed from
> office and indicted for the crimes now being charged against General Walker:
> seditious conspiracy and inciting insurrection in the State of Mississippi.

There is enough on the records to impeach Kennedy without the Mississippi invasion -
as treason in Cuba - UNLESS deserting our boys and throwing them, as it were, into
the lions den, is not treason.

FACTS FOR ACTION is published (5 times a year) by CHRISTIAN RESEARCH for the purpose
of alerting citizens to needed action to preserve our Christian Heritage. Editor:
Gerda Koch. Subscription $1.00.
Make checks payable to: CHRISTIAN RESEARCH, 2624-1st Ave. S., Minneapolis 8, Minn.

BACKGROUND OF ELECTED ASSEMBLYMAN ARNOLD ROSE – UNIVERSITY OF MINNESOTA PROFESSOR

SPECIAL RELEASE- CHRISTIAN RESEARCH - 2624-1st Ave. S., Minneapolis 8,Minn. Oct.28, '62
RE: ARNOLD ROSE, Candidate for the State Legislature,41st District. Revised Dec.4, '62

It is highly important for every voter to know for whom he is voting, especially
since the Communists are working to conquer enemy countries through legislation. -
In the book - AND NOT A SHOT WAS FIRED, the author, Jan Kozal, a Communist, puts
forth the plan of how to conquer any country through the legislative process!

We feel responsible to release the following information on Dr. Arnold Rose, Professor at the University of Minnesota and candidate for the State Legislator:
                                    ,Democratic Senator from Mississippi,
  1. Arnold Rose assisted the socialist Gunnar Myrdal with   the book THE AMERI-
     CAN DILEMMA. James O. Eastland, in his MODERN SCIENTIFIC AUTHORITIES IN THE
     SEGREGATION CASE (May 26, 1955) says of Rose's and Myrdal's AMERICAN DILEMMA:

         The American Dilemma was written in largest part by American Communist
         front members, such as E. Franklin Frazier, who contributed to 28
         portions of the book, and W.E.B. DuBois, (Now publicly announced as a
         Communist). See FACTS FOR ACTION NO. 25, p.2) who contributed to 82
         portions of the book. Altogether, the Communist front members identi-
         fied with Myrdal's AMERICAN DILEMMA contributed 272 different articles
         and portions of the book officially adopted by the Communist Party and
         by the Supreme Court as its authority for its racial integration deci-
         sion May 17, 1954. (Ed. See the Mississippi story, p. 2ff)

Sen. Eastland mentions 17 other Communist fronters and left-wingers as co-authors of
the book. He did not mention Dr. Rose, but Dr. Rose may be one of those who keep
their names out of Communist fronts but be very useful to them at the same time.

  2. Gunnar Myrdal, Co-author with Dr. Rose, was known as a "Swedish Socialist."
     In 1958 when he spoke at the University of Minnesota, Myrdal was asked
     if he knew that his associate and helper Ralph Bunche in all probability,
     had been a Communist some time in his life according to the testimony of
     Manning Johnson. (The question was based on the article "Who and What is
     Ralph Bunche?" by Lord Harold Varney in the AMERICAN MERCURY 5-'56). Dr.
     Myrdal was highly provoked at the question and said, "Why do you ask me
     that question?" Dr. Arnold Rose came to his rescue and the question remained
     unanswered. The questioner did not know at that time that Dr. Rose was the
     co-author of the book AMERICAN DILEMMA and therefore also associated with
     Ralph Bunche, and W.E.B. Du Bois.

  3. The following is from the government document entitled "LIMITATION OF AP-
     PELATE JURISDICTION OF THE UNITED STATES SUPREME COURT - HEARING BEFORE
     THE SUBCOMMITTEE TO INVESTIGATE THE ADMINISTRATION OF THE INTERNAL SECURITY
     LAWS OF THE COMMITTEE ON THE JUDICIARY - UNITED STATES SENATE - 85th CONGRESS -
     Second Session - S 2646. Appendix IV to Part 2 - A STUDY ENTITLED - "THE
     SUPREME COURT AS AN INSTRUMENT OF GLOBAL CONQUEST" by SPX RESEARCH ASSOCIATES
     AND SUBMITTED TO THE INTERNAL SECURITY SUBCOMMITTEE IN CONNECTION WITH ITS
     HEARINGS ON S 2646. Feb. 19-21. 25-28 March 3,4, 1958. (Available from
     Christian Research)

Colonel Tom Hutton, SPX Research Associates, said "This is the government document
the Communists do not want the American people to read." We quote:

    (a) Destruction of internal security from within (almost an invariable prerequi-
    site) has marked pressure patterns of every government overthrown by the Communist
    Global conquest in the past 15 years -- Of ten cases bearing on internal security
    of the United States reviewed by the Court in the past 19 months, all 10 have been
    decided against enforcement of internal security laws and/or administrative regu-
    lations...(We omit parts b,c,d,e,f, & g. and continue with h, page 8.)

                                      237

(h) No pressure pattern of the Communist global conquest is more familiar than of well-placed Communist and pro-Communist advisors to free government policy-makers and agencies having paralytic potentials.

Revealing then, not surprising is the Court's acknowledgment of the influence of a notorious Swedish Communist, Gunnar Myrdal, as an "authority" in its May 17, 1954, segregation decision in Brown v. Board of Education (347 U.S. 348) which has triggered racial conflicts in the United States like those envisioned by Stalin in his "American Black Belt" program of Negro domination. (10) (We feel the footnote important enough to add here:)

> (10) The "Black Belt" plan which emanated from the Sixth World Congress contemplated confiscation of all white property, seizure of all government agencies in the Southern States, and merger of the States into a Negro Soviet. See The Communist, February 1931 pp. 153-167; W. Z. Foster, The Negro People in American History. H.Rept. 2244, pp 265-276.

Arnold Rose's official election flyer states that he "is known for his sociological researches throughout the world" and author of "scientific articles." The AMERICAN DILEMMA was perhaps his only book of national and "international" "fame," a book which was more of a cause than a cure for the problems: A report reached us that another printing will be made! More trouble can be expected.

By the way SPX means Soviet Principle Number X, which concerns itself with the application of "paralysis as a principle of Soviet Global warfare, within the American government structure..." We continue to quote the third paragraph under (h) above:

> As a conscious and effective instrument of the Communist global conquest, less subtle than Krishna Mennon of India (Ed.Note: Defense Minister of India. According to the WANDERER 11-8-'62 "under the heading "We Should Fire Our Krishna Menons by Robert Morris "he has oriented Indian policy toward the Soviet bloc..." Nehru finally fired him.) but more able than Ludwig Rajchman of Poland, the same Gunnar Myrdal is so important to Moscow that the Soviet made his appointment as executive secretary of the United Nations Economic Mission for Europe a condition of Kremlin participation. (11)
> (Ed. Note: Again we feel the note is so important that we add it right here:)

> (11) Gunnar Myrdal, expelled from office as Swedish Trade Minister for double-dealing with Moscow, is the author of An American Dilemma, to which the Supreme Court referred to in footnote 11 of its segregation decision, along with other modern authorities, "quite a few of whom were on Federal subversive lists." (Congressional Record p. A 407 A).

If Sweden dismissed Gunnar Myrdal when it discovered this man's "double-dealing with Moscow" should Minneapolis voters take a chance and elect this man's co-author and co-"expert", Arnold Rose, to a legislative office in a free American state?- We think that George Washington's order at Valley Forge is timely today: "Let Only Americans Stand Guard Tonight!" -- and now (Dec. 5 '62) Rose is elected. WILL OUR STATE legislature and MINNESOTA CITIZENS GRANT HIM A SEAT IN OUR HONORED MINNESOTA LEGISLATURE? - That depends upon what you will do!

Minnesotans, WRITE our Governor and your state representative, and protest the seating of Arnold Rose in the legislature-and get at least five others to do the same. If you do not know who your representative is, call your city hall, library or newspaper.

* * * * * * * *

Additional copies of this sheet 20¢; 5 for 25¢; 25 for $1.00.
Order from: CHRISTIAN RESEARCH, 2624 - 1st Ave. S., Minneapolis 8, Minnesota

We plead for contributions to help us send this sheet to all state officials and leaders.

I AM A LIBERAL

Dear Sleepy Joe,

I call my self a liberal. The name "socialist" or "communist" is not yet popular in the United States.

I do not like a republican form of government as provided for in the Constitution of the United States as it keeps the control and power in the hands of the people.

The Constitution provides that the duty of the executive branch of the government is to execute the laws and policies enacted by the legislative branch.

These things I do not like. Therefore, I am working to change the government into a democracy, which provides for a strong central government with the policy-making powers in the hands of the President. I have been so successful at this that now we hear the President asking us to elect a Congress to please <u>him</u>.

I am working to get control of every area of your life. I plan to do this through socialized medicine, urban renewal, "Fair Housing" laws, Metro government, the trade expansion act, federal aid to education, disarmament, etc.

I have persuaded you that the best way to fight communism is to support it through foreign aid.

My left-wing senators and representatives in Congress are diligently working for these issues.

If you object to these plans and issues, I will smear you with Communist-coined smear words. I am an expert at using smear words such as "fanatics," "alarmists," "extremists," "lunatic fringe," an d "the noisy minority."

I talk a great deal of "going forward" and "progressing," but I do not tell you that this means going forward into more socialism.

I talk much of peace, but I do not tell you that by "peace" I mean "conquering you without war" and that "the end of war is the control of a conquered people." (From the Communist Manual of Instructions of Psychopolitical Warfare.)

I am working for international interdependence (not independence) and a Communist-approved "one-world government" through the United Nations and related world organizations.

Don't wake up before it's too late!

Yours for going forward peacefully,

Lefty Louie

(Permission to use granted by "Wide-Awake" Joe.)

- -

Additional copies of this sheet - 15¢ postpaid. 8 copies 25¢, 40 for $1.00. Order from: CHRISTIAN RESEARCH, 2624 First Avenue South, Minneapolis 8, Minn. We are contemplating printing this in leaflet form. Remarks, which we will share with the author, will be appreciated.

HOW YOU CAN HELP:

A. SUBSCRIBE to FACTS FOR ACTION. $1.00. BE INFORMED. Why not get a good book for Christmas? See bibliography below. Order from: CHRISTIAN RESEARCH. Address below.
B. WRITE
It is important that we get a card or note off quickly when an issue arises. "I am greatly encouraged and heartened" wrote a senator. He had received "hundreds of letters" regarding his stand on the Alger Hiss matter and the Am. Broadcasting Co. Letters of protest are also needed. We are joining thousands over the land ---
C. Re Dr. Charles E. Smith, the Chief psychiatrist of the Federal Prison System, who is "beholden to the Attorney General". Without an examination, without having talked or even seen General Walker, upon his statement based on "various news reports" he committed, or rather imprisoned General Walker in a mental institution! (Read the Mississippi story, pages 1-6 in this issue). We are asked to write to:

Dr. F. J. L. Blasingame, Exec. Vice President
American Medical Association
535 North Dearborn Street
Chicago 10, Illinois

Dr. William L. Baughm, President
Association of Amer. Physicians
and Surgeons
1635 West 25th Street
Anderson, Indiana

Ask them that they censure Dr. Smith's action and use their influence to remove him from his job. Write them that Smith's action is giving the whole medical profession a black eye IF they allow this to go uncensored. Write them that you believe it was a violation of the Bill of Rights the way they treated General Walker and IF that is not stopped, none of us will be secure if we are critical of the administration
D. CHRISTIAN RESEARCH
Surely you can serve God and your nation in one or more of the following:
1. Join our family of monthly pledgers. - We need typists and can use more workers also. We are so grateful for an accountant who came to us this week!
2. We would like to clear away a balance of $55.00 due in November on our new mimeograph machine.
3. BUILDING: We are sorry that the building we had contemplated buying does not meet the legal requirements for our center. Pray for a suitable building.
E. COMMUNIST IMPORTS: Thanks to the TWIN CITY COMMITTEE TO WARN OF THE ARRIVAL OF COMMUNIST IMPORTS for their fine work they are doing to expose this Communist traffic that the State Department allows. For more information write (name above) Box 6811, Edina Branch, Mpls. 24. They, like we, need workers and contributions.

BIBLIOGRAPHY: (We regret that we had to cut this) Order from CHRISTIAN RESEARCH.
1. AMERICA LISTEN - Frank L. Kluckhohn.. $ .75
2. BRAINWASHING: A Synthesis of the Russian Textbook on Psychopolitics........ 1.00
3. HOPE OF THE WORLD, The: Dan Smoot 2.00
4. THE INVISIBLE GOVERNMENT: Dan Smoot 3.00
5. OXFORD-A WARNING FOR AMERICANS - Mississippi Junior Chamber of Commerce ... Free
6. SECRET GOVERNMENT, OF THE UNITED STATES, The, by Mary Davidson 1.00
7. DAN SMOOT REPORT - Weekly - $10.50 a year.
   Order from: Dan Smoot Report, P.O. Box 9538, Lakewood Station, Dallas 14, Texas
8. SPX RESEARCH REPORT ..... AMERICAN BAR ASSOCIATION REPORT ...... each ..... .25

FROM OUR READERS: ...enclosed check of $100.00, which I hope will be of some help to you...I agree with you that Fulbright is...a disgrace to the U.S." - A businessman.

"I see you are still hitting hard. More power to you. I have to admire you as a heroic woman talking out, whereas so many maintain a craven silence."-Retired Pastor

OPEN HEARING- COURT HOUSE- 11:00 A.M., Dec. 21. RE-DEVELOPMENT IN SEWARD DISTRICT. This is all part of the total Marxian disease in our nation. ATTEND and OPPOSE it!

Additional copies of this issue: 25¢; 5 for $1.00;
Order from: CHRISTIAN RESEARCH, 2624 - 1st Ave.S., Minneapolis 8, Minnesota

F A C T S   F O R   A C T I O N

To   Preserve   Our   Christian   Heritage

APRIL-MAY-1963   VOL. I,NO. 24

CONTENTS:

ARNOLD ROSE, MINNESOTA UNIVERSITY PROFESSOR AND STATE LEGISLATOR, COLLABORATES WITH COMMUNISTS AND COMMUNIST FRONTERS

In our present calamity we find our federal government, instead of protecting and
serving the American people, actually serving the Communist conspiracy within our
nation and in foreign countries. Let us admit first of all that we have been dis-
obedient to God. We have been sound asleep - too long.

Former F.B.I. agents say again and again that our Universities are the breeding places
for Communists. Communists are not made overnight, but the socialist professors at
our Universities see to it that the Communists are "made" in schools which once
honored God and produced "soldier(s) of Jesus Christ." A student from the University
told this writer "I believe we should have many more Communists in this country."
This is the meaning, if not the exact words, as witnesses can testify. That was the
young man's convictions. Let's not blame the youngster, but ourselves. We have allowed the Communists and Communist collaborators at our University and are allowing
them at present. Refugees who have come from Czechoslovakia say, they were amazed
when Czechoslovakia turned Communist, how many professors from the University turned
out to be Communists!! And today we have a "collaborator" at the University who is
at the same time a legislator at our state capitol! Will we learn before it is too
late?

CLEAN   OUT   THE   UNIVERSITY ! ! !

Dr. Isaac Koltoff (chemistry) with 35 Communist front associations was allowed to
teach at the University 35 years - one year for each front! Cyrus Barnum (chemistry)
is listed in 6000 EDUCATORS as having 12, Guy Stanton Ford (retired - history) with
eight fronts. Space forbids more. Legislators maintain that they cannot dictate to
the University. IF legislators have a responsibility to see that people are not deliberately poisoned or killed, have they less responsibility to stop subversion and
the destruction of our free institutions?? We say: THEY HAVE. Taxpayers should
write and telephone their Congressmen and the board of regents and EXPECT the University to CLEAN OUT Communists, fronters and collaborators.

Rose worked with Du Bois, Myrdal and Bunche. Du Bois has contributed to the DAILY
WORKER and has been a fronter for years and was recently publicly declared a Commu-
nist. For Myrdal see pages 2, 3 and 6 of this issue. For Bunche, whom Dr. Kenneth
Goff, ex-Communist, calls the "Butcher of Katanga" see pages 5 and 6.

Dr. Rose's first position was "Research Associate at Carnegie Corporation of New York,"
(1940-1943) the years he worked with Gunnar Myrdal on their AMERICAN DILEMMA, the book
which triggered the racial agitation in this nation. The same Carnegie Incorporation
gave financial assistance to the Council on Foreign Relations to organize committees
in many cities. (Smoot: INVISIBLE GOVERNMENT.p.8) St.Paul and Minnesota have such a
committee. John Cowles, Jr., Vice President of the STAR, Wilbur Elston, Robert W.
Smith and other past and present staff members from the STAR and TRIBUNE and ST. PAUL
DISPATCH AND PIONEER PRESS, Prof. Harold Deutsch, W. C. Rogers, Director of World

(Continued on page 7)

241

LIMITATION OF APPELLATE JURISDICTION OF THE
UNITED STATES SUPREME COURT

(The "Suppressed" Report)

HEARING
BEFORE THE Senate Subcommittee
ON
S. 2646

APPENDIX IV TO PART 2

A STUDY ENTITLED "THE SUPREME COURT AS AN IN-
STRUMENT OF GLOBAL CONQUEST" BY SPX RESEARCH
ASSOCIATES AND SUBMITTED TO THE INTERNAL SECU-
RITY SUBCOMMITTEE IN CONNEXION WITH ITS
HEARINGS ON S. 2646

"This is the government document the Communists
do not want the American people to read."
Col. Tom Hutton, SPX Research Associates

Below is from S/099.

(a) No pressure pattern of the Communist global conquest is more familiar
than that of well-placed Communist and pro-Communist advisors to free govern-
ment-policymakers and agencies having and wishing paralytic potential.
Reward as, then, but not surprising is the Court's acknowledgment of the influence of [notorious] Swedish Communist, Gunnar Myrdal, as an "authority" in its May 17, 1954, segregation decision in Brown v. Board of Education
(347 U.S. 348), which has triggered racial conflicts in the United States like
those envisioned by Stalin in his "American Black Belt" program of Negro
domination.

"As a conscious and effective instrument of the Communist global conquest less
mobile than Krishna Menon of India but more able than Ludwig Rajchman
of Poland, this same Gunnar Myrdal is so important to Moscow that the Soviet
made the appointment as Executive secretary to the United States Nations Economic Mission for Europe a condition of Kremlin participation."

* "The the courts, use the judges, use the constitution of the country * * * (Con-
gressional Record, 85/1, No. 102, p. 4664).
* Speech before the Ohio State Bar Association, May 17, 1957. President Eisenhower
had stated the same premise in other verbiage in his Governors Conference speech at
Seattle in 1953.
* See Byrnes, supra, and Jones, Congressional Record No. 103.25, 85/1, No. 1697 (Stencil).
* Documented examples are given in the equation found in the following section (XII)
China: Lattelin, Curry, Dexter White to Secretary Morgenthau in the financial debacle of
how coming under area VIII pressure from Moscow. See SPX Bradicer, Morgenthau
reports, and other publications of Senate Judiciary Subcommittee on Internal Security.
* Gunnar Myrdal, from behind the screen of an Internal Revenue Department
confiscation of all white property, seizure of all government agencies, Kingdom
States, and merger of the States into a Negro Soviet. See The Communist, February 1931,
pp. 265–276: The Negro People in American History, p. A1074.
† Gunnar Myrdal, expelled from office as Swedish Trade Minister for double-dealing with
Russia: It is the author of An American Dilemma, to which the Supreme Court referred in
footnote 11 of the segregation decision, since with other modern authorities, "quite a few
of whom were on Federal substantive lists" (Cong. Rec., p. A1074).

See "Myrdal's Contempt for the Constitution p.3b

AN

AMERICAN

DILEMMA
(HARPER & BROTHERS PUBLISHERS—NY-LONDON)
The Negro Problem
and Modern Democracy

by   Who is Gunnar Myrdal?

GUNNAR MYRDAL
WITH THE ASSISTANCE OF
RICHARD STERNER

ARNOLD ROSE

Volume II   Sociology Professor at
U of Minn.
Legislator—4?? District

Do Minnesotans want a teacher at its
University and a lawmaker at its capitol
who collaborate with a Communist
and with Communist fronters??

See Reading p.8. Also Facts For Action No. 22.

242

The Supreme Court's "Modern Scientific Authorities" in the Segregation Cases

Speech of
Hon. James O. Eastland
of Mississippi

In the
Senate of the United States

Thursday, May 26, 1955

Let us consider the so-called modern authorities on psychology cited by the Court as its authority to change and destroy the constitutional guaranties of the reserved natural right of the people of the States of the Union to freedom of choice and of the States to regulate their public schools.

MYRDAL'S AMERICAN DILEMMA

The Court cited and adopted generally, and without reservation, as its leading authority on modern psychology, Myrdal's book An American Dilemma, when it said—and I quote from Chief Justice Warren's opinion: "And see generally Myrdal, An American Dilemma, 1944."

Let us take a look and see what the Court adopted as its leading authority on modern psychology as the basis for its racial integration decision, when it adopted Myrdal's An American Dilemma.

In 1937 the Carnegie Foundation brought over Dr. Gunnar Myrdal, pro-

fessor in the University of Stockholm. He was described by the corporation as a social economist. He called himself a social engineer. He was a Socialist who had served the Communist cause. He admitted he had no knowledge of the Negro question in the United States. He was hired to make an investigation of race relations in this country; was given an ample staff and funds for that purpose, and was told to publish his findings. On this project Myrdal naturally found himself in the company of those recommended in the Carnegie Foundation, of Alger Hiss fame.

MYRDAL'S CONTEMPT FOR U. S. CONSTITUTION

Myrdal has an utter contempt for the principles upon which the United States was founded and for the political system to which the people adhere. It is incredible that the Supreme Court could have overlooked, if they read it at all, certain remarks that are contained in his book, on which the Court mainly bases its decision. Myrdal stated that the Constitution of the United States was "impractical and unsuited to modern conditions" and its adoption was "nearly a plot against the common people." This is purely Communist propaganda, which was cited by the Supreme Court, and on which the Chief Justice of the United States based a very far-reaching decision looking to the destruction of our form of government. I have often wondered what was the source of the pro-Communist influence in the Supreme Court.

Myrdal shows that he did not write this 1,400 page book himself. He hedged himself about with many self-imposed restrictions and "value premises," so that the book has no scientific validity, either from the standpoint of biology, sociology, or psychology.

THE COOPERATING SOCIAL EXPERTS

Myrdal shows that this book was the work of several so-called social experts furnished him by the Carnegie Founda-

tion, of Alger Hiss fame. It would be more in keeping with the facts, if, when Myrdal gave the names of most of these Carnegie Foundation "social experts," he had said that they were taken right out of lists of members of Communist and subversive organizations dedicated to the overthrow of our Constitution and the United States Government, because that is the actual fact.

If Chief Justice Warren had only taken the time and trouble to refresh his memory from his own State's officially printed reports and records of his own administration as governor of his own State, he would have found, and he can still find, the names of these Myrdal "social experts" in the fourth report on un-American activities. In California, 1948, and the sixth report published in 1951 on Communist front organizations by The Joint Fact-Finding Committee to the 1948 and 1951 regular California Legislature, when the Chief Justice was governor of the State of California.

Certainly Judge Warren cannot claim unfamiliarity with his own State official reports on such an important subject.

I shall give 16 names furnished by the Carnegie Foundation as "social experts" to Gunnar Myrdal, the Swedish "social engineer," for the writing of "An American Dilemma," adopted in full by the Court and their Communist connections according to the official 1948 California report, made at the time the Chief Justice was Governor of California.

The tenor of that book is to the effect that the American form of government has outlived its usefulness, and that the Constitution of the United States is a plot against the common people of this country. That was the message of the principal authority relied on by the Chief Justice of the United States in this far-reaching decision.

NAMES AND ORGANIZATIONS

The names and organizations with which the Myrdal advisers were affiliated are as follows:

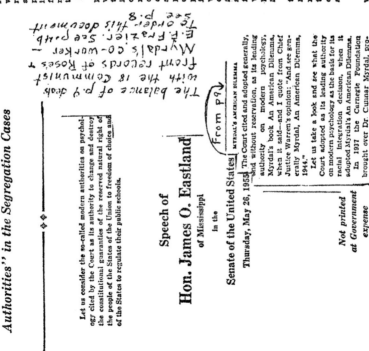

From p.9

The balance of p.9 deals with the 18 Communist front records of Rose's + Myrdal's co-worker E. Frazier. See pub. To order this document see p.8

3-a

Not printed at Government expense

946518—54674   United States Government Printing Office, Washington : 1955

Frank Boas was 1 of 17 liberal leaders who signed a letter addressed to American Civil Liberties Union, supporting the Soviet Union; chairman of the American Committee for Democracy and Intellectual Freedom, successor to the Communist front, the Scientists' Committee; affiliated with the American Committee for Protection of Foreign Born; member of the American Committee To Save Refugees; affiliated with American League for Peace and Democracy; member of the National Council of the American Peace Mobilization; affiliated with the Citizens Committee To Free Earl Browder; affiliated with Committee To Defend America by Keeping Out of the War; member of the Provisional Committee of the Conference on Constitutional Liberties in America; an advisory board of Films for Democracy; member of John Reed Clubs; member of National Emergency Conference for Democratic Rights; associated with National Federation for Constitution Liberties; affiliated with People's Peace; supported the Stalin-Hitler Line Committee To Defend America by Keeping Out of War; member of Russian War Relief, Inc.; signer of the statement defending the Communist Party; and listed as a well-known Communist and sponsor of Young People's Records.

All these Frank Boas organizations were shown to be Communist or Communist-front organizations in the official 1948 California report.

W. E. B. DuBois was a member of the National Committee of All-America Anti-Imperialist League; member of American Committee for Indonesian Independence; affiliated with American League for Peace and Democracy; sponsor of China Conference Arrangements Committee; affiliated with Citizens Consultant to Committee for a Democratic Eastern Policy; contributed to the Committee for Protection of Foreign Born; contributed to the Communist official organ, the Daily Worker; and a

signer of the Golden Book of American Friendship With the Soviet Union.

These organizations are listed as Communist or fronts.

Alain Locke was affiliated with American League for Peace and Democracy; sponsor of China Conference Arrangements Committee; sponsor of Conference on Constitutional Liberties in America; signer of Golden Book of American Friendship With the Soviet Union; among the instructors and guest lecturers of Jefferson School of Social Science; associated with National Federation for Constitutional Liberties; signer of Statement Defending the Communist Party; and member of Board of Sponsors of People's Songs, Inc.

All these are listed as Communist fronts and Communist organizations.

Ira de Reid was affiliated with American Committee for Protection of Foreign Born; affiliated with Citizens Committee To Free Earl Browder; member of national board of National Sharecroppers Funds; and affiliated with National Citizens' Political Action Committee; American Committee for Protection of Foreign Born; American League Against War and Fascism; Citizens Committee To Free Earl Browder; National Federation for Constitutional Liberties; and Southern Conference for Human Welfare.

All these organizations are listed as Communist or Communist fronts.

Doxey Wilkerson was consultant to the Committee for a Democratic Eastern Policy, which is listed as a Communist-front organization.

Ruth Benedict, according to the Daily Worker of March 31, 1947, page 11, was the coauthor of a pamphlet The Races of Mankind, which the War Department banned.

Charles S. Johnson was national vice chairman of National Share-Croppers Fund; affiliated with American Committee for Protection of Foreign Born;

National Federation for Constitutional Liberties; and Southern Conference for Human Welfare.

These organizations were listed as Communist fronts.

Clark Foreman was one of the initiators of a National Congress on Civil Rights, out of which emerged the Civil Rights Congress; speaker at conference and vice chairman of National Committee To Win the Peace; and vice chairman of Progressive Citizens of America.

These organizations are listed as Communist fronts.

Arthur Raper was a member of national board of National Sharecroppers Fund; affiliated with Council of Young Southerners; League of Young Southerners; and Southern Conference for Human Welfare.

These organizations were listed as Communist fronts.

Lewis Webster Jones was national sponsor of the National Council of American-Soviet Friendship, successor to the discredited Communist front, the Friends of the Soviet Union.

Ross Nelson was listed as Communist or Communist fellow-traveler, and textbook writer for use in public schools.

Sterling Brown was affiliated with League of American Writers, which is a Communist-front organization.

Eveline Burns was listed as Communist, textbook writer, and member of Citizens' Committee for Better Education, a Communist front.

Thomas Jones was advocate of United Negro and Allied Veterans of America, cited as a Communist-front organization.

T. Arnold Hill was cooperator-sponsor of Social Work Today which is a Communist periodical.

One of the so-called social scientists who also contributed to the writing Myrdal's An American Dilemma, adopted by the Supreme Court as its authority on modern psychology, was none other than E. Franklin Frazier,

whose 18 Communist organizations connections I have already given.

An American Dilemma was written in largest part by American Communist front members, such as E. Franklin Frazier, who contributed to 18 portions of the book, and W. E. B. DuBois who contributed to 32 different portions of the book. Altogether the Communist front members identified with Myrdal's An American Dilemma contributed to different articles and portions of the book officially adopted by the Communist Party and by the Supreme Court as its authority for its racial integration decision of May 17, 1954.

That is the true picture presented by an analysis from the records of the decision of the United States Supreme Court in the school segregation cases.

How can the Court expect the American people to accept its decision to change the accepted meaning of the fundamental principles of our Constitution when its decision is contrary to every other decision of the United States Supreme Court on the same question, and when its decision is now based on its adoption of memoirs of Communist organizations and Communist writings as its authority to change fundamental principles of the Constitution?

This same Gunnar Myrdal has recently appeared in the news as directing the staff of the United Nations Economic Commission for Europe in the preparation of a report regarding the foreign operation of the American Oil Industry. Myrdal's Commission feels that American oil companies "overcharged" their European customers for Middle Eastern oil, and hinted that some sort of international price control is the indicated remedy.

SATURDAY EVENING POST COMMENT ON MYRDAL

The Saturday Evening Post comments editorially that Myrdal is a Swedish Socialist. I quote:

The author of a report on the race problem in the United States, in the course o

See p.8

Cont'd on p.7

Congressional Record

None Is So Blind As He Who Will Not See

SPEECH

OF

HON. JAMES B. UTT

OF CALIFORNIA

IN THE HOUSE OF REPRESENTATIVES

Monday, January 15, 1962

pro-mp-5 WHO MANAGES THE U.N.?

Now, Mr. Speaker, let us look at the present management of the United Nations. Russia had been demanding a troika to supplant the U.N. Secretariat after the death of Hammarskjold. The failure of Russia to secure this troika was hailed as a great victory for the West, but was it? U Thant of Burma, a self-styled Marxist, was chosen and he agreed to invite a limited number of U.N. under secretaries "to act as my principal advisers on important questions." So far as he has indicated two: George P. Arkadov, a Communist from the Soviet Union, and Ralph Bunche of the United States. This was a Communist victory in that Russia now has its troika; one an avowed Marxist, the second a dedicated Communist, and the third with a pro-Communist bias. A résumé of Dr. Bunche's record, prepared by Archibald B. Roosevelt, son of Theodore Roosevelt, includes this paragraph:

Dr. Bunche was part of the editorial apparatus of an openly Communist magazine, Science and Society, for over 4 years. He contributed to this publication and added his name and prestige as a professor of Howard University even after the Communists in their publication, The Communist, openly stated that Science and Society maga-

zine had as its function "to help Marxward moving students and intellectuals to come closer to Marxism-Leninism; to bring Communist thought into academic circles."

In a Senate probe by the Internal Security Subcommittee it was brought out that Dr. Bunche had repeatedly pressured persons in charge of U.N. employment to hire a notorious Communist agent, in spite of the fact that here was a derogatory report against the individual by a security agency of the Government.

Dr. Bunche was a high official in the Institute of Pacific Relations, an organization investigated thoroughly by the Senate Internal Security Subcommittee and described as follows:

The effective leadership of the IPR used IPR prestige to promote the interests of the Soviet Union in the United States.

The object of this IPR was, in 1944, to force the Chinese Government to adopt reform measures and make concessions to the Chinese Communists which would pave the way for seizure by Soviet forces.

The IPR leadership sought to bring into public discussion at a vital meeting internal conditions in China so that Chiang Kai-shek would be criticized for the internal situation in China.

Dr. Bunche is on record as supporting the position of the IPR leadership in this matter.

It is my considered opinion that Dr. Bunche must be considered a security risk for our country in any position which he may hold.

This "troika" arrangement, engineered by the Communists, is frightening and devastating when you consider the United States of America has no foreign policy of its own except the United Nations.

"Lincoln once said:

If destruction be our lot, we ourselves must be the author and finisher.

This is it, Mr. Speaker. If this Republic is to perish, we ourselves, within our own household, will be the architect and finisher of our fate.

WHO IS RALPH BUNCHE?

The following is from H.L. Varney's — WHO... IS RALPH BUNCHE? —The AMERICAN MERCURY. MAY 1956.

WHETHER he had become a card carrying Communist member before this time is a fact known only to Bunche and to the Communist Party. The fact remains that Manning Johnson, who was present at the conference as a representative of the Negro Communist, has declared in an affidavit that he was introduced to him at Howard as "Comrade Bunche." Later, Johnson states that he encountered the professor at a top caucus meeting of conference delegates attended only by party members.

Subsequently, when James W. Ford, top Negro Communist leader, gave his report on the Howard University conference to the Negro Commission of the party, he stated that he had had some difference with "Comrade Bunche" based on the new Communist policy of using non-Communist leaders in "united front" organizations. At a later Commission meeting, Ford reported that the Bunche disagreement, had been straightened out.

Significantly, Bunche's name appears in the official account of the launching of the National Negro Congress written by William Z. Foster, chairman of the Communist Party (History of the Communist Party of the U.S., page 308). Foster's account is worth quoting:

"The rising spirit of struggle among the Negro people during these years reflected itself in the National Negro Congress, organized in Chicago, February 14–16, 1936. The NNC grew out of a conference held previously under the auspices of Howard University and the Joint Committee on National Recovery. Among those present were such notables as Ralph Bunche, W. E. B. DuBois, A. Philip Randolph, R. A. Carter, John P. Davis, James W. Ford, and others."

It was not long before Bunche publicly identified himself with another all-out Communist venture. This was the party magazine, Science and Society, A Marxian Quarterly.

For Rose's connection with Bunche, Myrdal and Du Bois see FACTS FOR ACTION, NO. 22 & pp.1—4 of this issue (24) 25¢ each. Order from CHRISTIAN RESEARCH, Inc. 2621 1st Ave. S. Mpls.8, Mi

245

in the Thirties, that richer fields were beckoning to him among the New Deal "Liberals." The turning point in his life was probably his meeting with Gunnar Myrdal, the Swedish Socialist.

Myrdal is an obscure figure to most, but few men have played a more important behind-scenes role in the ideological history of our war and post-war period. It is not an exaggeration to say that Myrdal blueprinted the whole race-equality policy which has been adopted *in toto* by the United Nations and by two administrations of the United States. He was quoted by Chief Justice Warren as the authority on American Negro problems in his historic desegregation decision. At present he is executive secretary of the UN Economic Commission for Europe.

Myrdal was commissioned in 1938 by the Carnegie Foundation to make a $300,000 survey of the American Negro problem. His survey lasted four years. It culminated in the book, *The American Dilemma*, which has become something of a bible on the subject among American "Liberals."

BUNCHE spent two years with Myrdal between 1938 and 1940, preparing a section of the final report. In this section, he found it advisable to differ with the Communist Party, specifically criticizing the 1939 Ribbentrop-Molotov Pact. Since then he has never been publicly identified with the Communists.

Myrdal, who, as a challenger of the Hitler race theories was the darling of the interventionists of the pre-Pearl Harbor period, undoubtedly showed the ambitious Bunche the richness of the rewards which the internationalist political and social coterie, and the foundations can bestow upon their favorites. It is a fact that ever since this period, Bunche has been a complacent follower of the approved internationalist line. He has long since outpaced his teacher in the skill with which he has cultivated the internationalist garden.

The war years saw Bunche widening out his activities onto the world field. He was appointed as a "social science analyst" on Africa in the war-time OSS. He rose rapidly to become chief of the Africa Section of the OSS in 1943. He transferred to the Department of State in 1944.

Here he came under the influence of Alger Hiss. Hiss was then riding high in the Department. It was the period later described by ex-Assistant Secretary of State Adolf A. Berle as the one of struggle in the Department between the pro-Russian and the non-appeasement factions. He described it:

"In the fall of 1944, there was a difference of opinion in the State Department. I felt that the Russians were not going to be sympathetic and cooperative ... The opposite group in the State Department were largely the men — Mr. Acheson's group of course, with Mr. Hiss as his principal assistant in the matter. At that time Mr. Hiss did take what we would call today the pro-Russian point of view."

Now the significant thing about Bunche is that, entering the State Department at this time, he became a Hiss man. The association paid off in gratifying rewards. He was Hiss's assistant secretary at the Dumbarton Oaks Conference in Washington in August-October, 1944, which set up the framework of the United Nations. He accompanied Hiss to San Francisco in March, 1955, as an adviser to the American delegation at the UN organizing conference. (His was secretary of the delegation, and did the hiring and firing.)

Later, when the UN was set up, Bunche, after several preliminary chores, was appointed to the important post of director of the Division of Trusteeship in 1946. His appointment record shows the name of Hiss as one of his sponsors. United States in which a Ralph Bunche can soar to Hall of Fame heights is not a United States in which a Booker T. Washington or a George W. Carver could win recognition, with their solider claims to greatness. It is not a United States which is attuned to political courage.

It is a United States in which the "upstage honor awards go to the man who is most calculatingly astute in his ideological affiliations and in his choice of sponsor. Such astuteness Ralph Bunche possesses in exceptional measure. He will continue to shine in his stellar lustre as long as the United Nations, and its gonfaloniers, write American foreign policy.

Archibald Roosevelt, only living son of Teddy Roosevelt, documents the Communist and pro-Communist connections of Ralph Bunche in a 48-page letter protesting Bunche's receiving the Theodore Roosevelt medal for distinguished service. The May AMERICAN OPINION in an article "RALPH BUNCHE" states "While Hammerskjold was directing the overthrow of Katanga from the North, Myrdal was organizing support for subversive movements in Rhodesia to the South; yet in the end it was Bunche who had to follow through." (See "Gunnar Myrdal-Expert for the Communists" FACTS FOR ACTION No. 24, p.2) Bunche was a high official in the subversive Institute of Pacific Relations. The Mpls. Tribune (1-20-63) tells of an "Elite Group to Take Part in N. Y. Parley." Myrdal met with this "elite group", most if not all of whom were members of the Council on Foreign Relations. (CFR) Is the C.F.R. a new form of the sinister old subversive I.P.R.? Ralph Bunche, too, is a member of the C.F.R., The Invisible Government of the U.S.A.

THE INVISIBLE GOVERNMENT - DAN SMOOT - $3.00. The SECRET GOVERNMENT OF THE U.S. -$1.00 Order from: CHRISTIAN RESEARCH, 2624 1st Ave. S. Mpls. 8, Minn. Additional copies of this sheet 15¢ postpaid. 8 for 25¢. 40 for $1.00

The clipping at top (Congressional Record excerpt) reads:

this "monumental work." Myrdal described the adoption of the United States Constitution as "mainly a plot against the common people." It asks, is Myrdal the best authority a U. N. agency could rely on for a completed study of the oil industry?

It is a tragic commentary on the intelligence and judgment of the members of the United States Supreme Court that they would override the Constitution on the alleged evidence and opinion of such a "psychological" authority. It is the final indication as to the decree and extent that the Court has been "brainwashed" by pressure groups and is willing to sacrifice the people, the Constitution, and established law to communistic and socialistic dogma and principles.

Mr. President, it is evident that the decision of the Supreme Court in the school segregation cases was based upon the writings and teachings of pro-Communist agitators and other enemies of the American form of government. The Chief Justice of the United States actually cites as authority for his decision a book, the thesis of which is that the Constitution of the United States is "impractical and unsuited to modern conditions" and its adoption was "nearly a plot against the common people." Our country has come to a sorry state of affairs when the Chief Justice of the Supreme Court, speaking for all the members of the Court, should cite, as his authority for a decision, a book compiled by an alien who advocates the destruction of the American form of government—the very form of government which this Chief Justice and this Court are sworn to uphold.

SOUTH WILL NOT OBEY DECISION

Mr. President, the question is asked, Will the South obey this decision of the Supreme Court? Who is obligated morally or legally to obey a decision whose authorities rest not upon the law but upon the writings and teachings of pro-Communist agitators and people who have a long record of affiliations with anti-American causes, and with agitators who are part and parcel of the Communist conspiracy to destroy our country? From the beginning of the Republic, the Judiciary, the Congress, the executive branch of the Government, and all the States have recognized that a State has the power under the Constitution to segregate children in its schools because of race. The Supreme Court of the United States has consistently so held throughout the years. Any person is credulous indeed to believe that southern people will permit all this to be swept aside by a Court who relies for its authority not upon the law but upon pro-Communist agitators and enemies of our system of government.

Mr. President, for the welfare of America, the resolution to investigate this setup should be adopted.

Mr. JOHNSTON of South Carolina. Mr. President, I wish to join the Senator from Mississippi in sponsoring the resolution.

Mr. EASTLAND. Mr. President, I ask unanimous consent that the name of the distinguished Senator from South Carolina [Mr. JOHNSTON] be added as a co-sponsor of the resolution.

Mr. JOHNSTON of South Carolina. I make the request in view of the fact that the Subcommittee on Internal Security has been making a study of the subject.

The PRESIDING OFFICER. Without objection, it is so ordered.

345516—5467A

ARNOLD ROSE – COLLABORATOR WITH COMMUNISTS AND COMMUNIST FRONTERS

(Continued from p. 1)

Affairs Center, O. Meredith Wilson, President, and others from the University of Minnesota. 27 Out of 78 members are from Minnesota's colleges and the Metropolitan newspapers – almost 35%.

The Carnegie Foundation, besides financing the Myrdal-Rose AMERICAN DILEMMA, supported the subversive INSTITUTE OF PACIFIC RELATIONS, responsible for China's fall AND the Social Science Research Center, of which the well-known socialist Harold Laski said "AT BOTTOM, AND STRIPPED OF ITS CAREFULLY NEUTRAL PHRASES, THE REPORT IS AN EDUCATIONAL PROGRAM FOR A SOCIALIST AMERICA." (See this issue p. 8– FOUNDATIONS). This same foundation that gave Rose his first position is perhaps the source of most of the subversion in the social sciences in education in this country today!

Rose wrote other books on the race issue, one of them AMERICA DIVIDED, which deals with minority groups. In reading portions of his AMERICAN DILEMMA, the writer is reminded of Max Lerner's AMERICAN CIVILIZATION. While the writers purport to describe a culture or civilization, they actually bore and whittle away from within at the very foundations of that civilization. In other words, they divide and destroy.

Arnold Rose serves on the following committees: Education, General Legislation, Metropolitan and Urban Affairs, Administrative rules and Procedures, etc. He is a member of the Unitarian Society, which sponsored the notorious Communist, Corliss Lamont, and other extreme radical and left-wing speakers.

Do you want a man who worked with Communists, pros and with a man of whom the Honorable James B. Utt says "he must be a security risk for our country in any position he may hold."? (See p. 6) Isn't Arnold Rose, too, a security risk for Minnesota and for the nation?

THANK YOU all who attended and helped make our first dinner meeting a success! For those who could not be with us: Dr. Frederick Fowler, member of the board of CHRISTIAN RESEARCH spoke on "Saving a Nation." He spoke on the concept of sin and the need of man's redemption. He brought out the need for Integrity, for Hope and for Security, in our individual lives and for our government. "I H S spells - CHRIST."

About 100 attended. We are grateful to those churches who announced our meeting. The MINNEAPOLIS STAR gave a good resume' of Dr. Fowler's talk. However, when Dr. Fowler said, "We give billions to save a Godless apparatus that had already declared its main purpose of destroying (us)" he referred to Soviet Russia and not to the Social Security system, as the paper indicated. Dr. Fowler did say, quoting Prof. Lewis Haney, that social security was "perhaps the greatest hoax ever put over on the American people (and a) racket carried on by their government..."

"This was a real eye-opener," and "Will you have another meeting like this soon?" were responses from various groups. Our answer: "We can IF we get more help." We were happy to be able to pay all the expenses and to gain about a dozen new subscribers. The work of Christian Research started five years ago this fall. We could plan a meeting with the purpose of raising the $500.00 we now have for a down payment on a much needed building to $1500 or $2000. Pray, but also give. Let us move forward in raising a standard against the enemy!!

NOTICE! Three people enclosed money for subscriptions for FACTS FOR ACTION, but no name. Please, contact your friends and help us get these names and addresses!
PRAYER REQUEST: Rev. Harold McClure, chairman of CHRISTIAN RESEARCH board, is entering the DEACONESS HOSPITAL Monday, May 20 for a serious operation. Pray for Healing.

HOW YOU CAN HELP:
1. "A CALL TO ACTION!" E.D. Kiselev, Ass't. Sec. General for Security Affairs, really "commander in chief of U.N. Military forces, is dead." We join the AMERICAN COALITION...in "URGING YOU TO WRITE and get others to write, telephone, or telegraph at once members of Congress demanding that our Government insist on appointment of a U.S. Citizen to (that office.)" We ought to demand this appointee be cleared by our security committees! -Write city and suburban press.
2. VOTE: June 11. If you wish to keep your voice in the choice of many public officials and not let one man appoint them, Vote NO on the new charter! For help in voting for city aldermen call FE 6-9228.
3. SUBSCRIPTIONS: Is yours due? Please, check date above your name on envelope. Friends who contributed $10.00 or over will find only the year when we last heard from you. We would like to hear from all of you again. See address below.
4. STATE FAIR: Aug.24-Sept.2: NEEDED: 1.HELPERS. 2. $300.00 - Please call TA 2-4428.
5. READING:
   (1) S P X RESEARCH REPORT - 20¢ postpaid. 7 for $1.00.   (COMMON SENSE - $1.00)
   (2) MANNING JOHNSON, negro, former Communist, author of COLOR, COMMUNISM AND
   (3) JAMES O. EASTLAND: "The Supreme Court's 'Modern Scientific Authorities' in
                          (the Segregation Cases." 20¢ postpaid. 10 for $1.00.
   (4) THE INVISIBLE GOVERNMENT by Dan Smoot - $3.00
   (5) WHY KENNEDY SHOULD BE IMPEACHED - M. Fagan 50¢ Series of 5 - Timely -$2.00.
   (6) FOUNDATIONS by Rene' Wormser. $7.50 - A book our congressmen should have!

FROM OUR READERS: "I was happy to hear you on radio...I have been getting anti-communist literature from the west coast...but didn't know of any place here...I will tell my Christian friends about your paper..." (We are grateful for the increase of voices on radio. - Thanks to those who mentioned our address for literature. Our sales have (been increasing.
FACTS FOR ACTION is published five times a year by CHRISTIAN RESEARCH, Inc. for the purpose of alerting citizens to needed action to preserve our Christian Heritage. Editor: Gerda Koch. The work of CHRISTIAN RESEARCH, Inc. is supported by literature sales, contributions, pledges and subscriptions. ($1.00) Club Membership is $10.00. Make checks out to: CHRISTIAN RESEARCH, 2624 - 1st Ave. South, Minneapolis 8, Minn. Additional copies of this issue - 25¢ -- 5 - $1.00. Write for quantity prices.

STATEMENT · SPECIAL RELEASE · CHRISTIAN RESEARCH
2624 1st Ave. S., Minneapolis 8, Minn.

RE: ARNOLD ROSE

It is highly important for every voter to know whom he is voting for, especially since we KNOW that the Communists have been working to conquer enemy countries through legislation. They have succeeded far more in the U.S.A. than the average American realizes. — In the booklet "AND NOT A SHOT WAS FIRED," Jan Kozak, a Communist, puts forth the plan how to conquer any country through the legislative process!

We, therefore, feel it pertinent to release the following information on Dr. Arnold Rose, candidate for the State legislature of the 41st legislative district:

1. Dr. Arnold Rose is co-author with Gunnar Myrdal of the book THE AMERICAN DILEMMA. James O. Eastland in his "SUPREME COURT'S 'MODERN SCIENTIFIC AUTHORITIES' IN THE SEGRE- GATION CASES" (May 26, '55) says of Myrdal's AMERICAN DI- LEMMA:

   The AMERICAN DILEMMA was written in largest part by American Communist front members, such as E. Franklin Frazier, who contrib- uted to 28 portions of the book, and W. E. DuBois, who contributed to 82 different portions of the book. Altogether the Communist front members identified with Myrdal's AN AMERICAN DILEMMA con- tributed 272 different articles and portions of the book officially adopted by the Communist Party and by the Supreme Court as its authority for its racial integration decision May 17, 1954." He mentions 17 other communist fronters and left wingers as co-authors.

2. Gunnar Myrdal was known as a "Swedish Socialist." In 1958 when he spoke at the University of Minnesota, Myrdal was asked if he knew that his associate and helper Ralph Bunche, in all probability, had been a com- munist some time in his life, according to the testimony of Manning John- son. Question based on "Who and What is RALPH BUNCHE?" by Harold Lord Varney. AMERICAN MERCURY May 1956) Dr. Myrdal was highly provoked at the question and said "WHY do you ask me that ques- tion?" Dr. Rose came to his rescue and the question remained unanswered. The writer who put the question, did not know at that time that Dr. Rose was the co-author of the book, and therefore, was also associated with Ralph Bunche.

3. The following is from the "LIMITATION OF APPELLATE JURISDIC- TION OF THE UNITED STATES SUPREME COURT — HEARING BEFORE THE SUBCOMMITTEE TO INVESTIGATE THE ADMIN- ISTRATION OF THE INTERNAL SECURITY LAWS OF THE COM- MITTEE ON THE JUDICIARY UNITED STATES SENATE — 85th Congress — Second Session — S. 2646. Appendix IV to PART 2, A STUDY ENTITLED — "THE SUPREME COURT AS AN INSTRUMENT OF GLOBAL CONQUEST" BY SPX RESEARCH ASSOCIATES AND SUBMITTED TO THE INTERNAL SECURITY SUBCOMMITTEE IN CONNECTION WITH ITS HEARINGS ON S 2646. Feb. 19-21, 25-28 March 3, 4, 1958. Colonel Tom Hutton, SPX Research Associates said

"This is the government document the Communists do not want the American people to read." We quote from mp. 1078 and 1079.

(a) Destruction of internal security from within (almost an invariable prerequisite) has marked pressure patterns of every government overthrown by the Communist global conquest in the past 15 years. Of ten cases bearing on internal security of the United States reviewed by the Court in the past 19 months, all 10 have been decided against enforcement of internal security laws and/or administrative regulations . . .

(b) No pressure pattern of the Communist global conquest is more familiar than that of well-placed Communist and pro-Communist advisors to free government policymakers and agencies having paralytic potentials.

Revealing then, but not surprising is the Court's acknowledgement of the influence of a notorious Swedish Communist, Gunnar Myrdal, as an "authority" in its May 17, 1954, segregation decision in Brown v. Board of Education (347 U.S. 348) which has triggered racial conflicts in the United States like those encisioned by Stalin in his "American Black Belt" program of negro domination.

The flyer for Arnold Rose states that he "is known for his sociological researches throughout the world" and author of "scientific articles." The AMERICAN DILEMMA was perhaps his only book of national "fame." We continue to quote the SPX RESEARCH REPORT: "As a conscious and effective instrument of the Communist global conquest, less subtle than Krishna Mennon of India but more able than Ludwig Rajchman of Poland, the same Gunnar Myrdal is so important to Moscow that the Soviet made his appointment as executive secretary to the United Nations Economic Mission for Europe a condition of Kremlin participation." (11) We add the footnote here again:

Gunnar Myrdal, expelled from office as Swedish Trade Minister for double-dealing with Moscow, is the author of AN AMERICAN DILEMMA, to which the Supreme Court referred in footnote 11 of its segregation decision, along with other modern authorities, "quite a few of whom were on Federal subversive lists." (Cong. Rec. p. A 407 A)

If Sweden dismissed Gunnar Myrdal when he discovered his "double-dealing with Moscow" should Minneapolis voters take a chance and elect Gunnar Myrdal's co-author Dr. Arnold Rose to a legislative office in a free American state? — We think that George Washington's order at Valley Forge is timely today: "Let Only Americans Stand Guard Tonight!"

APPENDIX II. *Bills introduced into the Minnesota State Legislature in 1963 on which Rose was co-author and which were claimed by another legislator to indicate sympathy toward Communism*

A RESOLUTION MEMORIALIZING THE UNITED STATES SENATE TO RATIFY THE UNITED NATIONS GENOCIDE CONVENTION

WHEREAS, in many parts of the world today, despite the ugly examples of genocide we saw during World War II and prior to the war, there is still evidence that many racial, ethnic, religious, and national groups are being subjected to systematic terrors and pressures that aim at the destruction of these groups; and

WHEREAS, the United Nations' Genocide Convention which was completed in 1948, largely through United States efforts, was unanimously adopted by the General Assembly on December 9, 1948, the United States becoming a signatory to that Convention; and

WHEREAS, the Convention remains ineffective as to the United States until it has been ratified by the United States Senate; and

WHEREAS, this Convention was referred to the Senate Foreign Relations Committee and has remained in committee for over a decade; and

WHEREAS, the Convention embodies a basic principle upon which our nation was founded, namely, that an attack on human rights and individual freedoms is an attack on the body politic itself that must be thwarted by every legitimate means; and

WHEREAS, the Genocide Convention has become the most widely ratified United Nations agreement with the exception of the United Nations Charter itself, 64 nations having already adopted the Convention; and

WHEREAS, the failure of our own nation to become a party to the Convention has exposed us to allegations of insincerity in the struggle for human dignity, has embarrassed our friends and allies abroad who look to us for leadership, and has seriously weakened the Convention's effectiveness as an international instrument; and

WHEREAS, genocide can be abolished only where there is effective international cooperation; and

WHEREAS, the people of Minnesota, through their own support of legislation to eliminate discrimination, have set in our country an example of citizen participation in the fight for human rights; and

WHEREAS, the Minnesota State Legislature, representing the people of the State of Minnesota, desire to be in the forefront of a nationwide effort to obtain Senate ratification of the Genocide Convention; now, therefore,

BE IT RESOLVED, that the Minnesota State Legislature express in the strongest terms its sentiment that the Senate Foreign Relations Committee should act favorably and speedily on the report of its Special Subcommittee recommending ratification of the Genocide Convention; and

BE IT FURTHER RESOLVED, that the Secretary of State transmit copies of this resolution to the President of the United States, all members of the Senate Foreign Relations Committee, and the United States Senators from the State of Minnesota.

A BILL FOR AN ACT RELATING TO BIRTH CERTIFICATES OF ILLEGITIMATE CHILDREN

BE IT ENACTED BY THE LEGISLATURE OF THE STATE OF MINNESOTA:

Section 1. Where the birth certificate of a person indicates that his father is unknown, the person, if he is 18 years of age or older, or his mother or legal guardian if he is under 18 years of age, may petition the district court of the county of his residence for an order requiring the state registrar to prepare a supplementary certificate naming a fictitious person as father. The surname of the fictitious father shall be the same as the surname appearing on the birth certificate. The first name may be any suitable name requested by the petitioner. The state of Minnesota shall be recorded as the state of birth of this fictitious person, and his age be recorded the same as that of the mother.

Sec. 2. If it shall appear to the court to be proper, it shall grant the petition and issue its order accordingly. The clerk shall file such order, and record the same in the judgment book. The order shall not be filed, nor any certified copies issued, until the petitioner shall have paid to the clerk the cost of such proceedings. The costs shall be provided by law.

Sec. 3. When the state registrar receives a certified copy of such an order, he shall prepare a supplementary certificate naming the fictitious person set forth in the court's order as father, and specifying that the birth is legitimate, if that fact is recorded on the certificate released for public use. The state registrar shall seal and file the original certificate of birth with the certified order of the court attached thereto. Such sealed documents may be opened only upon order of the court or, if absolutely necessary, by the state registrar.

A BILL FOR AN ACT AUTHORIZING CERTAIN PUBLIC CORPORATIONS TO PROVIDE MUSICAL PERFORMANCES FOR STUDENTS

BE IT ENACTED BY THE LEGISLATURE OF THE STATE OF MINNESOTA:

Section 1. Subdivision 1. For purposes of this act, "public corporation" means and includes any county, independent or special school district, city, village, or borough, and "wholly professional musicians" means persons who derive most of their earned income from the performance and teaching of music.

Subd. 2. The governing body of any public corporation may contract with any nonprofit corporation or association for the performance of music having a cultural and educational value by one or more wholly professional musicians, such performances to be given for students who attend schools which satisfy the requirements of compulsory attendance. Such corporation may charge an admission fee to defray all or part of the cost of the performance.

Subd. 3. In connection with any such performance, a public corporation may lease suitable space therefor and provide transportation for children.

APPENDIX III. *Letter sent by the Faculty Legal Protection Committee to all members of the University of Minnesota faculty and enclosure on background of libel suit*

Dear Colleague:

This letter is written to enlist your support in a matter of concern to our entire University community. During the past half year repeated irresponsible and reckless charges have been made against both specific members of our faculty and the University in general. In most instances these have involved the claim or inference that our ranks are studded with "communists," "communist collaborators," or whatever may be understood under "leftists." Though much relating to these accusations has been reported in the media of public communication, many of the most vituperative and scurrilous charges have circulated more privately within extremist circles or have been addressed wholesale to regents, university administrators, and legislators. Thus the full extent of the damage to the image of the University may well have escaped your attention.

The response of the University has so far centered very properly in the Regents' splendid statement on academic freedom. In this we take pride as a definition that should stand for academic generations. Yet, defining and indicating the limits of academic freedom, however necessary and appropriate, cannot completely respond to the requirements of the present situation. The issue is not merely what is or is not permissible in terms of academic freedom. Ways must also be found to guard ourselves from untrue and libellous charges against colleagues, entire departments, or organs of the University. Society fortunately provides one procedure that involves public examination of such attacks and is effective in discouraging their continuance.

Professor Arnold M. Rose of the Department of Sociology is one member of our faculty who has recently been under severe attack. The group responsible for this assault consists of extremists guilty repeatedly of distributing literature which responsible attorneys find to be false and libellous. Professor Rose has engaged the services of an attorney of high reputation in Minneapolis, Mr. Norman Newhall, Jr., who is filing a libel suit against the group. Mr. Newhall is confident of winning the case but estimates that it will cost about $3,000.

This situation has made innumerable claims on Professor Rose's time and energies. We, the undersigned members of an informally constituted committee, consider it our duty to see to it that he does not carry this burden alone. We are prepared to assist him with our counsel and to give him moral and financial support. We hope you share our conviction that his cause is that of each and all of us, and that we owe him much for his willingness to undertake this arduous task in our common interest. The coming libel suit should serve to discourage the kind of reckless attacks made on the University in recent months and reveal them in their true light. It should also serve to impose greater restraint on elements which in legislative years make extravagant charges in the attempt to influence negatively the support given the University.

We invite you to assist us as your means may permit to help defray the expenses of the suit. Our main concern is to achieve a resounding demonstration of faculty solidarity and whatever you can afford will be most welcome. Checks should be made out to the Faculty Legal Protection Committee and sent in the enclosed envelope to our Secretary-Treasurer, Robert H. Beck. If the total amount donated exceeds Professor Rose's legal expenses, the surplus either will be deposited for a permanent Faculty Legal Protection Committee (possibly administered by the University chapter of the American Association of University Professors) or will be returned to donors on a pro rate basis, if such return is requested. The same procedure will be followed for a sum equivalent to the actual expenses as a first charge against any damages that are recovered.

With warm appreciation for whatever you can do to support this cause,

Sincerely,

Faculty Legal Protection Committee
　　Francis M. Boddy
　　Richard K. Gaumnitz
　　Donald Hastings
　　Richard C. Jordan
　　Stanley V. Kinyon
　　William P. Martin
　　Alfred O. Nier
　　Grover C. Stephens
　　Harold C. Deutsch, Chairman
　　Robert H. Beck, Secretary-Treasurer

Background of Libel Suit; Professor Arnold M. Rose, Plaintiff

(for distribution to the U. of M. faculty only; not before Feb. 1, 1964)

Two issues of FACTS FOR ACTION, a mimeographed propaganda sheet distributed by Christian Research, Inc., of Minneapolis, attack the University of Minnesota, and Professor Arnold M. Rose particularly. In its issue of October 28, 1962 (revised December 4, 1962), FFA accuses Rose of being a Communist collaborator because of co-authorship of AN AMERICAN DILEMMA (a comprehensive study of the American Negro problem, sponsored by the Carnegie Corporation, published in 1944). The "Communists" Rose is alleged to have collaborated with are Gunnar Myrdal (senior author of the book), Ralph Bunche, and W. E. B. DuBois. In fact, DuBois had absolutely nothing to do with the book, and Rose never had the slightest association with him. His writings are referred to frequently, as he was a major scholar on Negroes for some sixty years, but so is every other writer on American Negroes referred to in this 1483-page book. (DuBois became a Communist at the age of 93, in 1960, 16 years after the publication of the book). Bunche had an early association with the preparation of the book, when he was a professor at Howard University, and Rose has had minor contacts with him. He is currently Undersecretary of the United Nations, formerly a high-ranking Department of State official, and recipient of the highest American civilian medal of honor from President Lyndon Johnson. Myrdal is the only one with whom Rose has worked closely; he is an anti-Communist, a world-famous professor of Economics, a former Minister of Commerce in the Swedish government, and former director of the Economic Commission for Europe of the U.N.

The April-May 1963 FFA repeats the above charge, but then goes on to say "CLEAN OUT THE UNIVERSITY." It specifically mentions the following faculty members as being associated with "Communist fronts": Isaac Kolthoff, Cyrus Barnum, Guy Stanton Ford. One such "Communist front" mentioned is the Council on Foreign Relations, and the following are listed as members: "John Cowles, Jr., Vice President of the STAR, Wilbur Elston, Robert W. Smith... Prof. Harold Deutsch, W. C. Rogers, Director of the World Affairs Center, O. Meredith Wilson, President, and others from the University of Minnesota. 27 out of 78 members are from Minnesota's colleges and the metropolitan newspapers -- almost 35%." The same sheet makes further attacks on Ralph Bunche, "the Butcher of Katanga," and Gunnar Myrdal.

When these sheets were circulated to members of the Minnesota Legislature in March 1963, Rose denounced them as false and libelous from the floor of the House, thus giving warning against their further dissemination. Yet it was on the basis of these documents that an Anoka citizen, an associate of Christian Research, attacked Rose's invitation to speak at the Anoka County Library on January 7, 1964. The Minneapolis STAR disseminated the charges to the public, but at first failed to report the Anoka County Attorney's finding that there was no basis for the charges, and otherwise distorted its news reports.

259

Christian Research, Inc., is a local distributor of national publications of the "Impeach Earl Warren" and "Eisenhower is a leading Communist" variety. Its goal is not merely restraint of academic freedom at the University of Minnesota; it seeks nothing less than the revolutionary transformation of American life and institutions. Few Minnesotans know about this organization, but already it has had significant influence on the Minnesota Legislature and on the Minneapolis City Council. It has no more than one hundred members, but they are dedicated and hard-working. The Minneapolis press has given them some publicity.

Professor Rose has retained the services of a Minneapolis law firm to represent him in a libel action against those responsible for the publication and distribution of this material. Because the court dockets are crowded, the case will not come to trial for many months. Libel suits are difficult because the defendant's right to free speech must be protected. But because the defamation in this instance is so blatant and has such significant consequences, this seems to be a valid and enforceable libel claim.

Christian Research, Inc., is involved with the sponsors of other recent attacks on the University of Minnesota. For example, it provided a forum for a talk by Kenneth J. McDonald, commander of the Third American Legion District, on "Atheism-Communism at the University of Minnesota" on January 17, 1964.. McDonald is the one who started this year's attack on academic freedom at the University. Various nation-wide extremist groups work in the Twin Cities through, or in collaboration with, Christian Research, Inc.

APPENDIX IV. *Letter sent by Paul B. Hurley to the clerk of the Minnesota House of Representatives, March 9, 1963, and interrogatories filed by Mr. Hurley with the clerk of the District Court on February 3, 1964*

Paul B. Hurley   407 18th Ave. North   Mpls. 11, Minn.   3-9-63

Minnesota House of Representatives   SUBJECT: Dr. Arnold Rose and his
Minn. State Capitol   SUBTLE Genocide Bill(PLOT) 1 P.M.
St. Paul, Minnesota   Scheduled Meeting, Room #2,3/12/63

EXHIBIT H-1
Marge Knudson
Reporter

Minnesota State Legislators (House)   Proper
    W A R N I N G ! ! ! !   Committee

Enclosed, please find tract "The Genocide Plot" which will give you
some insight into how these eternal tormentors of humanity "DUPE" the "STUPID-GOY".
Also, enclosed, please notice my famous "Jew-nitarian expose' and
Background of Elected House-member...Dr. Arnold Rose.
Wanted...circular...distributed during last election, etc..

At first glance Dr. Rose does not appear very dangerous , yet, in my
humble opinion...Dr. Rose is one of the most dangerous men in America
including "The nine men against America."

These PHONEY-FALSE advocates of truth and justice want to SILENCE all
opposition. The obvious purpose is to prevent their exposure by those whom they know
...know what the REAL score is.
       (or)
It(THE PROPOSED ROSE BILL) on GENOCIDE is patterened after along the
same lines as the United Nations "plan" (see enclosed tract). (THE GENOCIDE PLOT)

Keep an eye on this fellow Rose. I suggested that the House give the
"boot" to him and his deceiving smile (previous correspondence).

I wont be able to attend the meeting(committee) Tues., March 12, 1963
at one o'clock. I did want you to have this information so that you can "QUASH" any action on this bill. A Mr. Harris will be there who may have a copy of "Mind Tapping"....
A reprint of two separate articles dealing with a dangerous new weapon of the prosecution
and the courts in American criminal law.
    Article I. Pre-trial Mental Examination: A Dread Weapon by Robert Morris

    Article II. Mind Tapping...Psyshiatric Subversion of Constitutional Rights

These two articles give you some insite as to how these children of
the devil , as Jesus Christ Himself , referred to them; and as numerous great men of
history have denounced them. We will mention one in passing...Martin Luther who took
time out from his important work to denounce them.."All their hearts' wailing(today..
like that deliberate lie about the 10 million Jews said to have been liquidated by Hitler
)and longing terminates in the effect they someday might deal with us as they did in
Esther's time in Persia. And how the Jews love the Book of Esther which is so suitable to
their blood-thirsty, revengable, murderous appetite and hope ! The sun has never set nor
shone on such blood-thirsty and vindictive people who cherish the idea of murdering and
strangling the heathen." " No other men under the sun are more greedy than they have
been and always will be as one can see from their accurced USURY. They console themselves
that when the Messiah comes, He will collect all the gold and silver in the world and divide it among them. " " One should destroy all prayer books and copies of the "TERRIBLE"
TALMUD in which they learn such Godlessness(Benjamin Freedman, a former Jew..exposed in
his famous "Facts Are Facts" $1.00, Christian Ed. Assoc., Union, New Jersey and his World
War III records...can get all 3 for $5.00 now) Will send the rest by Harris because I
only have a few minutes to get this into the mail as a certified letter.

    Thank you,

    Signed...................
    Paul Benjamin Hurley
    407 18th Ave. N.
    Mpls. 11, Minn.

STATE OF MINNESOTA

COUNTY OF HENNEPIN

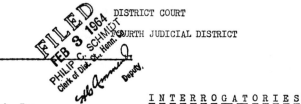

DISTRICT COURT

FOURTH JUDICIAL DISTRICT

Arnold Rose,

     Plaintiff

Gerda Koch, Christian Research, Inc. ,

     Defendant

I N T E R R O G A T O R I E S

-1- Are you a Jew Dr. Arnold Rose ?

-2- Have you ever studied the reprehensible so-called Jewish Bible , the "terrible" Talmud as exposed by the former Jew, Benjamin Freedman in his "Facts are Facts" and his electrifying "World War III" speech ?

-3- Are you now a member of the Unitarian Church ? Do you attend regularly ?

-4- Did you attend the Memorial Lecture to Dr. John Dietrich, Sat. Eve. at 8 P. M. , Dec. 1, 1958 ? Do you subscribe to the philosophy of Dr. Dietrich and the somewhat contrversial speaker that evening Dr. Corliss Lamont..."Humanism in religion is the shifting of emphasis from God to man, making the enrichment of human life, rather than the glorification of God, the object of our allegiance and consecretation." ?

-5- Compare the basic philosophy of Unitarianism with Karl Mark's(a Jew)"Religion is the opiate of the people, people directing toward a visionary other world, the thoughts and purposes that should be devoted to this world. ?   "REAL" ?

-6- Now, Dr. Arnold Rose, as a great educator and sociologist and author("An American Dilemma", including the "Great" "Sweat" experiments : , and other race-mixing books, under the heading Civil Rights and so-called, possibly, for political expediency or , maybe, as a Jew, the promotion of the Rabinovitch theme as expounded by Rabbi Emanuel Rabinovitch in 1952, " the goal towards which the Jews have been striving for over three thousand years"....namely, the peaceful domination over a "happy", bastardized earth, in which the most dangerous enemy...the polar opposite....of Jewr Jewry...the Aryan, will,(in the Rabbi's own words) be "nothing more than a memory" .....IS WITHIN HAND'S REACH ! " ? What are your real motives Dr. Arnold Rose in "pushing" Civil Rights which is number 1 on the Communist program for taking over America as exposed in my famous "Beware of Humphrey and Freeman Ho(cus) Po(cus)" on file with the F.B.I. (?) You Jews promote race-mixing for the "stupid-goy" as you call us in your filthy Talmud but yo do not practice that which you so eloquently preach ? Refer: Mpls. Tribune, Aug. 3, 1963 "Rabbi Says Jews Dating Non-Jews is "DANGEROUS" and Mpls. Star , Sat. , (11-A), 2-1-64, "Challenges of Judaism Presented ...Rabbi David Lieber, President of the University of Judaism, Los Angeles, Calif. Steve Litton statement DISRESPECT NON-JEWISH GIRLS INSOFAR AS MARRIAGE CONCERNED ?

-7- Can you define the terms(dictionary)American, Americanism, Democracy, Democrat, Republic, Communism, Socialism, Fascism ?) The latter is for nationalism and opposed to internationalism. You couldn't be considered a fascist ? for American Nationalism ? For the American Constitution ? American and Americanism as defined in the dictionary ? Difference between socialism and communism ? Are you a socialist ? Don't you advocate socialized medicine and other means of socialized control from Washington and World Government ...the aim of the Zionist Jews and isn't communism merely a "TOOL" of the international Zionism which you advocate Dr. Arnold Rose ?

-8- If you are a 100 % American(not belonging to one of the aboriginal races, native or inhabtant of the Western Hemisphere, devotion or "loyalty" to the United States, its customs, traditions, peculiar to the United States, a thing considered typically American(The Supreme Court bases their "infamous" integration decision on your book, Dr. Arnold, "An American Dillema" Rose and this was not nor ever has been American custom nor American tradition until, using your book as a guide, socialized justice and American tradition and American custom as a continuation of the policy of FDR ...of COOPERATION WITH JEWISH COMMUNISM ...selling out...the majority white race for Jewish gold, power, and political expediency(the block Jew-Negro vote, they and you know, Dr. Arnold Rose, controls national elections and metro-govt. elections).....)? Why do you, Dr. Arnold Rose, if you are such a "GREAT" American "push" the Un-American , pro-communist platform as do your JEW-NITARIAN friends with their support of numerous Communist "FRONT" organizations ...WILPPF...NAACP...ADA...ADL...UL...ACLU.. CORE...(Socialist and Conscientious Objectors...not while he was training in Israel. ...Zev Aleony..however ?) Twin City Secularist Society, etc. ?

-9- When are you ...TRAITORS...to the American "IDEA" going to accept the challenge of Mr. Benjamin Freedman to debate the truth or falsity of the ZIONIST WORLD CONSPIR⁂ ACY and its SCHEMES for WORLD CONTROL and WORLD GOVERNMENT(Rose-Naftalin-Scheiner)?

NOTES AND INDEX

NOTES

Chapter 1. Overview: Big Issues Mirrored in Little Events

1. F. P. Keppel, "Foreword" to Gunnar Myrdal, with the assistance of Richard Sterner and Arnold Rose, *An American Dilemma* (New York: Harper, 1944), p. vi.

2. *Ibid.*, pp. vi–vii.

3. Smith v. Allwright, 63 S. Ct. 1325 (1944).

4. John Gunther, *Inside U.S.A.* (New York: Harper, 1947), p. 683.

5. A recording was made of Myrdal's speech for a subsequent radio program, but no recording was made of the question period. Both Rose and Miss Koch agreed on the events occurring during the question period, however, and reported these events at the 1965 libel trial, so they are described here in some detail.

6. Elections to the Minnesota State Legislature are nonpartisan — that is, there is on the ballot no party designation for candidates — and candidates for the House of Representatives sometimes run in two-member districts. Thus Rose and the opponent mentioned were both Democrats, though only Rose had the Democratic-Farmer-Labor (DFL) party's endorsement, and they were running in a field of four candidates for two seats in the legislature. The legislative district they were campaigning to represent has more than 100,000 inhabitants.

7. Rose had written, or had participated in writing, a dozen other scholarly books after *An American Dilemma*, but these were never referred to.

8. It is against Minnesota law to circulate any campaign literature without identifying the person whose candidacy is being supported. It was apparently this fact which motivated the opponent mentioned to distribute very few copies of it.

9. Christian Research was not formally incorporated until February 1963, several months after the first two sets of leaflets were distributed.

10. The mimeographed leaflet was originally pages 7 and 8 of a ten-page issue of *Facts for Action*. This issue became plaintiff's Exhibit A in the trial. The printed leaflet which had no identification of the candidate on whose behalf it was being distributed became plaintiff's Exhibit D. They are reproduced in Appendix I.

11. This became plaintiff's Exhibit B. See Appendix I.

12. Anoka County is a suburban area adjacent to Hennepin County, in which Minneapolis is located.

13. A description of this meeting was provided to the author by the county attorney, who offered to repeat it as sworn testimony on the witness stand.

14. Grinde's letter became plaintiff's Exhibit C.

15. Reproduced in Appendix III.

16. Rose had been "accused" by Miss Koch and some of her followers of being a Unitarian; Rose testified in court that he happened not to be a Unitarian, although he had lectured to the Minneapolis Unitarian Society twice in the past fifteen years, just as he had lectured at two Roman Catholic seminaries during the preceding two years without being a Catholic. Daly called him non-religious; Rose testified that he was a Jew, and not an atheist.

17. The historian Richard Hofstadter used this term to characterize the style of writing and speaking among right-wing extremists. See his *The Paranoid Style in American Politics and Other Essays* (New York: Knopf, 1965).

18. 385 U.S. 388, 87 S.Ct. 1975, 18 L. ed. (2nd) 1094.

Chapter 2. A Study: "America's Single Most Important Domestic Problem"

1. Arnold M. Rose, "Distortion in the History of American Race Relations," in *Assuring Freedom to the Free*, edited by Arnold M. Rose (Detroit: Wayne State University Press, 1964), pp. 27–44.

269

2. W. E. B. Du Bois, the leading Negro spokesman in the period 1910–1935, used this analogy: "It is difficult to let others see the full psychological meaning of caste segregation. It is as though one, looking out from a dark cave in a side of an impending mountain, sees the world passing and speaks to it; speaks courteously and persuasively, showing them how these entombed souls are hindered in their natural movement, expression, and development; and how their loosening from prison would be a matter not simply of courtesy, sympathy, and help to them, but aid to all the world. One talks on evenly and logically in this way but notices that the passing throng does not even turn its head, or if it does, glances curiously and walks on. It gradually penetrates the minds of the prisoners that the people passing do not hear; that some thick sheet of invisible but horribly tangible plate glass is between them and the world. They get excited; they talk louder; they gesticulate. Some of the passing world stop in curiosity; these gesticulations seem so pointless; they laugh and pass on. They still either do not hear at all, or hear but dimly, and even what they hear, they do not understand. Then the people within may become hysterical. They may scream and hurl themselves against the barriers, hardly realizing in their bewilderment that they are screaming in a vacuum unheard and that their antics may actually seem funny to those outside looking in. They may even, here and there, break through in blood and disfigurement, and find themselves faced by a horrified, implacable, and quite overwhelming mob of people frightened for their own very existence." *Dusk at Dawn* (New York: Harcourt, Brace, 1940), pp. 130–131.

3. Ray Stannard Baker, *Following the Color Line* (Garden City, N.Y.: Doubleday, Page, 1908).

4. In 1948, Rose published a 325-page updated summary of *An American Dilemma*, under the title *The Negro in America*. This was republished in 1956 and again in 1964, with new introductions.

5. Rose did not agree with Myrdal in accepting Charles Beard's interpretation of the Constitution as a document expressing only the interests of the upper classes of 1778. It is ironic that some of Beard's work, especially his interpretation of America's entry into World War II, is accepted as gospel truth by the right-wing extremists. See Charles A. Beard, *An Economic Interpretation of the Constitution of the United States* (New York: Macmillan, 1913); *President Roosevelt and the Coming of the War* (New Haven, Conn.: Yale University Press, 1941).

6. This was one of the first large-scale studies undertaken in the social sciences, so the participants may be excused for having higher expectations about the work that should be done in a given period of time than would be true today. Much more money is spent today, and deadlines are much more lenient.

7. Stouffer also was to complete the study of Negro population characteristics left unfinished by the resignation of one of the staff members.

8. Doxey A. Wilkerson in Herbert Aptheker, *The Negro People in America* (New York: International Publishers, 1946), p. 9. One of the many peculiarities of Communist thought and expression is illustrated in this passage. Wilkerson uses the phrase "corporation-financed" as though he meant business-financed, to imply that American businessmen found it expedient to hire a foreign scholar to whitewash their mistreatment of Negroes. As Wilkerson well knew, since he had accepted regular salary checks from the same "corporation" without doing much work, the study had been financed by the Carnegie Corporation of New York, not a business but a philanthropic foundation. He also knew that the book was not a whitewash of American business. But it is part of the Communist creed that one should lie, in small ways as well as big ones, to advance the interests of "the party."

9. Rose's mentor at that time, Professor Samuel Stouffer, was one of the few who did not share the negative image of Myrdal, but he had had only one personal contact with Myrdal, in May 1940.

10. Sterner's book was later published under the title *The Negro's Share: A Study of Income, Consumption, Housing and Public Assistance* (New York, Harper, 1943).

11. Myrdal had spent that summer at Dartmouth College in Hanover, New Hampshire, and Miss Moulik and Rose had first joined him there. Myrdal's selection of Hanover and Princeton was based on the fact that they had good college libraries, were pleasant communities to live in, and were accessible to New York City, where the Carnegie Corporation had its offices.

12. Alva Myrdal, *Nation and Family* (New York: Harper, 1943).

13. This point of view was delineated in Appendix 2 of *An American Dilemma*, in the preparation of which Rose worked closely with Myrdal. Rose received much criticism, as well as some praise, for his work on this aspect of the book from his fellow sociologists.

14. It was not until 1959 that another sociologist would take the thesis of "moral dilemma" seriously enough to give it an independent test. Then he published his article in a journal read mainly by psychologists: Robert W. Friedrichs, "Christians and Residential Exclusion: An Empirical Study of a Northern Dilemma," *Journal of Social Issues*, 15(no. 4):14–23 (1959). The first independent test published in a sociological journal did not appear until 1965. See Frank R. Westie, "The American Dilemma: An Empirical Test," *American Sociological Review*, 30:527–538 (August 1965). Also see Rose's response to the Westie study: "On an Empirical Test of *An American Dilemma*," *American Sociological Review*, 30:103 (February 1966).

15. Almost immediately after the book appeared, the publisher — Harper and Brothers — published a 16-page condensation. Shortly afterward, Maxwell Stewart wrote a 32-page summary, published under the title *The Negro in America*. Rose was not able to publish a systematic summary until he was released from the Army, finished with his doctor's degree, and established in his academic career — in 1948. However, his *The Negro in America* also became an authoritative, if less scholarly, work that continued to be widely read through the 1960's.

Chapter 3. The Right-Wing Extremists: An Upper Midwest Variation

1. Goldwater's sentence, with apparent reference to the segment of his followers referred to in this book, was "Extremism in the defense of liberty is not a vice, moderation in the pursuit of justice is not a virtue." Those who oppose the extremists, among both Democrats and Republicans, doubt that they favor either liberty or justice. While most extremists supported Goldwater, not all extremists are Republican, and no such implication is intended here.

Rose's interpretation of Goldwater was that he himself was never fully a "Goldwaterite," but that he found it expedient or compelling to accept support from such a devoted following. Some right-wing extremists were not enamored of Goldwater — they called him a "socialist." There is a tendency among extremists to bicker among themselves and for some to claim that they are purer or more extremist than others.

2. Richard Hofstadter, *The Paranoid Style in American Politics and Other Essays* (New York: Knopf, 1965), Chapter 1.

3. An American Institute of Public Opinion poll released in February 1962 indicated that 8 per cent, of the 53 per cent aware of the John Birch Society, were favorable toward it. The Birch Society is the best organized of the current right-wing extremist organizations. See J. Allen Broyles, *The John Birch Society: Anatomy of a Protest* (Boston: Beacon Press, 1964) and B. R. Epstein and Arnold Forster, *The Radical Right* (New York: Random House, 1967).

4. The Roman Catholic Church has outlawed, and otherwise disassociated itself from, various of the fundamentalist groups that have grown out of it — such as the Father Feeney movement of Massachusetts and the Father Coughlin movement of the 1930's. The Church has also denounced the John Birch Society, but it tolerates

certain other groups that are within the orbit of right-wing extremism. The struggle over this issue within the Catholic Church is suggested by Edward T. Gargan, *Radical Catholics of the Right* (Omaha, Neb.: Catholic Council on Civil Liberties, 1962).

5. On the relationship between religious fundamentalism and right-wing extremism, see Hofstadter, *The Paranoid Style in American Politics*, pp. 72–77, and David Danzig, "The Radical Right and the Rise of the Fundamentalist Minority," *Commentary*, 33:291–298 (April 1962).

6. Ray Carroll, *Jesus a Capitalist* (Billings, Mont.: American Council of Christian Laymen, 1952), p. 4.

7. With one post-hoc exception: After a dentist in the Army was discovered by the military authorities to have been a Communist, McCarthy claimed the dentist was on his list. But he never claimed to have submitted his list to the military authorities or even to the FBI.

8. On the historical role of the "Jews" in the thinking of right-wing extremists, see Oscar Handlin, "American Views of the Jew at the Opening of the Twentieth Century," *Publications of American Jewish Historical Society*, No. 40, Part 4 (June 1951), pp. 323–345, and John Higham, "Anti-Semitism in the Gilded Age: A Reinterpretation," *Mississippi Valley Historical Review*, 43:559–578 (March 1957).

9. While the chief verbal targets of the extremists have been these powerful and "distant" persons and organizations, the specific practical targets against which the extremists have been most successful in their attacks have been the local libraries, the local schoolteachers, and the PTA's — what Alan Westin calls the "soft underbelly of democracy." See Westin's chapter in Daniel Bell, ed., *The Radical Right* (Garden City, N.Y.: Doubleday, 1963), especially p. 251.

10. Hofstadter subsumes both of these tendencies under what he calls the Manichean element" in right-wing extremism — that is, the tendency to think of all events as reflecting a struggle between good and evil. Edward Shils — in his *The Torment of Secrecy* (Glencoe, Ill.: Free Press, 1956) — concentrates on the tendency of the right-wing extremists to oversimplify matters, which he deals with as the main characteristic of the Populist tradition.

11. Theodore H. White, *The Making of the President* (New York: Atheneum, 1965).

12. The best analysis of this has been written by the "true conservative" Peter Viereck, in Chapter 8 of Bell, ed., *The Radical Right*.

13. For a history of the latter, see Hofstadter, *The Paranoid Style in American Politics*, Chapter 7.

14. Bell, ed., *The Radical Right*, p. 16.

15. Hofstadter, *The Paranoid Style in American Politics*, p. 23.

16. *Ibid.*, p. 29.

17. *Ibid.*, p. 31.

18. *Ibid.*, p. 39.

19. A considerable number of retired generals are on the fringes of the right-wing extremist movement. The reasons for this are analyzed by Morris Janowitz, *The Professional Soldier* (Glencoe, Ill.: Free Press, 1960); see especially pp. 429ff.

20. Alan F. Westin, "Anti-Communist and the Corporations," *Commentary*, 36: 479–487 (December 1963).

21. There is a strong parallel between right-wing extremism in its Upper Midwest form and the Strasser-Roehm "Socialist" wing of the German National Socialist party.

22. See Hofstadter, *The Paranoid Style in American Politics*, "Introduction." See also S. M. Lipset, "The Sources of the Radical Right," in Bell, ed., *The Radical Right*, pp. 307–372.

23. S. M. Lipset, *Agrarian Socialism* (Berkeley: University of California Press, 1950), p. 10.

24. *Ibid.*, p. 29.

25. Arnold M. Rose, "Anti-Semitism's Root in City Hatred," *Commentary*, 6: 374–378 (October 1948).

26. Oscar Handlin, "American Views of the Jew at the Opening of the Twentieth Century," *op. cit.*, pp. 323–345.

27. *Ibid.*, p. 341. Bryan was not uniquely a product of the Upper Midwest, but his most devoted followers and successors were.

28. *Ibid.*, pp. 341–342.

29. *Ibid.*, pp. 329–344.

30. Carl C. Taylor, *The Farmers' Movement 1620–1920* (New York: American Book, 1953), p. 489.

31. Arnold M. Rose, "A Theory of Social Organization and Social Disorganization," in *Theory and Method in the Social Sciences* (Minneapolis: University of Minnesota Press, 1954), Chapter 1.

32. Charles P. Loomis and J. Allan Beegle, "The Spread of German Nazism in Rural Areas," *American Sociological Review*, 11:724–34 (1946), at p. 725.

33. Rudolf Heberle, *From Democracy to Nazism* (Baton Rouge: Louisiana State University Press, 1945), p. 79.

Chapter 4. The University: Professorial Dignity and Student Ribaldry

1. This campus has one section in Minneapolis and another (for agriculture) in St. Paul. These operate as a unit, with buses to convey students the two and a half miles between their respective centers. The university also has a campus in Duluth, with 4405 students in fall 1965, and a new one in Morris, with 984 students. The total university was fifth largest in the United States, ranking behind the State University of New York, the California college system, the University of California, and the City University of New York, all of which have more than four campuses.

2. There have always been separate teachers' colleges, in addition to the College of Education at the university. About 1955, these colleges became four-year liberal arts colleges, and now provide some competition at legislative sessions for the higher-education dollars. But the rivalry has been nowhere near as great as in those states — like Michigan, Iowa, and Illinois — where there are several state universities, or even in California where the superstructure of one university administration is relatively nominal.

3. Many other discoveries and inventions came out of the University of Minnesota that were important to the economy of the state: a means of controlling wheat rust and the corn borer; genetic improvement of the hog, the apple, the raspberry; significant advances in heart surgery; etc.

4. Minnesotans are careful to refer to it as the *Joe* McCarthy era, because one of their own senators happens to be named McCarthy also. Suffice it to say that Eugene J. McCarthy of Minnesota is almost the antithesis of the late Joseph McCarthy of Wisconsin.

5. These charges were mainly made orally and were presented on television or reported in the press. But see also *Facts for Action*, No. 11 (September–October 1960), pp. 2–9; *Highlights of Christian Research Activities, 1960–1961*, pp. 3–4.

6. *Facts for Action*, No. 17 (November–December 1961), p. 3.

7. Persons who are the objects of attack by the right-wing extremists have regularly been subjected to similar harassment in recent years. Governor Nelson Rockefeller of New York, in his speech to the Republican National Convention in 1964 (which was noisily booed by the Goldwater supporters at the convention), referred to threatening telephone calls in the middle of the night. Tom Braden, president of the California State Board of Education, described the full-scale attack on him in his article "I Was the Target of a Hate Campaign," *Look*, 27:54–60 (October 22,

1963). In January 1966 a radio announcer in New Jersey who criticized the right-wing extremists was beaten up by three unknown assailants even as he was making announcements over the radio. Only three months earlier the attorney general of New Jersey ordered an investigation into what he said was a well-armed, under-ground, right-wing organization (*New York Times*, October 23, 1965, p. 32), but apparently it was not effective in breaking up the group. Examples of this sort of extralegal violent activity can be multiplied.

8. It should be noted here, as it was not in any discussion at the university or elsewhere in the state, that until it was proposed that he be dismissed from the uni-versity, Sibley's freedom of speech was being attacked, not his academic freedom. The attack on Rose, for his work on *An American Dilemma*, as a scholarly publica-tion, was an attack on academic freedom from the start.

9. The Minnesota Poll is the product of a reasonably scientific polling agency sponsored by the Minneapolis Star and Tribune Company.

10. One of the many letters to the editor concerning the Sibley-Rosen debate came from a responsible Minneapolis clergyman who said he got a sick feeling in his stomach when he heard the jeers of students putting to scorn a man "who was cer-tainly no intellectual match for Prof. Sibley, but who at least had the courage of his convictions." He felt that by remaining silent in the face of such advocacy he and others like him were helping to destroy the principles and practices on which this country was founded. (*Minneapolis Tribune*, January 14, 1964, p. 4.)

11. *Minneapolis Tribune*, January 31, 1964, p. 1.

12. Alfred O. C. Nier, in the *Minneapolis Tribune*, January 13, 1964, p. 6.

13. Some students, acting at the suggestion of the dean of students, formed a "truth squad" in February 1964, to carry correct information about the university back to their home communities throughout the state. Their call for volunteers be-gan: "The University has been called Communist, Godless, immoral, irresponsible! The real University is being masked by false accusations. The misunderstanding of the University is typified by the reaction to the Sibley-Rosen confrontation. WE MUST RESPOND TO THESE INAPPROPRIATE CHARGES AND INNUENDOS MADE AGAINST THE UNIVERSITY OF MINNESOTA." The students who responded to this call were not nearly as numerous as those who jeered at the earlier Sibley-Rosen debate.

14. From what the author has read of the Berkeley affair it would seem that the students started out with a justified grievance against the university administration, and the latter mishandled their complaint. Later, however, some of the students condoned public obscenity in the name of freedom of speech, and their leader pub-licly said that a leading Birchite attacking the university was better than the presi-dent who allegedly said one thing at one time and another thing at another time. The extreme "purity" of many young people is both factually hypocritical and an ex-pression of inexperience and immaturity.

Chapter 5. The Minnesota Legislature: The Political Response

1. See Chapter 3 for a fuller discussion of right-wing extremism in the Upper Midwest states.

2. Olson was elected governor in 1930, took office in 1931, was re-elected twice, and died of cancer at the end of 1935.

3. The full story of the 1960 Democratic National Convention is only gradually coming out as President John F. Kennedy's close associates write their memoirs. Ap-parently what happened was that Kennedy personally preferred Freeman as his run-ning mate but recognized that Lyndon Johnson would be more likely to help him win the election, and in any case "deserved" the post more.

4. Stassen retained a good deal of influence in Minnesota until he failed in his efforts to move onto the national scene in 1952. Even before that, he had moved out

of the state, and his subsequent activities had no more than a curiosity interest for Minnesotans.

5. These four factions do not have exact parallels on the national scene, although the DFLers come close to being equivalent to the northern Democrats in Congress (including former Senator Hubert Humphrey and Senator Eugene McCarthy). The "dissident Liberals" would have parallels in Senator Frank Lausche of Ohio and former Representative Howard W. Smith of Virginia. The Republican faction of Minnesota's legislature would be similar to former Governor Elmer L. Andersen of the state and to most of the New England Republicans (not as liberal as Senator Jacob Javits or Clifford Case). The "Conservative" faction in Minnesota would be most like Senator Everett Dirksen, except that they are estranged from their party while Dirksen is at the heart of his party.

6. Rose's first participation in the work of a campaign was in 1954, when he did some house-to-house campaigning for Humphrey, Freeman, and Donald M. Fraser, then in his first race, for a state Senate seat. Fraser is now the United States congressman from the Fifth Congressional District and one of the ablest young politicians in the United States. In that campaign, Rose also spoke at home coffee parties for Senator Humphrey.

7. Freeman had appointed Naftalin as state commissioner of administration after his gubernatorial victory in 1954. Later, in 1961, Naftalin was elected mayor of Minneapolis. Others who were members of the Second Ward Club at one time or another included Walter F. Mondale, who became Minnesota attorney general in 1959 and United States senator in 1965 when he was appointed to serve out Vice President-elect Humphrey's unexpired term (Mondale had earlier been a student in one of Rose's classes), and Karl F. Rolvaag, who was elected lieutenant governor in 1954 and governor in 1962. Mondale and Rolvaag had never been leaders of the Second Ward Club as had Humphrey, Freeman, Fraser, and Naftalin.

8. Rose worked so hard in that campaign that he made the mistake of believing he didn't need the help of many other possible volunteer helpers. In the last two weeks of the campaign, the Republican state chairman put over fifty workers into the ward on behalf of Rose's opponent. Election day in June was one of the hottest in Minnesota's history, and more Republican voters were motivated to go to the polls than Democratic voters.

9. This was a heritage of the same split within the DFL that had existed since Humphrey organized the party. Those who opposed the Humphrey-Freeman type of liberals in the party were ensconced in the Minneapolis Central Labor Union. These union leaders made special efforts to defeat Rose, raising a large fund to campaign against him; they helped elect a Republican whom they later found to be their vigorous enemy. They thought of Rose as a lieutenant of Humphrey and Freeman, which he was, but not on as high a level as they supposed, and some of them also hated Rose as a Jew and an intellectual. These same labor leaders had defeated other liberal candidates, although they were nominally DFLers and although they could rarely get any of their own labor candidates elected. They thus operated to split the party and throw many city elections into the hands of the Republicans, until the DFL party leaders persuaded AFL-CIO President George Meany to look into their financial mismanagement of the Central Labor Union. He dismissed the president of the CLU, and the receiver appointed by the AFL-CIO got some of the other leaders to promise to be good. A few broke away from the CLU and continued to oppose the DFL as "dissident Liberals." It was one of the members of this group, a long-time legislator and dismissed local union president, that Rose fought against in the 1962 election and defeated.

10. Many of the people at the university call this the "university district" because the university is physically located in it, but the district is far larger than university people realize. Only 7 to 9 per cent of the voters of the 41st Legislative District

are university-connected — most of the faculty and staff live away from the university, in better class neighborhoods; in addition most of the students and many faculty don't vote in local elections.

11. Rose took a leave of absence without pay from the university during the five months of the legislative sessions. Since this was five-ninths of the academic year, he lost five-ninths of his academic salary, which was much more than he earned during his entire two years as a legislator.

12. In voting on minor bills, unless he happens to know something about them, a legislator looks for guidance to his leaders, including committee chairmen and ranking committee minority members. More than 2000 bills were introduced into the 1963 session of the Minnesota legislature, and more than half of these came to the stage of being voted on, so no legislator could read all he had to vote on, much less study them. The notion that a conscientious legislator knows the contents of most of the bills he has to vote on is a pious public myth — one of the hundreds surrounding elected officials.

13. The only important bill Slater brought his crowd out to oppose was one to increase the number of low-cost public housing units in the state, but this was later in the session.

14. There was another possible objection that the illegitimate individual might seek to claim to be the heir of some deceased person who had the same name as his putative father. Of course, the difficulty here was no greater than in the case of a legitimately-born person whose father had the same name as the rich deceased person. Rose met this objection in his bill by providing that any judge, as well as the state commissioner of public welfare, would have access to the original birth certificates which would reveal illegitimacy when that was the fact.

15. It was late in the session, hence difficult to arrange for a committee hearing in the Senate. However, Rose got one of the House Conservative co-sponsors of the bill — Rep. John T. Anderson — to make a personal appeal to the Senate majority leader for a hearing. When the latter called for a presentation of the bill in committee, at the very last possible moment in the session, the Senate chief author of the bill was unprepared to present it. He, a DFLer like Rose, had not thought it possible that this "minor" bill — authored by a DFLer — could get a hearing from the Conservatives at this difficult time, and he had not prepared himself. So the bill failed to get through the Senate.

Chapter 6. The Irresponsible Press: A Deeper Problem

1. This would, incidentally, imply that Gardner Cowles, the publisher of *Look* magazine, and brother of the publisher of the *Minneapolis Star*, was also a "notorious Communist" supporter, since *Look*, on November 19, 1963, published an article by Gunnar Myrdal and paid him for the article.

2. The only distortions of the Anoka County incident to appear in the *Tribune* were three repetitions of the statement — apparently taken out of the newspaper's files, which the *Tribune* shares with the *Star* — that the Anoka County Board *ordered* an investigation of two professors. In two of these news stories, the two professors were erroneously identified as Sibley and Rose.

3. Kennedy especially was a master of public-image building, but no one has yet studied his skills. Few have created the image of so much achievement while having actually accomplished very little — due, in Kennedy's case, to real barriers placed in his way by Congress and by other nations. Nevertheless, the facts will show that as representative, as senator, and even as President, he had relatively few solid accomplishments for the years he spent in those offices. His capacity for relating himself to the mass media, however, was almost unparalleled.

There are other things a politician learns to do to manipulate a newspaper reporter besides offering his own dramatic angles, of course: (1) He must always act like a warm human being toward a reporter. He may actually be a reserved, shy, or dignified person, and so appear to most of his constituents and associates, but to a newspaper reporter he must be a "buddy," acting without "airs." This the politician does by such things as offering a drink or a smoke to the reporter, removing his jacket and tie while talking to him, telling him little jokes or purely private experiences (concerning his wife, for example) which he knows the reporter will not print anyway. (2) The politician must pretend to "level" with the reporter. He may tell the reporter that his career will be harmed or ruined if the reporter prints what he is about to tell him, but he is going to tell him anyway and leave his reputation to the tender mercies of the reporter. Or the "victim" may be someone else. But a "true and secret" story must be given to a reporter in addition to a news release; otherwise there is the danger to the politician either that the news release will be shelved or that the reporter will invent his own dramatic angle for it.

4. One careful study, conducted by University of Illinois social scientists, shows that the public has considerably more accurate knowledge of mental illness than the image of the mentally ill portrayed in the mass media. The mass media systematically distort and stereotype the mentally ill person, but occasional direct contacts keep many members of the public better informed. See Jum C. Nunally, *Popular Conceptions of Mental Health* (New York: Holt, Rinehart, and Winston, 1961).

5. Ralph Turner and F. J. Killian, eds., *Collective Behavior* (Englewood Cliffs, N.J.: Prentice Hall, 1957); Kurt and Gladys Lang, *Collective Dynamics* (New York: Crowell, 1958).

6. Hadley Cantril, *The Invasion from Mars: A Study in the Psychology of Panic* (Princeton, N.J.: Princeton University Press, 1940).

7. *Minneapolis Tribune*, October 2, 1965, p. 15.

Chapter 7. The Law of Libel: A Right Decision and Dangerous Dicta

1. Increasingly, as in the *Rose v. Koch* case, fourteen jurors will be impaneled at the beginning of a trial, so as to avoid a mistrial if one of the jurors becomes incapacitated. Just before the jury goes out, the extra jurors are dismissed.

2. See David Riesman, "Democracy and Defamation: Fair Game and Fair Comment," *Columbia Law Review*, 42:1085–1123 (1942), on libel law in Britain and other countries. For the South African case, see the *Minneapolis Star*, June 17, 1967, p. 7A.

3. Minnesota law was not so far out of line with the Supreme Court's decision of March 1964 as was that of most other states. Minnesota had always had an especially weak law on libel — requiring proof of malice as well as proof of falsehood from a public official suing for libel.

4. This was at least true of Justice Black's concurring opinion, with which Justice Douglas associated himself. Justice Goldberg's separate concurring opinion (with which Douglas also associated himself) was somewhat more cautious, in that he distinguished the private life of a public official from his "official conduct" and would have eliminated libel suits for the latter alone.

5. Anthony Lewis, "Libel and the Constitution," *New York Times*, March 11, 1964, p. 19.

6. One such was the criminal libel case of *Garrison v. Louisiana*, decided on November 23, 1964, by the United States Supreme Court in almost the identical way the *New York Times* case was decided. Another was a libel case against Aaron E. Henry, a Mississippi Negro civil rights worker, reversed by the United States Supreme Court on March 29, 1965. At the time of the *New York Times* decision, that newspaper reported (April 4, 1964, p. 12) that there were seventeen similar suits — involving a total of $288 million in damages — pending. If all of these had been

decided in favor of the respondent (plaintiff), several newspapers and magazines — including the *New York Times* — would probably have had to go bankrupt.

7. Justice Black was no doubt incensed by Alabama's flagrant violation of the Court's previous Brown decision to desegregate the public schools, as well as the trivial grounds for the libel suit in the *New York Times* case. But there would still be danger if his statements quoted above were to become law. Justice Brennan's ruling decision is more than adequate to give full protection for freedom of speech and press, without being so "absolute."

8. A person running for public office could, by easy extension of the *New York Times* decision, be legally considered a public official, even if he is not elected. The United States Supreme Court here favorably cites a Kansas decision to that effect: Coleman v. MacHennan, 78 Kan. 711, 98 Pac. 281 (1908).

9. *New York Times*, April 20, 1966, p. 1, and April 24, 1966, editorial section.

10. However, one of her witnesses — former legislator Dan Slater — thought that Rose's support for an anti-genocide resolution to the United States Senate was evidence of Communist sympathy, as also was Rose's bill to grant a full birth certificate to illegitimate children. See Appendix II.

11. John Henry Faulk, *Fear on Trial* (New York: Simon and Schuster, 1964); Louis Nizer, *The Jury Returns* (Garden City, N.Y.: Doubleday, 1966), Chapter 4.

12. There were other matters of law that Newhall had to do research on before the trial. But they were technical in nature and need not concern the reader who is not a lawyer: (1) Whether the charges made by Miss Koch against Rose were "libelous per se." Newhall decided they were. (2) Whether the libels published while Christian Research was unincorporated were attributable to the whole group individually or only to Gerda Koch, who did all the actual work on the paper. As we have seen, Newhall decided to follow through only against Miss Koch and Grinde, who were the only ones personally to write the libels, and to dismiss the suits against the other members of her committee and against the incorporators of Christian Research. (3) Whether *Facts for Action* was a newspaper within the meaning of Minnesota's statutes. If it were a newspaper, Newhall would have had to give Miss Koch a formal "notice of request for retractions" before he could sue (and if she had published a retraction he could not sue). Newhall decided that *Facts for Action* was not a newspaper, and Judge Barbeau agreed with him on this, but the Minnesota Supreme Court later did not, although it let the issue alone because Daly did not raise it.

Chapter 8. The Trial, I: The Defense Becomes a Prosecution

1. An "expert witness" is one who testifies as an expert about the general or background facts pertaining to a case, and he need not know the party on whose side he is testifying.

2. *Congressional Record*, Vol. 101, Part 6 (May 26, 1955), pp. 7119–7124. 84th Congress, 1st session.

3. *Congressional Record*, Vol. 108, Part 1 (January 15, 1962), pp. 214–216. 87th Congress, 2nd session.

4. Herbert Aptheker, *The Negro People in America* (New York: International Publishers, 1946), p. 66.

Chapter 10. The Trial, III: The Jury Renders Judgment

1. *Time*, 86:67–68 (December 10, 1965). Reprinted by courtesy of *Time*; © 1966 by Time Inc.

Epilogue: Lessons from a Lawsuit

1. Donald T. Barbeau, "Memorandum" to Order Rejecting Defendant's Plea for a New Trial, April 25, 1966.
2. Brian J. Coyle (senior student), "President Asks for Recognition," *Minnesota Daily*, January 7, 1966, pp. 4–5.
3. Richard Hofstadter, *The Paranoid Style in American Politics and Other Essays* (New York: Knopf, 1965), Chapters 1 and 4.
4. It is difficult to say whether the right-wing extremists themselves are aware of the point. Probably some cynical leaders among them are, but it is doubtful whether someone like Gerda Koch understands it.
5. Louis Nizer, *My Life in Court* (Garden City, N.Y.: Doubleday, 1961), on the case of Quentin Reynolds, and Louis Nizer, *The Jury Returns* (Garden City, N.Y.: Doubleday, 1966), on the case of John Henry Faulk.
6. Judge Barbeau in instructing the jury on the definition of malice not only quoted the *New York Times* decision but added that the jury could consider evidence of personal ill-will, the exaggerated language of the document, the extent of its publication, or any other factors that the jury might regard as equally relevant. This instruction was drawn from the earlier Minnesota case of Friedell v. Blakely Printing Co., 163 Minn. 226, 203 N.W. 974. It was several U.S. Supreme Court decisions issued after the Rose-Koch trial which prohibited trial judge Barbeau from citing this earlier Minnesota case, as explained in the text.
7. 385 U.S. 388, 87 S.Ct. 1975, 18 L. ed. (2nd) 1094.
8. 383 U.S. 75, 86 S.Ct., 15 L. ed. (2nd) 597.
9. 385 U.S. 374, 87 S.Ct. 534, 17 L. ed. (2nd) 456. The Court of Appeals for the Eighth Circuit reached the same result in Pauling v. Globe-Democrat Pub. Co., 362 F. (2nd) 188. The court considered Pauling to be a public figure because he was a scholar and scientist of international prominence who had written and spoken extensively and had undertaken to provide leadership among scientific and other academic people on the controversial subject of nuclear testing. Justice Peterson also cited the case of Clark v. McBaine, 299 Mo. 77, 252 S.W. 428, decided in 1923, which "although not squarely in point, applied the concept of qualified privilege to adverse comment upon the fitness of a state-supported university faculty member." Justice Peterson said he did not have to rule whether all state-supported university faculty members were public figures because Rose clearly was a public figure by virtue of his eminence in his field and his participation in public affairs even outside the legislature.
10. 379 U.S. 64, 85 S.Ct. 209, 13 L. ed (2nd) 125.
11. 379 U.S. 74, 85 S.Ct. 216, 13 L. ed (2nd) 133.
12. 383 U.S. 84, 86 S.Ct. 675, 15 L. ed (2nd) 204.
13. Minnesota Supreme Court, No. 79 Hennepin County, Peterson J., in the case of Arnold Rose, respondent, v. Gerda Koch, and Christian Research, Inc., appellants, filed October 20, 1967, p. 36.

Olson, Floyd B., 71, 275n2
Oman, Rev. Mr., 197
Orwell, George, 39
Osborn, Frederick, 24, 159–160, 185, 206

Paine, Thomas, 176, 205
Pape, Frank, 116
Parent-Teacher Association, 102, 272n9
Park, Robert E., 185
Pauling, Linus, 116, 279n9
Pearson, Drew, 116
Perez, Leander, 46
Peterson, C. Donald, 220–223, 279n9
Peterson, Harry, 219
Populism, and right-wing extremism, 46, 48, 71, 218, 272n10
Porth, A. J., 194
Postlethwaite, Deane, as witness, 175
Public figures, and libel, 18, 116–117, 120, 279n9
Public officials, and libel, 18, 110–111, 113–117, 120, 186, 211, 219–225, 278n8
Public opinion polls, 19, 59, 272n3, 274n9

Rahm, Adina, 178
Randolph, A. Philip, 206
Raper, Arthur, 185, 244
Reagan, Ronald, 41
Reid, Ira De A., 185, 244
Reporters, psychology of, 96–101
Republican party, 159, 174, 177, 202:
    and right-wing extremism, 36, 40, 99, 103–104, 108, 114, 125, 216, 219, 271–272n1; in Minnesota, 72–74, 141; regarded as subversive, 162
Reuter, E. B., 24
Reynolds, Quentin, 219
Riggins, Don, 200
Right-wing extremism: identified, 3, 4, 13, 17, 20, 25, 33–34, 215–216; of Daly and Gerda Koch, 35, 164–165, 173, 216; and Democratic party, 36, 162; and Republican party, 36, 40, 99, 103–104, 108, 114, 125, 216, 219, 271–272n1; religious fundamentalism and, 36–37, 272n4; early history, 36, 41–42; not opposed to Communism, 37–39, 217–218; irrationality of, 39; leaders of, 40–41; and class, 41–42, 44–45, 46; conspiratorial mode of, 43–45; variants of, 46–47; agricultural depression and emergence of, 47–52; and

harassment, 58–61, 191, 274n7; and legislature, 77, 80, 81–84, 86; and *Minneapolis Herald*, 94–95; Hurley and, 126; literature of, 183, 190, 215, 231–248
Robeson, Paul, 206
Rockefeller, Nelson, 274n7
Rockwell, George L., 46, 60
Rogers, William C., 241, 259
Rolvaag, Karl, 14, 62, 275n7
Roman Catholic Church, and fundamentalist groups, 272n4
Romney, George, 216
Roosevelt, Archibald, 46
Roosevelt, Eleanor, 233
Roosevelt, Franklin D., 3, 98, 173
Rose, Arnold M.: background and beliefs, 4, 6, 34, 140–142, 147–148, 160, 161–165, 192–193, 269n7, 269–270n16; chairman of Myrdal lecture, 6–7; attacked in legislative campaign, 7; attacked in legislature, 8, 77, 82–84; Anoka County incident, 8–12; demand for *Star* retraction, 12, 88–93, 103–104; harassment of, 12, 58, 146; hires attorney, 13; support from faculty, 13–14, 63–64, 68–69, 257–260; said to have leading role in Communist conspiracy, 15, 206; wins suit, 16, 209–210; connection with Myrdal study, 26–32, 142–145, 160–161, 191; early political experience, 75–76, 275n6, 275n8; affiliation with Democratic party, 75, 141, 149, 160, 162, 166, 174, 177, 179–180; elected to legislature, 76; and Slater, 77–82, 193–196; fellow legislators support, 84; relations with attorney, 92–93, 107–108; memorandum on *New York Times* decision, 121–123; preparing for trial, 124–128; testimony of, 140–145, 158–165, 191–193; witnesses for, 148–149, 152–153, 161, 166, 170, 174–180; invitation to White House, 193; decision overturned, 220–222; Minnesota Supreme Court affirms vindication of Rose's character, 222–223; text of attacks on, 237–238, 241, 242, 243, 247, 249–250; bills introduced by, 253–254; income reduced during session, 276n–11; *et passim*
Rose, Caroline B., 32, 305
Rosen, Milton, 57, 59, 60, 61, 62, 67, 93, 105
Rosenberg, Ethel, 206

286

University of Minnesota, 4, 6, 8, 10, 12, 17, 95, 225: World Affairs Center of, 9, 11; and legislature, 12, 54–55, 60–67; faculty defense fund, 13, 14, 63, 257–259; campuses and enrollment, 53, 273n1; general town-gown relations, 53–54; support of academic freedom at, 55–56; attacks on, 56–62, 86, 133, 165, 216–217, 235, 237–238, 241, 247; response of faculty to Rose's libel suit, 63–64, 66–67; reaction on campus to trial, 68–69; and Anoka County Board, 88; and *Star*, 104–105; social science faculty of, 171; legislative district of, 276n10

Utt, James B., 135, 137, 231, 241–245

Vance, Rupert B., 24
Varney, Lord Harold, 237, 241, 245
Vietnam war, 206, 217
Viner, Jacob, 185

Walker, Edwin, 46, 171, 234–236, 240
Walker v. Associated Press, see *Associated Press v. Walker*
Wallace, George, 46, 60
Wallace, Henry, 72

Ward, Harry, 175
Warren, Earl, 4, 5–6, 104, 138, 181, 217, 243–247, 260
Welch, Robert, 162, 163, 199, 204, 205
Wells, H. G., 100
Wenberg, Stanley, as witness, 175
Wentworth, T. C., 231
Wheeler, Burton K., 47
White, Harry Dexter, 38
White, Richard H., 161
White, Walter, 185
Whitten, Richard B., 185
Wilkerson, Doxey, 27–29, 145, 158, 185, 190–191, 197, 244, 271n8
Williams, Faith, 185
Wilson, Harold, 109
Wilson, O. M., 67, 259
Winona Daily News, 104–105
Wirth, Louis, 24, 30, 185
Wood, L. Hollingsworth, 24, 185
Woofter, Thomas J., Jr., 24
Wormser, René, 248
Wright, Donald O., 60
Wright, Richard, 21

Yale Law Review, 117
Young, Donald, 24, 166, 175
Youngdahl, Luther, 72